# LIFE IN TUSCANY.

# LIFE IN TUSCANY.

BY

MABEL SHARMAN CRAWFORD.

FROM THE LONDON EDITION.

NEW-YORK:
SHELDON AND COMPANY, 115 NASSAU STREET.
1859.

TO

WILLIAM SHARMAN CRAWFORD,

**This Volume**

IS

AFFECTIONATELY DEDICATED

BY HIS

DAUGHTER.

# INTRODUCTION.

At the present moment, when Italy is the central point of interest to the whole of Europe, no apology, it is hoped, will be necessary for the contribution of any information tending to throw a light upon the character, condition and ideas of the people of that land. The classic and historical associations of Italy, its architectural remains, and the treasures of ancient and modern art contained in its churches, museums and picture galleries, have been the theme of so many eloquent writers, that it would be superfluous, if not presumptuous, for any one not highly qualified by learning and research, to treat of such subjects. Avoiding, therefore, topics to which, under any circumstances, no interest arising from novelty can now possibly attach, I venture to hope that these impressions of the aspects of "Life in Tuscany," derived from a ten months' sojourn in that country, will prove neither trite nor unacceptable.

Tuscany, it is true, with barely two millions of inhabitants, constitutes but a small section of Italy, which counts a population of twenty-five millions; but the part which this petty State may enact, in the event of an insurrectionary movement throughout the land, will certainly exercise a powerful influence over the destinies of the Italian Peninsula. For Tuscany, small though it be, is far from an insignificant province of Italy, embracing as it does several cities and towns of considerable importance —Florence, Pisa, Sienna, Lucca, Leghorn, Pistoia, and Arezzo; and thus it possesses a power and influence far beyond what it would derive from its limited population and extent of territory. For cities, important and influential in every country, are especially so in Italy: in them are concentrated the entire wealth, intelligence, commercial enterprise, and intellectual activity of the provinces. Were it not for Milan and Venice, Lombardy would lie supine beneath the iron heel of Austria; the destiny of the States of the Church depends on the will of Rome; and Naples gives the law to that kingdom of which it is the metropolis. Everywhere in Italy cities dominate: it is only by their power that tyranny, domestic or foreign, can or will be overthrown.

In addition to the power and influence that Tuscany derives from its cities, Florence, indissolubly associated as it is with glorious recollections of past greatness, gives to the province of which it is the capital, a distinguished position among other Italian States. Proud memories of the fame, the power, the riches and conquests of Florence in bygone times—of the great names which have shed lustre on its literature, arts, science and arms—foster the bright hopes and lofty aspirations in which Italians indulge, of the future of their native land.

Judging from the past as well as from present indications, Tuscany will not remain inert if a struggle for freedom should begin in Northern Italy. The people, united by a bond of common grievances proceeding from the same source, will join in the cry of "Down with the Austrians;" and the first cannon shot from the fortress of Milan will be echoed from the ramparts of Florence.

As unforseen and sometimes trivial occurrences frequently give an unexpected turn to affairs, no prediction of the course and result of future events can be relied upon: still—as the liberal cause was lost, during the late revolution in Italy, mainly through democratic violence and want of unity of action—should the Italians now unite, as they seem disposed to do, and fight for their freedom under the banner of the King of Sardinia, hope may not unreasonably be entertained that the issue of the apparently impending struggle will be widely different from that of the last. Wise, indeed, it is for the people of a country which has long been oppressed, to renounce the idea of a form of government demanding for its due administration qualities to which oppression does not give birth—and wisely will they act in seeking to acquire the power of self-government under the guidance of a constitutional monarch.

M. S. C.

*Crawfordsburn,*
*March 23d.*

# NOTE TO THE AMERICAN EDITION.

---

The prophecy contained in the author's introduction has proved true. On the breaking out of the late French-Sardinian war with Austria, a bloodless revolution at once took place in Tuscany. The Grand Duke, not waiting to meet the indignation of his people, fled to the protection of his Austrian master. After the battle of Solferino had decided the fate of the war, he abdicated in favor of his son Ferdinand; but the Florentines utterly refused to accept again the House of Lorraine as rulers, and have established the same form of government which was adopted in 1848. What will be the issue, depends on the brave hearts of the Tuscans, and the *laissez faire* policy of Napoleon III.

# CONTENTS.

# LIFE IN TUSCANY.

## CHAPTER I.

### BATHS OF MONTE CATINI.

LITTLE as Tuscany can compete with some of the small German States bordering on the Rhine, in regard to variety and abundance of mineral waters, it yet possesses several medicinal springs that enjoy a high local reputation for their sanative properties. For those afflicted with rheumatic affections, the sulphureous Baths of Pozzolenti, adjoining the town of Leghorn, are considered beneficial. In the same locality also are the springs of Monte Nero, containing a large proportion of salts of magnesia, much frequented in the summer months, for drinking merely. Near Pisa, the Baths of San

Guiliano afford, or at least profess to afford, a means of relief or cure for various ills that afflict suffering humanity. The Baths of Lucca enjoy a still more distinguished and wide-spread reputation —a reputation, however, probably much enhanced by their agreeableness, in point of scenery and shade, as a summer place of residence. But of all the mineral waters of this part of Italy, none rank so highly in popular estimation—either as regards internal or external application—as those of Monte Catini, a small watering-place, situated in the northern part of Tuscany. These springs, which are Crown property, bring in a considerable revenue to the State, from the large annual export of the waters that takes place to the principal cities of the Grand Duchy. On most occasions of trifling indisposition, the citizens, both rich and poor, of the Tuscan towns, instead of having recourse to doctors' drugs, are wont to avail themselves of those which nature has compounded, and swallow huge draughts of Monte Catini water: which, however, as far as pleasantness of flavor is concerned, has little to boast of over the medicaments which load the shelves of the apothecary.

In point of beauty, the situation of the Baths of Monte Catini has much to recommend them. Placed on the verge of the rich Val Nievole, where the plain terminates abruptly in a range of well-wooded heights, the Baths offer on their northern side a series of highly attractive views. Immediately above, perched like an eagle's nest on the very summit of the declivity, is seen the small town of Monte Catini, crowning the steep sides of the hill from which both it and the Baths below derive their name. To the right and left, other hills, forming a portion of the same northern chain, with picturesquely-varied forms and outlines, enhance the attraction of the scene. But though the Baths offer some very charming views, these sink into insignificance in point of beauty compared with those which the sides or summits of the adjacent hills afford. Ascending even a slight elevation in the vicinity, and looking southward, the eye wanders over a far-reaching, fertile plain. In proportion as the step ascends, so does the prospect gain in beauty and extent; till from the summit of Monte Catini, or the contiguous heights, a view is gained which well repays the fatigue and toil the steep ascent involves.

Below, gleaming in the bright light of an Italian sun, stretches out the rich vale of Nievole, blending in the distance with the still richer vales through which the Arno runs. Amidst fields teeming with the rich products of a fertile and well-cultivated soil, amidst olives, mulberries, vines and figs, gleam forth the numerous dwellings of the peasantry, interspersed with white glistening villages and small country towns. Here and there rises up a chapel tower; here and there, too, amidst the sea of verdure, the country palace of a nobleman may be seen. To the south and east a range of undulating hills, wearing the misty veil of distance, closes in the view; to the west, towering above the calm waters of the small lake of Bientina, is seen a mountain, forming a portion of the Pisan group, advancing boldly into the plain; and to the north a chain of lofty hills—here separating into gentle slopes, there parting into steep ravines, crowned not unfrequently with villages and ruined towers, rising out of groves of chestnut and olive trees—combine to form a grand, imposing framework for the rich and smiling scene.

Like most parts of Tuscany, the whole country in the vicinity of the Baths of Monte Catini wears quite a garden-like aspect of cultivation, neatness and care. Not a crooked fence, not a useless hedge, not a weed, not a waste patch of ground is visible any where. Vines fastened to stakes, or trailing their graceful branches from tree to tree, form the boundaries of fields and farms. In the early summer months a vast variety of wild flowers are to be seen, many of which attain to the dignity of garden plants in England. Amidst the long, slender stalks of wheat, the beautiful purple gladiolis springs up abundantly, and is succeeded, a little later in the year, by a bright-colored kind of lupin; while at the same time the gumcistus may be seen on every side, showering its delicate white blossoms on the turf around. Towards the end of June the orange lily becomes a common ornament of the woods and fields; whilst with July the crowning glories of Italy's floral riches appear in the sweet-scented clematis, and the still more fragrant and beautiful myrtle; both springing up under the sole care of a kindly nature; both doomed for the most part to bloom neglected and unseen, and to yield their perfume solely to the passing breeze.

Like the mineral waters of Germany, those of Monte Catini are, during the summer season, much used for bathing purposes. Hither, particularly during the months of July and August, flock from all parts of Tuscany a health or pleasure-seeking crowd.

Those who may have seen the Baths of Monte Catini during the winter, will, if subsequently visitants at the springs in the fashionable bathing months, find a wonderful difference in their aspect. Without shops, without trade, without the slightest pretension to anything that might be called a town, the Baths of Monte Catini may be considered to have, for at least nine months in the year, a merely nominal existence. The whole permanent population of the place consists but of the keepers of a few lodging-houses and hotels. In the vast, palace-like Government structure, which absorbs within its capacious centre and wings the greatest portion of the migratory summer throng, spiders and ghosts may for a large portion of the year revel in silence and darkness unmolested. The stranger, whom curiosity should at such a season allure to the spot, would find his meditations almost as secure from interruption from the world without, as if, like a hermit of the olden time, he inhabited a cell in some rocky wilderness. Beneath the long avenue of trees leading to the principal spring, he will hear no voice save that of the strolling mendicant, or the more agreeable accents of the peasant, who, with a courteous "felice giorno," passes on; and to the few inhabitants of the locality or the neighborhood he may chance to meet, he will find himself an object of curiosity and surprise, and a phenomenon as rare and extraordinary as that which might be presented by the sight of a swallow in the depth of the winter season.

Even so late in the year as the month of May, when all Italian nature is thoroughly awake, when the fields are green with waving corn, the trees in leaf, the sky serene, the air warm, and the birds in full song, the Baths of Monte Catini still wore to my eye, on my arrival there, the aspect of a place asleep: not in a profound sleep, however, for symptoms of an approaching animation, a coming awakening, were beginning to be visible at this time. Through the open doors of long-deserted houses, the voices of workmen were to be heard, as they painted here, and whitewashed there, in preparation for the opening of the bathing season. Into long-darkened rooms sunlight and air were allowed to penetrate once again, whilst sweeping, dusting, and polishing of the furniture actively went on. The roads were cleaned, the walks were weeded, while garden-plots or pleasure-grounds were, in accordance with the happy inspiration of some moment, re-arranged. An air of business was visible everywhere: I heard the note of preparation for the rising of the curtain on the scene. As the month rolled on, the signs of activity and of animation increased; the very frogs, who had been exerting their voices pretty freely for some time previously, seemed to croak more loudly as June drew nigh: from every pool, and brook, and water-course, arose a clamor that, especially in the night-time, filled the air. Out came the fire-flies as the day expired, and lit up the roads and lanes with their bright, flashing lamps, vieing with the stars above in number and brilliancy. Thus May died out, and with the 1st of June Monte Catini may be said to take off its nightcap; for the bathing season has then officially begun.

But though the place has nominally entered on a new stage of existence, for three weeks at least it bears in its aspect the signs of its old drowsy, yawning, lethargic state; in spite of its newly-arranged electric telegraph, its freshly-opened post-office, and its grand grocer's shop, whose shelves display a goodly array of imposing canisters. Until after Midsummer-day, it is only drop by drop that the Baths of Monte Catini fill. With July, however, when the bathing mania in all parts of Tuscany sets in, the stream of population, which has been flowing so languidly during the preceding month towards the Baths, grows strong and deep; to the infinite satisfaction and advantage of the keepers of lodging houses and hotels. With the increase of visitors, beggars multiply in number; a numerous concourse of the blind, the halt, the maimed the sick, and ragged, all ply their trade with zeal.

Beneath the long avenue of overarching trees, a motley throng of promenaders may be seen in the cool morning and evening hours. Representatives of almost every class of Tuscan society may be distinguished there, from the cringing beggar to the haughty peer. The peasant woman, with her blue cotton dress and handkerchief covering her dark hair, looks with unconcealed curiosity and surprise at the many-flounced skirt and fashionable bonnet of the Florentine belle. The petty shopkeeper of the provincial town and the Leghorn merchant, with their wives and families; the lawyer and Government official; all swell the morning and evening concourse at the springs. Long-robed ecclesiastics abound, from the humble country priest to the pompous prelate boasting the dignity of an archiepiscopal see. Carriages dash along the drive, at a rate that none but Italian coachmen ever think of forcing their horses to achieve. Itinerant shopkeepers set up their stalls, and solicit the passer-by with eager looks and words to buy their wares. From the tent erected by the migratory showman, there issues forth a troop of dancers and athletes, bedaubed with paint, bedecked with tinsel finery, and who, to the sound of drum and fife, parade about with the view of attracting spectators to performances announced in stupendous capital letters to be the most wonderful in the world. On every side, life, noise and animation prevail. The butterfly, that has just issued from its chrysalis, affords an apt illustration of the changed aspect which the Baths of Monte Catini presented to my view, on my return there in July after a short absence.

The several mineral springs of Monte Catini vary somewhat in equality, but their elementary nature is much the same. All are saline: the Rinfresco slightly, the Tetuccio more, and the Fortuna most of all. In public estimation the Tetuccio ranks the first; the visitors to this spring exceeding infinitely in amount the frequenters of the other two. The morning scene which the Tetuccio presents, is a gay and animated one. Beneath an awning, covering a portion of a small garden whose roses and oleanders are in full bloom, may be seen a motley company, some standing, but the most part sitting, in groups of three or four, around small circular marble tables covered with glasses, destined to be repeatedly filled from the large reservoirs of tepid mineral water close at hand. Nauseous as is the beverage, it is wonderful to see the equanimity with which it is swallowed down; not in one great draught, as inclination would prescribe, but sip by sip, in pursuance of the physician's command. Old and young, all have their glasses before them, or in their hands, whilst animated conversations are carried on. New groups arrive, familiar faces depart; there is a perpetual bowing of heads, an interminable shaking of hands. By nine o'clock, however, the morning drama is at an end, and the drinkers have disappeared: around the marble tables, covered with empty glasses, are seen circles of untenanted chairs, and the plash of falling water is the only sound that breaks upon the ear.

The ordinary routine of existence at Monte Catini taxes the energies of both mind and body but in a slight degree: life seems to pass away in a kind of blissful indolence there. The "dolce far niente," so dear to an Italian heart, is indulged in to its full extent. The water-drinking business of the morning coming to an end, the company separate, and retire to their respective rooms, to drive away with a cup of coffee or a substantial meal, the lingering flavor of the Tetuccio spring. Between breakfast and the bathing time, which varies from eleven to one, a gentle doze is taken, either on bed or sofa, as convenience or inclination may suggest. Dinner at two o'clock evokes signs of energy and animation on every side, which continue for an hour or an hour and a half, till, the great event of the day being concluded, the last glass of wine swallowed, the last apricot eaten, the company formally separate, with the polite wish, mutually expressed, that each may enjoy a sound repose; whereupon, ladies and gentlemen repair to their respective sleeping apartments, doff their outer garments, close the shutters, adjust their pillows, and enjoy two hours of blissful unconsciousness of all the trials and miseries of life, as attested by the loud nasal sounds that may be heard issuing from the darkened rooms.

Not more surely, however, does the light of morning arouse the lark to life and animation, than do the shades of evening put an end to the afternoon slumberer's dreams. The gentleman resumes his coat, and the lady makes her toilet afresh, as the sun sinks downward to the west, and between five and six o'clock the whole population of the Baths is out of doors again; for the most part bending their steps onward towards the Rinfresco spring, where, after a glass or two being drank, they stroll about, some here, some there, exchanging salutations with their friends; talk of the heat, repeat the latest news, and tell of the last wonderful cure that the waters of Monte Catini have performed. Carriages dash up and down beneath the avenue of trees; and horses decked out with feathers and gay trappings are stimulated to a frantic speed. With the vanishing twilight vanishes also the gay scene, and between eight and nine, when the darkness of night comes on, the voice of the cicala, a huge species of locust, reigns supreme.

Within doors, however, considerable animation prevails, for the hour of supper has arrived. That meal being ended, those of the company who do not feel themselves overpowered by the exertions of the day, repair to the casino, a suit of rooms assigned to the purposes of amusement. Here, in a large apartment, brilliantly lit up, is to be found every evening a considerable assembly. Some talk, some play at cards, some read French or Italian newspapers; others stake a paul in a game of chance, called the Tombola, a particular kind of lottery: of which species of amusement all Italians seem to be enthusiastically fond. Music also generally lends its aid to make the hours pass by pleasantly and fleetly. In a nation gifted with such musical tastes as are the Italians, in every assemblage, amongst the upper and middle classes, will certainly be found both gentlemen and ladies possessing no mean skill as vocal or instrumental performers. Thus, at Monte Catini, scarcely an evening elapses without some black-moustached, dark-haired amateur sitting down at a fine piano forte, with which the casino is furnished, to favor the company with a sonata; and occasionally a philanthropic lady will minister to the general happiness by singing an opera air, for which act she is sure to be rewarded by a shower of "bravas" at the end. Dancing, too, occasionally affords to the juvenile portion of the assembly an amusement of a still more attractive kind; rising in dignity from the impromptu waltz, suggested by the enlivening strains of some musical amateur, to the more solemn occasions when ladies and gentlemen in full ball dress perform their varied evolutions to the accompaniment of a full band. But be it ball, or dance, or song, or cards, or simple talk that crowns the labors of the day, the company separate at an early hour, to prepare, by several hours of sleep, for a repetition on the morrow of the exertions undergone the preceding day.

Though a favorite resort of the inhabitants of Tuscany in general, the Baths of Monte Catini number few foreigners amongst their visitors. Amid the crowd of dark-eyed and dark-complexioned Italians, that lounge along the walks or cluster at the springs, a ruddy English face, though so familiar a sight in the chief towns of Tuscany, is rarely to be seen. France and Germany contribute, also, but little more than England to swell the bathing crowd, which pours in so freely during the months of July and August, from Florence, Leghorn, Pisa and the minor provincial Tuscan towns. The absence of the English element, at least, is easily explained. To the native of the British Isles, bred up to activity of body and mind, the indolent, drowsy kind of life, which almost every rich or well-born Italian likes to lead, must ever be uncongenial. To an Italian, the one short, solitary, shady walk or drive, of which the Baths of Monte Catini can boast, is amply sufficient for every purpose of exercise. To lounge morning and evening under the one avenue of overarching trees, or to drive up and down, criticising new faces, remarking new dresses, seeing and greeting acquaintances or friends, contents, as far as bodily exertion is concerned, the Italian's utmost desire. But it is not so with the English visitor; who, even in amusement, craves exercise of a more varied, active kind — a craving which the Baths of Monte Catini can hardly satisfy during the hot months of August or July, from the absolute want of agreeable shady walks, rides or drives. For rich, and indeed beautiful, as is much of the scenery in the vicinity of the Baths, the roads and walks are all too much exposed to the hot glare of a July or August sun, to admit of driving, riding, or walking being indulged in until the sun is down; an hour too late to allow of pleasure excursions being made of any but the most limited description. For this reason, therefore, the Baths of Monte Catini are but in little favor with the numerous members of the active Anglo-Saxon race, who, either from motives of economy or of pleasure, have taken up their abode in Tuscany. Thoroughly Italian, therefore, is Monte Catini, and thoroughly Italian it will probably remain to the last hour of its existence, however much the migratory English may multiply in Italy.

Though liberality is somewhat a rare attribute of the Government of the present Grand Duke of Tuscany, this quality is certainly displayed by it in so far as regards its acts in connection with the amusements of the summer visitors to this locality. Freely may the stranger enter the brilliantly lit up casino; freely may he join in the dance, or listen to the performance of a well-trained band; freely do the French and Italian papers lie at his command: the light music and journals being supplied at the cost of the "Administration," as the presiding power in this place is called. This liberality, however, is far from being of a disinterested character; as, the greatest portion of Monte Catini being Crown property, the Grand Duke's revenues are materially augmented by there being a numerous resort of visitors to the springs. The liberality, therefore, displayed in providing amusement gratis for the guests, may be compared to the sowing of a bushel of corn with the assured hopes of receiving back an abundant harvest in return. That the policy thus pursued is a wise and profitable one there can be little doubt; for Italians generally, both of the upper and middle classes, have fortunes of a very moderate amount: and probably many of those families who come to Monte Catini during the fashionable bathing season, have to economize in various ways for some time previously in order to provide the funds necessary for a summer trip. To persons such as these—to persons, too, endowed by nature with a keen love of pleasure, as for the most part all Italians are—the offer of amusements free of cost will prove in itself a lure of a very effective kind to draw visitors to the baths, all sanitary considerations apart; but when, in addition, the highly reputed medical properties of the mineral waters are taken into account, it is no wonder that the place should overflow with visitors: to the benefit not only of the Grand Duke, whose huge hotel is amply filled, but to the profit also of the poor peasant of the neighborhood, who lets his humble apartment for, to him, the handsome sum of threepence or fourpence a night.

Short, however, is the harvest season, for either peasant or Grand Duke. Towards the end of August, the morning convivial gatherings at the Tetuccio spring dwindle down considerably in numbers; by the first week in September most of the company have departed, and the remainder are preparing to take a flight; and on the 15th, when the Baths are formally closed, the last lingering remnants of the bathing crowd have left. The crack of the vetturino's* whip is then no longer heard,

*Hack-driver.

and the drive echoes no more with the roll of carriage wheels and the tramp of horses. The awning at the Tetuccio is taken down, the marble tables vanish from the scene, and the hotel-keeper sits down to count his gains, and compare the profits of the season just expired with those of former years. The careful mistress of the lodging house, with a sigh at the transitoriness of sublunary joys, takes down the curtains of her untenanted beds, folds up her table-covers and quilts, consigns her delf and china to the cupboard, and closes the window-shutters of her deserted rooms: all signs of life and animation disappear, and the Baths of Monte Catini once more lie buried in their habitual nine months' sleep.

Long, however, before the close of the fashionable season, I left the place, consequently my description of its autumnal aspect is derived, not from the results of personal observation, but from information afforded me by some of the very few permanent residents at the Baths. In the height of their summer gaiety I went away, bearing with me many pleasant remembrances of the place—remembrances of quiet strolls, through fields and lanes, to humble dwellings, where I was always a welcome guest—of soft summer nights, when the sparkling stars yielded in brilliancy to the fire-flies' flashing light — of rambles through groves, where the myrtle offered its beautiful white blossoms to my sight; and, above all, remembrances to which I shall ever fondly turn, of courteous acts, kind wishes, and friendly looks and words.

"We go to bed at five o'clock in the evening in the winter months, because it is cold, and we have nothing in the world to do," said the mistress of a small inn at Monte Catini to me; and I thought that nothing could depict more forcibly than these simple words the utter stagnation of life prevailing during the winter months in that locality.

## CHAPTER II.

### VIAREGGIO.

ABOUT fifteen miles from Lucca there lies on the shores of the Mediterranean a small sea-port town called Viareggio. Insignificant in point of size, almost destitute of trade, save that connected with the fishermen's pursuits, the existence it leads is, for the greatest part of the year, of the very quietest and most monotonous description. The surf breaks upon an almost untrodden strand; the sunset glow upon the magnificent mountains of Carrara, arrests no wandering stranger's admiring gaze; and the tramp of horses' feet and the roll of carriage wheels are almost unknown sounds in the streets of Viareggio.

But it is not always thus; for a short season of gaiety and animation annually chequers the ordinarily quiet life of the inhabitants of this locality. Soon as the bathing movement has fairly commenced in Tuscany, Viareggio, like the Baths of Monte Catini, emerges in the hot sun of summer like a butterfly from its chrysalis. Brief, however, is its period of festivity, for, unlike the bathing towns and villages on the coasts of the British Isles, which enjoy a succession of visitors, from May until October, the bathing towns and villages on the shores of Italy, can count upon but a two months' influx of strangers. According to Italian ideas, to bathe in May savors strongly of insanity; to bathe in June is deemed an act considerably more rational, but still one that sense and prudence must condemn; and it is not till the *sol leone* (the lion sun) of July is glowing overhead, that public opinion in Italy sanctions a rush into the sea. August is looked upon also with considerable favor in reference to its sea-bathing qualifications, but is far from being so highly thought of in this respect as its predecessor July. September puts the whole flock of bathers everywhere to flight; except those eccentric foreigners, the "Inglese," who, notwithstanding the decreasing temperature, still continue their daily immersions in the waves. October finds the bathing boxes closed, the hotels deserted, and the lodging houses consigned to darkness, silence and solitude.

It was in the middle of July, in the very height of the Italian bathing season, that I first made acquaintance with Viareggio. The approach to it from Lucca, is characterized by considerable beauty of scenery. The road, for the first few miles, lay through a country where vines, trained so as to form festoons from tree to tree, encircled fields that looked like gardens in point of neatness and care of cultivation. In the ground, where but ten days before the reaper's sickle had been at work gathering in sheaves of golden grain, young plants of maize had already sprouted, and through the line of trees that fringed the road, one caught glimpses in every direction of the red tile-roofed dwellings of the peasantry.

Scenes such as these, however, soon gave place to others of a different character. On reaching one side of the plain in which Lucca stands, the road began to wind up through a kind of gorge in a chain of hills covered with a perfect forest of chestnuts; vines, fields and houses disappeared from view, and all the eye now saw was the bright blue sky overhead, and the steep declivities of the winding glen below, clothed with the bright green foliage of that tree which is, to the inhabitants of the district where it grows, what the bread-fruit tree is to the South Sea islanders. The ascent, though steep, is not a lengthened one; and before long, the horses, after a short pause at the summit to take breath, commenced to descend rapidly the other side of the mountains. The road wound backwards and forwards, curve after curve, in an extremely snake-like fashion; a course of proceeding highly to be commended, both as regarded considerations of safety and scenery: the latter especially, for the views which every turn disclosed, were of a very beautiful description, and of a highly varied character.

Below, at the furthest edge of the narrow plain, to which the chestnut-covered hills served on one side as boundary, lay the little town of Viareggio, gleaming brightly in the sunshine; while beyond, the blue waters of the Mediterranean, sparkling in the same bright rays, mingled in the distance with the still deeper azure of the sky. On another side, the fine mountains of Carrara rose up to view, their bald crags and precipitous peaks towering majestically, high above the calm blae sea and the tree-fringed coast, and the villages nestling amongst the chestnut groves, which closed the base and partially adorned the sides of the whole mountain range.

The immediate vicinity of Viareggio, however, is marked by a feature not of the most agreeable kind; for no sooner do we enter on the narrow plain which intervenes between the mountain chain and Viareggio, than there is to be seen on either side a marsh, which even Tuscan industry seems not to have been able to convert to any other use than the growth of osiers, that flourish in company with beautiful white water-lilies. Up almost to the very doors of Viareggio this swamp extends; a closeness of vicinity that, it appeared to me, must prejudicially affect the salubrity of the locality; but, according to the Italian doctrine on the subject, the sea-breeze blows away from Viareggio every kind of unwholesome exhalation.

Within the memory of man, Viareggio has made a great advance in dignity, having become at least trebled in size and population during the last fifty years; still, however, it will have to grow at the same rate for the next succeeding half century, before it can take a distinguished place amongst the towns of Tuscany. Yet, insignificant in extent as it is at present, Viareggio evidently pretends to a far higher grade in point of station than that of a mere fishing village. A capacious church, crowned with a large dome, daily invites, with open doors, the devout Catholic to enter; and a large, waste-looking piece of ground, covered with parched-up grass, and surrounded by a fringe of scrubby trees, proudly assumes the name of the "Piazza Grande." A canal, cut from the sea into the heart of the little town, allows boats to discharge their cargoes conveniently; and close to it, under a double row of mushroom-shaped trees, is the favorite lounge of the seafaring population, where neighbors meet to sit and talk together about their good or bad success in the take of fish, or the last news of the vine disease, or the conscription (a word of terror to the Tuscan peasant); and gossip also (for human nature is much the same amongst high and low) about the petty scandals of their circle—how Guiseppe and his wife fell out, and how all Tomaso's earnings are squandered away in cards and drink.

During the course of years, Viareggio, originally built at about a quarter of a mile from the shore, has been creeping seaward; and line after line of street has been added: one row of houses excluding the view of the sea from that which had been previously built, to be itself subsequently excluded by a new row in a like unpleasant fashion. The line of houses that now occupies the van—the post of pleasure, honor and profit, in the bathing season—has a sufficiently attractive and cheerful appearance. Though the dwellings are for the most part small, yet nearly all of every size, from the so-called "palazzo" of four stories to the peasant's dwelling numbering but two, are characterized by iron balconies, by walls of gleaming whiteness, and by windows embellished and shaded by bright green Venetian blinds, closing externally after the Italian fashion. Here it is that pilgrims to the salt water chiefly take up their residence; and here it was that my friend and myself resolved to fix ourselves during the two weeks' stay we wished to make at Viareggio. But moderate as were our requirements with regard to accommodation, we found that even an attic to let, commanding a view of the sea, was almost an unattainable luxury. "Tutta piena, tutta piena" (all full), was the unwelcome answer that awaited our inquiries, as we wended our way from door to door on our unexpectedly difficult mission. At length, when all hopes of success were nearly extinguished, we chanced upon a house in which there actually were two apartments unoccupied.

The house belonged to a "Contadino"—the name applied to a man of the peasant or working classes in Italy—but, both outside and inside, the dwelling was very unlike a Contadino's common residence, into which no person of civilized habits could dream of entering as a tenant. But yet, though light and cheerful, with whitened walls and large glass windows, the two vacant apartments had not a very inviting aspect, in connection with the idea of even a fortnight's residence in them. No sofa or arm chair offered to the tired or languid frame a luxurious lounge, and the eye wandered dejectedly over superannuated rush-seated chairs, invalided looking-glasses, which appeared as if they had just passed through a severe crisis of small-pox, and beds quite mountain-like in the altitude to which they rose. Still, as the sea stretched out before the windows so beautifully blue, as the air felt deliciously fresh, as the waves broke with such a melodious sound upon the beach, and as no other accommodation by the sea-side was procurable, a bargain was struck with the mistress of the mansion; and in a very philosophic frame of mind, making sage remarks on the subject of the superfluities of existence, we entered upon the possession of the rooms in question.

It must be owned that it did require some philosophy to submit cheerfully to the various discomforts of our habitation; but after all, our stock of equanimity was not put to the severe test which our first twenty-four hours' experience of life in the Contadino's house gave us reason to anticipate; for after some sharp passages of words with our landlady, of whom we thought we had reason to complain, our circumstances assumed a more smiling aspect.

"Abbia pazienza; siamo Contadini,"* was the apology put forward by Violante, our landlady, for every deficiency in her establishment complained of: when our dinner-table exhibited a very limited amount of spoons and forks, when our lamps nightly evinced a most uncontrollable propensity to go out, the same appeal to our forbearance was sure to be made—"Abbia pazienza; siamo Contadini." Notwithstanding, however, the Contadino plea, we enjoyed the benefit of a considerable redress of grievances: the lights increased materially in brilliancy and longevity, and the important spoon and fork question, as well as other matters that came under discussion, underwent before long a satisfactory settlement.

"But, Contadini as you say you are, how do you

* Have patience; we are peasants.

happen to have such an excellent house as this to live in?" I said one day to Violante, retorting upon her favorite exclamation of *Abbia pazienza.*

"The house was a gift to me from a lady with whom I lived for some years in service," replied Violante; "she was a countess, who had a fine house in Florence, and so, being very rich, and very generous and good, she had this house built expressly for my husband and myself, that we might earn money by it in the bathing season. A good lady she was indeed to me! *buon' anima*, may her soul rest in glory."

The munificent gift of the countess to Violante came most opportunely, for through its means she was able to support her family when her husband, a sailor, was incapacitated from working by an accident, which rendered the amputation of one of his feet necessary, and thus reduced him to the position of a cripple. True, the profits derived from letting the house in the short bathing season, were trifling, but as the expenditure of the peasant's family was on the same scale also, the one sufficed for the requirements of the other. A piece of bread served for their breakfast; a decoction of hot water and maccaroni, flavored occasionally with a bone, afforded, under the name of soup, materials for their dinner; and their supper consisted of a dish of kidney beans served up in oil: altogether, a style of living, it must be confessed, by no means costly.

Occasionally, however, the family fared in a more luxurious manner, as I had an opportunity of observing from my window, which looked down upon a small garden; there, underneath the shade of a spreading vine, the master and mistress of the mansion, with a son and two daughters, daily assembled around a small table to make their mid-day meal. The exceptions to the general rule only occurred, however, on saints' days and Sundays, when a dish of fish or of stewed tomatoes graced the board; but no matter what might be the style of dinner, no sooner did the master of the house, the one-footed sailor, perceive me at my window, than with a most courteous bow he would very hospitably request me to assist at the rural banquet that was going on below—a piece of politeness which was invariably responded to on my part by wishing the company a *buon appetito*,* a wish enjoined by good manners according to the established Italian form.

In one respect, our crippled landlord was quite a curiosity in appearance, for he exhibited almost an African tint of skin. Swarthy as is generally the complexion of the working classes in Italy, their swarthiness rarely amounts to a degree of darkness sufficient to raise doubts in the stranger's mind as to their claim to a European origin; but Moschardino,†

* Good appetite.

† A soubriquet; one of the very many in general use amongst the working classes of Italy. I have found sometimes a man's next door neighbors were unacquainted with his real name.

as our disabled host was usually called, might well have passed for one who had drawn his earliest breath by the banks of the river Nile or Ganges. However, it always remained a matter of speculation with me how far Moschardino's oriental complexion was due to the action of the sun, or how far ascribable to a cause easy of removal by the application of a little soap and water.

Our landlady, Violante, was a perfect specimen of the Tuscan Contadina, the most hard-working, indefatigable specimen of human nature anywhere possible to find. With the earliest dawn of morning, almost before the cock had begun to crow, I heard her voice; and she still was bustling about long after I had lain down. How such an amount of energy, of strength and endurance could have been put into any feminine form, appeared to me a matter of surprise; but in the lean, sinewy frame of Violante, and in her furrowed brow, one read, as in a printed book, a history of long years of toil.

"It is a hard, hard life, I lead," she said to me one day, in answer to a remark of mine; "but how can it be helped? My husband can do nothing now to earn his bread, and the burden falls on me to support him and our family. Ah! it was a great mistake I made when I was young, to marry; but I knew nothing then of what was before me—of the hard lot that falls to a wife and mother. And Guiseppe, too, though he is a good husband now, in former times used to get drunk and beat me. Ah! would to Heaven I had never married," she exclaimed, reiterating the wish I had so often previously heard uttered by the peasant women of Tuscany, "for the life I lead, still striving to earn a *quattrino* for my family's sake, whom I love too well, is a life of the hardest slavery."

The weather set in very warm at the beginning of the third week in July at Viareggio; yet, however powerful might be the mid-day sun, its great heat was always tempered by a gentle breeze blowing freshly from the sea; whose blue expanse, ever ruffled through this cause, never once assumed during my stay a mirror-like aspect. Still, morning, noon, evening, night, the air was filled with the sound of breaking waves, whose foam, glittering by day in the bright beams of an Italian sun, formed a sparkling snow-white fringe along the sandy shore. Nothing more tempting-looking for bathing purposes than the Mediterranean at Viareggio can be conceived; nor did the reality belie, in this respect, my most ardent anticipations of enjoyment; for indescribably delightful was it to plunge beneath the tepid sea, and to feel the warm spray of the breaking waves dash over head and face, as in quick succession their curving crests, bursting with a roar, dissolved in a sheet of milk-white foam upon the beach. Little can those whose salt-water experiences are confined to the seas that wash the British or Irish coasts, form a fair idea of the luxury of an ocean bath under the warm sun of Italy. No chilly waters arrest the breath, or send a shudder through the sensitive frame; and neither prudential motives, fears for health, dread of congealing blood, colorless flesh, nor shivering limbs, limit the bather's pleasure to a few minutes' time.

To do the inhabitants (both permanent and occasional) of Viareggio justice, they showed the utmost appreciation of the marine privileges they enjoyed; in particular, also, it must be recorded that the rising male population of the town evinced this feeling in the strongest and most unequivocal way. Happy boys of Viareggio! While your luckless cotemporaries in other places and other climes are stammering over dull books, puzzling their brains over sums in arithmetic, and inking their fingers in a laborious attempt to make well-rounded "o's" and straight-backed "t's," you are reveling in a salt-water elysium from morn till night—now in the tide, jumping, shouting, laughing, dancing, splashing, gamboling away—now taking a race, in Eden's primeval garb, along the beach—then rolling or tumbling in the hot sand, and again rushing off into the waves, to commence a new series of evolutions.

"How often do you bathe in the day?" I once asked an urchin of about ten years old, whom I met upon the shore.

"Six or seven times," he replied.

"And how long do you stay in the water each time?" I rejoined.

"Generally from one to two hours," he answered —a reply which will serve to give an idea of the amphibious kind of existence led in the summer months by the juvenile population of Viareggio.

A very much more limited allowance of bathing is that which custom prescribes for the grown-up portion of the community; two baths a day being the general amount indulged in by both ladies and gentlemen. The bath, however, is very variable in duration: some renounce their aqueous life at the end of twenty or thirty minutes; others extend their morning and afternoon bath each into a recreation of two hours. Small wooden houses, three in number, rising upon a foundation of piles above the water, a few yards distance from the beach, and communicating with the shore by a narrow bridge, are used as bathing boxes, by every bather who aspires to belong in any way to the aristocratic or affluent class. For a lower order—for those, in short, who find it inconvenient to pay the "Bagnetti" regulation price, which runs at the rate of threepence or fourpence a dip—the shore affords sheds, or rather screens of straw, to serve as dressing-rooms, at a still lower price.

But well frequented as are the precincts of the Bagnetti and straw screens, they are scantily peopled in comparison with the aspect of the shore, where no such articles of luxury are to be found, and where, from morning till night, a motley company is to be seen either going to, or returning from, the sea. Here, comes a troop of soldiers marching along with measured tread, and there, a swarm of shouting urchins; a guardian of the peace, in all the pomp of cocked hat and sword, is followed by a brace of Capuchin friars, with long brown cloth robes, cord-girt waists, bare feet, and heads protected from the scorching sun by hats of straw with ample brims. Day after day is the same scene displayed, as day after day the sun shines bright and warm, in a sky where only a few fleecy wreaths of vapor are seen to veil the glory of its clear deep blue.

Unimpeachable, however, as are the merits of Viareggio so far as its bathing prerogatives are concerned, it yet has two very considerable draw-backs to its agreeableness as a place of residence in the summer time. On the English coast, the absence of trees and shade is a circumstance of little moment for visitors to the sea in search of recreation or health, as the sun there exerts a comparatively mild sway, even in the height of his dog-day reign. But in Italy, on the shores of the Mediterranean, where for many successive hours of a long summer's day, a flood of light and heat is poured down uninterruptedly from a cloudless sky, shade becomes not only a luxury, but (for all above the peasant class) almost a necessity of existence. In Italy, in such places where no groves, no avenues of overarching trees, afford a protection from the glare and heat, a journey to and fro, or round a room, or an excursion up-stairs, down-stairs, or to a neighboring apartment, must perforce content the cravings of a restless spirit for motion, during eight hours at least of diurnal existence. Such being the case at Viareggio—there stretching inland for half a mile or more, a waste of sand, on which nothing but some prickly sea-plants and coarse grass will grow—a walk, or stroll, or lounge in the open air by day, takes rank amongst the list of unattainable enjoyments. Even, indeed, in the cool early morning and late evening hours, outdoor exercise could only be indulged in at the cost of an amount of toil and fatigue which rendered walking a kind of purgatorial performance; for in the loose, soft, dry sand, which covered the beach and extended far inland, the foot sank deeply. Thus, between the hot sun and the yielding sand, Viareggio enforced (except as far as the occupation of bathing was concerned) a very sedentary existence.

About twenty-three o'clock, as the hour before sunset is called in Italy, Viareggio, which looked as if it was indulging in a nap all day, begins to assume a wakeful aspect, and shows signs of life and animation. Bright green jalousies are thrown wide apart, whilst every balcony has its group of occupants, to enjoy the coolness of the evening air; and a little later, as the sun sinks lower in the west, from almost every house along the shore, the inmates issue to bid the day good-bye, from a favorite spot of rendezvous on the beach, or from a still more favorite wooden pier which stretches out beyond. The beach is the halting place of the most juvenile portion of the community, who, with wooden spades or spoons, dig caverns, raise mountains, build houses, make cakes or pies, and perform many wonderful labors in the damp sand; while mammas, still keeping a watchful eye over the movements of their Biancas or Giovannis, salute their passing friends, or exchange with one another a budget of domestic news. Here stalks "young Italy," in a light linen coat, with a cigar in his lips, and staring fixedly, as is the mode universally with Italian gentlemen, at every youthful feminine face he sees. Dressed out in the most extravagant style of an extravagant fashion, with bonnet hanging on her neck, with dress swelled out by flounces, hoops, and horse-hair to a wondrous size, the Italian lady sails proudly on, rejoicing in the thought that her attire is in complete accordance with the last Parisian mode. The Capuchin friar, in his brown cloth robe, wanders to and fro, and looks with a moody air and lustreless eye upon all around; while here and there a portly priest, having his head adorned by a large three-cornered hat, and his feet set off by a pair of large buckles in his shoes, seems from his genial air to participate largely in all the pleasant influences of the scene.

But few, however, are the loiterers on the beach compared with those who stroll onwards to the wooden pier, which offers a pleasant lounge, as well as numerous seats to the idle throng. Here friends walk to and fro together, or sit side by side engaged in careless talk, while before their unheeding eyes extends a scene that, once beheld, stamps itself indelibly on the stranger's memory. Almost on the verge of the ocean bed, in which it would seem about to sink to rest, is seen the sun, no longer a globe of fire casting forth a furnace glow of heat and light, but a ball of burnished gold, shedding a golden radiance on water, earth and sky. The windows of Viareggio flash like diamonds in the yellow light, and high above the town, and far extending towards the north, tower the splendid mountains of Carrara, with their bold summits and wooded slopes bathed in the most exquisite violet hues. Still further in the distance the bold headland of Cape Corvo, rising at the entrance of the Gulf of Spezzia, stands up in strong relief against the glowing sky. Lower and lower as the sun sinks towards the horizon, brighter and brighter glows the reflection of its golden hues in the flashing mirror of the sea; gaining, at length, the line, where sky and water seem to meet, one minute half its burnished surface is seen above the wave, in the next its rapidly dwindling crescent form has vanished from the sky, which slowly pales into a silvery gray, while the purple tints upon the mountains merge into a twilight gloom. Night comes apace; but even as its darkening shadow falls around, a faint roseate light begins to creep up the western sky, as if the departed luminary were returning on his track again. Slowly spreading, the soft suffusion rises up on high, till a large portion of the vault of heaven glows with a ruddy light, that tinges faintly the calm expanse of water underneath. North, east, and south the darkness deepens overhead, while the round orb of the moon grows bright and the stars appear. Some minutes pass, and then the west, seemingly loath to exchange the rich livery of the day for the sable hues of night, slowly, reluctantly, as it were, yields to the latter's irresistible sway. The outline of the distant headland melts into the darkened sky, and the nearer mountains seem to grow loftier in the deepening gloom. From the west the rich tints of sunset fade quite away; whilst the sea stretches out a dark expanse, save where the moonbeams fling a glittering trail; and in the illimitable depths of the dark blue vault above innumerable stars are sparkling brilliantly.

But beautiful as was the day in its decline, the night to which it yields possesses charms, though widely differing, of a not less attractive kind.

Through the heated air a sense of coolness is diffused by the light evening breeze, which wafts slowly towards the pier small fishing barks belonging to the seafaring population of the town. Like diamond-dust gleam the myriad stars of the Milky Way, whilst the nearer stellar worlds illuminate the dark vault of heaven with their bright, sparkling lamps. In unclouded majesty the full moon pursues her upward course, marking the sea beneath with a rippling silvery trail. High up the side of the lofty mountains numerous fires break into view, which increase and wane, till they successively expire. Mingled with the melodious roar of the breaking waves are faintly heard the joyous shouts and laughter of young girls, seen in the distance, by the bright moonlight, sporting in the waters of the surf-fringed sea. No sound that comes but falls melodiously on the ear, and not an object visible but seems to add to the soft beauty of the scene, from the mariner's distant warning light in the isle of Tino, scarcely visible to the eye, to the full-orbed moon shining through the clear depths of an Italian sky.

Beautiful as is the scene, however, there are few of the assemblage on the pier that give much heed to it, further than to remark on the pleasant coolness of the air; and before long, when conversational topics grow somewhat scarce, or those discussed become threadbare, a homeward movement takes place amongst the throng. Following the example set, we also swell the numbers of the retreating band, and halt with a considerable portion of its strength at a café, where, still in conformity with the mode, we take our seat at a small round table, one out of several which occupy the space immediately before the door. Knocking the table to arrest the waiter's attention—who is rushing about with a kind of frenzied haste, now to receive orders, now to receive money, now to execute the orders that have been received—we at length are fortunate enough to obtain a moment's audience, in which we intimate our desire to indulge in the luxury of an ice cream. The much toiling individual again hurries off amidst a volley of knocks resounding from every side; to which, to the credit of that important personage be it said, no attention is given until our behest has been obeyed; this done, however, he hastens off once more in quest of a supply of *gelati di pesca* and *di albicocca** to satisfy the popular demand.

Very rightly does public opinion at Viareggio flow in favor of refreshments of this kind, for ices, excellent even in cold northern climes, possess peculiar merits under an Italian summer sky. What a thrill of pleasure does the taste of the first cold morsel send through the heated, languid frame! and to what a keen sensation of regret does the sight of the empty glass give rise! Not that the ices of

* Peach and apricot ices.

Viareggio or of Tuscany in general have any pre-eminent merits of an artistic kind; and in a less sultry clime they would probably be found undeserving of particular eulogy. One merit, however, peculiar to this land, they do possess undoubtedly, for when, after looking steadily at my empty glass, which sanitary considerations forbid me to renew, I ask what is to pay, I find that six soldi (an amount which, translated into English, becomes about twopence halfpenny) will satisfy the demand.

Beautifully bright shines the moon as we slowly take our way towards our abode, and darkly shows each shadow, seen in contrast with the silvery whiteness that characterizes every object on which the moonbeams fall. The doors and windows of every house are thrown wide open to admit the warm, yet fresh-feeling evening air. Lights sparkle inside: here, voices engaged in eager conversation are heard; there, the chords of a piano mingle with a singer's rich harmonious tones. Outside the doors of the lodging-houses, belonging to the peasant class, the family of the *contadino* sit enjoying the fresh air.

We pass along a lengthened row of neat, well-whitewashed dwellings to where our temporary one, distinguished from its neighbors by an image of the Madonna decorating the front, invites our entrance with open doors. Before the threshold sit Moschardino and Violante, with different members of their family. There is Paolo, a youth of nineteen, who, to his mother's regret, is on the eve of marriage; and that, too, with Italian improvidence, to a woman poor as himself: there, also, is Caterina, a very handsome, dark-eyed girl, who thinks that human felicity consists in the possession of a silk dress and the wearing of a gold chain. There also stands lounging by, Mariana, a half-witted girl of sixteen, who looks as if an abhorrence of soap and water was the predominating feeling in her darkened mind. All rise at our approach, all wish us "*felice sera*" in a breath, and the ever hospitable Moschardino invites us to sit down, which invitation, as the old gentleman's conversation is somewhat unintelligible, from the extreme volubility of his utterance, I decline. Violante hastens to bring lights: we ascend the stairs, and after exchanging a few words with our fellow-lodgers, two Lucchese ladies, whose apartments adjoin ours, we follow their example in preparing to seek repose.

"Felicissima notte,"* says Violante, in the soft dialect of Tuscany; "Felicissima notte," I respond; and, presto, clambering up the steep altitudes of my couch, and gaining the soft and sheltered summit of my Mont Blanc, I wish *felicissima notte* to Viareggio and the whole world.

* Most happy night.

# CHAPTER III.

## LUCCA, AND THE BATHS OF LUCCA.

LUCCA rises out of a plain that is celebrated for its fertility; the natural productiveness of the soil being increased by a most perfectly arranged system of irrigation. Stimulated by the combined influences of heat and moisture, all vegetation assumes the most luxuriant aspect. A richer and a more productive country than that by which the walls of Lucca are surrounded, is, perhaps, not to be found anywhere.

Lucca, like the most of the Italian towns in the present day, derives now its sole interest from its past existence. Places characterized as the scenes of remarkable or stirring events always exercise a kind of spell over the imagination. The cell where the patriot has been confined, the square which has witnessed the martyr's agony, the ground which has been the theatre of a famous battle, all exert a powerful influence over the mind and fancy. It matters not though the cell be but four common bare stone walls, though the square be an ordinary paved court, surrounded by mean and insignificant dwellings, or the battle ground be but an uninteresting-looking expanse of cornfields, intersected by quickset hedges—a power resides in all these objects to attract the eye, to enlist the interest, and to touch the feelings. The captive comes before us with his pale, thin, careworn face; around the stake to which the hapless victim is attached rise up the glowing flames; and the din of a murderous conflict—the tramp of horses, the clash of contending weapons, the cries of suffering, and the roar of cannon, resound within our ears.

Though Lucca, however, appeals not by its history to our sympathies in any particular degree, either through the greatness of its power or the genius of its sons, it yet possesses a claim to our respectful consideration from the high position it occupied among the numerous republican towns of Tuscany. Here was silk first produced and manufactured in Italy—a circumstance which contributed materially for many years to the prosperity of the town; and from the energy and enterprise that characterized its citizens in all matters that related to commerce and trade, the epithet of "the Industrious" was attached to its name. Even under the Lombard Kings of Italy, whose power was subverted by the Franks in the eighth century, Lucca had risen to be a place of considerable importance; so much so that it became the capital and seat of government of princes of its own, who, under the title of Duke, exercised sovereign sway over the whole of Tuscany. The twelfth century found Lucca a free town, whose existence was as much disturbed by dissensions and feuds amongst its citizens as was that of any other republican city of Tuscany.

Hotly and eagerly, as in Florence, did the Guelph and Ghibeline factions engage in conflict within its walls; and it was whilst these were battling together in the streets that, in the fourteenth century, the Pisans entered, and took possession of the town. Throwing off the yoke of Pisa, after various vicissitudes through which it passed, from the grasp of a domestic tyrant into the possession of a Bohemian King, Lucca was only saved from being subjected to Florentine rule by once more falling into the possession of the Pisans, who defeated the rival republicans in a mighty battle which was fought in contention for the prize under the very walls of Lucca. To the Pisan supremacy succeeded that of Charles IV, and from that monarch the Lucchese purchased their freedom at an enormous price. Short, however, was the period marked by the enjoyment of the costly boon, for before thirty years had passed away, Lucca lay prostrate at the feet of Gian Galeazzo, the tyrant Duke of Milan. Recovering their liberty once more, the Lucchese did not recover with it the qualities of mind which in former times had rendered them worthy to exercise the prerogatives of self-government; for whilst the town still bore the name of a republic, it was tyrannized over by a narrow oligarchy of its citizens—an oligarchy, however, which, though hated by the people, maintained its sway until the year 1800, when the French took possession of Tuscany: an event which was followed before long by the entrance into Lucca of the Princess Elise, sister of Napoleon Bonaparte, as the sovereign of the town and adjoining territory. In the same month, and in the same year, Genoa, which formed with Lucca the last remnants of the ancient republican towns of Italy, lost its independence also.

But if Lucca lost its independence, it did not lose its dignity, for it continued to be the capital of a State, the residence of a court, and the seat of government during the rule of the French Princess, and of the succeeding house of Bourbon, down to 1847; when, in virtue of the treaty of Vienna, whereby the Allied Powers assumed to themselves the right of deciding on the destinies of small, powerless States, Lucca and the Lucchese territory passed into the possession of Leopold II, the present Grand Duke of Tuscany. Behold now Lucca—its liberty, its independence gone; its name as a State extinguished; its distinction as the seat of government, as the residence of a court, at an end: behold it dejected, grieving, burning secretly with indignation at the change, with the spark of disaffection and disloyalty smouldering in its breast, ready at the first favorable moment to burst out into a formidable flame.

Piety and wealth combined in Lucca, as in its neighboring republican cities, to raise noble and numerous temples to the Deity. Some of these, erected in the eighth century, serve as monuments of the existence of the Lombard kingdom, by offering to view the characteristic features of the Lombard architectural school. The cathedral, a handsome building, dates its existence from the eleventh century, and exhibits a facade adorned by several tiers of arches and rich inlaid work; the latter representing the somewhat inappropriate subject of the chase—huntsmen equipped with lance and horn, and accompanied by dogs, being depicted in the pursuit of a curious medley of wild animals, consisting of foxes, wolves, lions, boars and deer. The interior of the cathedral, compared with the interiors of the cathedrals of Pisa and Florence, is somewhat insignificant; for, though ornamented with fine stained glass, some rich Gothic tracery, and a ceiling where frescoes of saints show forth, on a ground of blue, it does not at all make up by such decorations for its inferiority to the Florentine and Pisan cathedrals in point of size. One distinction, however, the cathedral of Lucca enjoys over that of Florence or of

Pisa, in that it is the possessor of a relic which was venerated in former times in the highest degree throughout all Europe. Richly gilt and adorned is the small chapel that contains the *Volto Santo di Lucca*,*—a crucifix carved in cedar wood by the hand, it is alleged, of Nicodemus, and miraculously transported to Lucca in the eighth century. By the "Volto Santo di Lucca," under its Mediæval Latin name, did princes and nobles swear: the *per vultum de Lucca* being recorded as our second Norman King's most favorite oath, of the many with which he was accustomed to garnish his discourse and to give energy to his words. Yet, although this relic has lost its ancient celebrity, though princes and nobles swear by it no more, its sacred reputation still in this day prevails so far as to cause it to be shrouded from the public gaze; except on three great occasions of the year, when it is brought forth for adoration, with a sparkling jewel on its breast, and a gilt crown upon its head. Fortunately, however, for the passing stranger, who, except by special permission or rare good chance, cannot get a glimpse of the sacred work of art—a declared fac simile of the image is always exposed to view; which, if in very truth it be what it is professed, gives a most unfavorable idea of the artistic genius of Nicodemus.

Exclusive of the cathedral, there are eleven

* "Holy face of Lucca."

churches in Lucca, sufficiently remarkable in some way or other to entitle them to a place in the guide-book of every traveler. San Michele, venerable in years, dating its existence from the period of Lombard rule, displays on the summit of its richly decorated white marble front a colossal figure of the Archangel in whose honor the stately pile was reared. Some fine pictures by Fra Bartolommeo give interest to San Romano; and San Frediano, built out of the ruins of a deserted ampitheatre, commends itself to Irish sympathies, from its having been raised in honor, as well as bearing the name, of the highly venerated son of an Irish king. In not only spiritual, but also in manual works, did the Irish saint engage; for within this church an immense slab of marble may be seen, which was lifted (as an inscription testifies) by San Frediano and his canons from the quarry where it was dug, and transferred by the same hands to the car destined to draw it to the place where it now stands.

Of the merits, or of the characteristics, of the seven remaining churches of Lucca, it is not for me to tell; since sight-seeing becoming an intolerable toil under the influence of a July sun, I turned away from churches, Lombard or Gothic, or Lombard and Gothic intermixed, from sculptures, from dim frescoes, and from paintings of artists of more or less note, and bent my steps towards the ramparts of the town, to take a look at the works of the great

Artist, whose creations combine all that is lovely and sublime: creations before which those of the greatest Italian masters fade into insignificance.

The Piazza Ducale, through which I passed on my way to the city walls, is a handsome, spacious square, adorned with rows of trees, and derives its name from the adjoining Ducal Palace, before whose unfrequented gate a sentinel was pacing apathetically to and fro. In front of the now deserted building a monument stands, raised to the memory of a Duchess of Lucca, to whom the citizens owed the construction of a splendid acqueduct, which affords at this present day a plentiful supply of water to the inhabitants of the town. Square, palace or monument, however, possess but little power to arrest the stranger's steps under the influence of a July noonday sun, and, passing onwards, I gained in a few minutes the ramparts of the town, from whence there burst upon my view a prospect of which the Lucchese have reason to be proud. How strongly does the durability of nature contrast with the instability of all human glories. Fallen now as Lucca is from its ancient republican wealth, power and dignity—blotted out as now it is from the list of States, and degraded into the rank of a mere provincial town, its amphitheatre of hills is still as beautiful, and towers up as grandly in the air as when, in centuries long gone by, the churches of San Fre-

4

diano and San Michele sprang into existence under the dominion of the Lombards.

Echoing no longer with the clash of arms, with warlike shouts, or with the heavy tread of men-at-arms, the ramparts now are made to serve far different uses from those for which they were originally constructed; for, planted with trees, which overarch a broad and well-kept walk, they now afford a delightful promenade to the Lucchese, especially in the hot summer months. Delicious is the shade, as, emerging from the heat and glare of a July sun, I stand beneath the thick canopy of leaves, through which but two or three intrusive sunbeams here and there can force their way; and peacefully the murmuring sounds from the quiet town fall on my ear, as, in a solitude* unbroken by the sight of any living creature, I slowly stroll along this enduring monument of a sanguinary age, where human blood was shed like water to satisfy the cravings of ambition, the desire for plunder, or the thirst for vengeance.

Very beautiful is the view, on which from time to time I pause to gaze. A soft purple haze rests on the chain of hills, that like a natural rampart encircles the rich vale in which Lucca stands. Here a declivity high and bare, there a verdant slope, ar-

*Italians say that no living creatures, save mad dogs and English people, will voluntarily stir out of doors during the heat of the day in summer.

rests the eye, whilst everywhere the graceful varying outlines of the hills are seen to stand out in bold relief against the deep azure of the sky, and the rich plain glows and sparkles in the bright sunshine. From the walls of Lucca to the Pisan hills upon one side, or on the other to the more distant Appenines, a sea of verdure stretches out, thickly dotted over with villages and the dwellings of the peasantry. Vines, festooned from tree to tree, encircle fields in which the Indian maize has taken the place of the tall, waving, golden wheat, harvested more than a month ago. Art combines with nature to adorn the scene, from the rich green of the irrigated meadows to the lofty arches of the magnificent acqueduct, which, spanning a large portion of the plain, advances in close vicinity to the city walls.

But when the churches and the view from the ramparts have been seen, the stranger, who chances to visit Lucca during the months of July or August, hurries away impatiently from the town; for the heat is oppressively intense, in the full glare of the sun, and even in the shade there prevails a stove-like temperature. At this season of the year no Lucchese noble, or plebeian with independent means, continues in the town. Some go to ruralize in country villas for a while; others, destitute of such possessions, repair to Leghorn or to Viareggio for sea bathing, or to Monte Catini for health or recreation; but, singularly enough, very few frequent the baths to which Lucca gives the distinctive name, although distant but fifteen miles, and possessing in point of coolness and beauty an immeasurable superiority over every other summer retreat in Tuscany.

But if the Lucchese are indifferent to the charms of the Baths of Lucca, the foreigners belonging to that fair-complexioned race denominated "*Inglese*," who have taken up their temporary or permanent abode in Tuscany, show a thorough appreciation of the advantages and attractions of the place. As soon as the hot weather begins, carriages, laden outside with luggage, and filled inside with faces belonging unmistakably to the Anglo-Saxon race, may be seen, day after day, traveling along the road that leads from Florence to these Baths; and so many of these vehicles passed before my view at Monte Catini in the month of June, that the dusty highway, on which my sitting room windows looked, assumed the aspect, in a great degree, of an English thoroughfare. Fully prepared, therefore, as far as society was concerned, to find myself in a miniature England, I leave the broiling town of Lucca, in company with a friend, to spend the autumn months amidst the shade of chestnut-covered hills, in the most beautiful valley of Tuscany.

Almost from the very gate of Lucca through which we pass, the road to the Baths is distinguished by a considerable degree of beauty. Following the course of the Serchio, (a very ill-conducted river, whose propensity for overflowing can with the greatest difficulty be restrained,) we travel along a road, bordered on both sides with festooned vines, towards the rich valley through which the Serchio winds. The closer we approach the hills, which on the north side bound the luxuriant plain, the more attractive becomes the scenery. At a distance of little more than three miles from the town, stands Marlia, a summer palace of the Duke; and in its vicinity may be seen many handsome villas, which, though the property of Lucchese nobles, are, for the consideration of a reasonable amount of *scudi*, quite at the service of such persons as may desire to have them as their summer residences: a condescension of an extremely sensible nature on the part of the proprietors, if, as it is alleged, the hills keep off every cooling breeze, and hosts of musquitoes indulge without pity or remorse their sanguinary appetites. Not far from Marlia, the Serchio is crossed by a sandstone bridge, erected in 1832 to replace its predecessor, which was carried away by one of the rebellious outbreaks of the river thirteen years before. As a protection, probably, against the recurrence of such a catastrophe, the present structure, Ponte a Muriano, as it is called, is adorned with statues of saints of colossal size, which we hope will have the good effect of keeping the turbulent Serchio henceforth in order.

From Muriano to the Baths, the road, still continuing faithful to the left bank of the Serchio, gradually ascends through a fine valley bounded by lofty hills, on whose declivities, midst olives, vines and chestnut trees, a succession of picturesque villages appear. On the summit of a lofty eminence is seen the Convento degli Angeli (Convent of the Angels), founded by the Queen of Etruria, in 1815; but in accordance with the name, which harmonizes well with the aerial situation of the structure, it must be a subject of regret to those of its inhabitants who may have to pant and toil up the steep ascent, on their return from spiritual missions in the world below, that the angelic mode of locomotion, by means of wings, has not been conferred on them.

Hills, mountains, river, chestnuts, olives, vines, villages, farm houses, villas, continue to meet the view as we proceed; but, like objects seen in a kaleidoscope, to which the slightest motion gives variety of aspect, each advancing step we take, though the features of the scene remain the same, presents them in some fresh and ever beautiful combination. Villages bearing the old Roman names, which mark their distance from the Lucchese metropolis, in quick succession we pass by, and near the furthest one of these we see the place where stood, not many years ago, a bridge which the Serchio in one of its fierce bursts of passion, entirely swept away. The little town of Borgo, the emporium of the mountain commerce in silk, hemp and wool, comes soon into view, and close to it is seen an ancient and extremely singular looking bridge, to which, though rightfully bearing the name of *Ponte della Maddalena*, the appellation of *Ponte del Diavolo* (Devil's Bridge), has been popularly assigned. Not wholly undeserved, indeed, is the ill-omened name by which this structure is almost invariably called, since, to the superstitious eye, it well might seem to owe its existence to some impish freak; for, constructed in utter opposition to ordinary rule, its central arch is raised to such a height above the other four that, at its summit, the narrow causeway forms an angle too acute to admit of any carriage crossing it. Thanks to the great altitude, however, as well as to the wide span of the centre arch, the Ponte del Diavolo has borne repeated bursts of the fitful fury of the Serchio for centuries, unscathed.

Shortly after passing Ponte del Diavolo, the Serchio, just previous to turning off into another valley, is joined by the Lima, a tributary mountain stream, by whose side we journey onward. In spite, however, of the very mild and inoffensive aspect of our new friend, which murmurs on musically over its rocky bed, it would seem to partake of the Serchio's turbulent character, for on its banks rise up the towers of an unfinished suspension bridge, intended to replace a bridge of stone which fell a victim to the river's violence in 1836. Still traveling by the Lima, along a road overhung by chestnut trees, and bordered on one side by vines, the first houses of Ponte a Seraglio, the metropolis of the bathing district, soon appears. On the very outskirts of the village rises up *La Maison de la Grande Betragne*, as if to arrest the onward movement of the British traveler by an appeal to his patriotic feelings. A few steps further on, the *Albergo di Londra* advances a similar claim on the cockney's sympathies; and within a few yards' distance "Pagnini's Hotel," written in gigantic characters on the front of a large house directly opposite "Cordon's Store," confirms the English character of the locality. Dashing along at the Italian's favorite frantic pace, through two short narrow streets, we reach the bridge which gives the distinctive name of Ponte a Seraglio to the small cluster of houses that extend for a short distance on either bank of the river.

But, the bridge being gained, our progress was arrested by a military band, that occupied (at the further side of the stream) a small piazza through which we desired to pass. Except for tired travellers, the delay would have been an agreeable one, for the scene had many features which could scarcely fail to be attractive to the stranger's eye. To the right and left, the view is closed in by wooded heights, at whose feet the river runs in a narrow winding valley; and high above the village rise up precipitous hills, clothed with the bright green foliage of the chestnut, amidst which here and there white gleaming villas are seen. Nearer, the view presents the animated scene which life in a fashionable bathing-place always offers in the frequented season of the year. Around the band, whose members seem to do their best to display the full powers of their instruments, is assembled a gay and motley company. Before the doors of three cafes of which the small piazza boasts, are ranged a number of small tables, where lovers of music and ice creams sit and indulge at the same time in their two favorite luxuries. Young ladies with large straw hats, brown, gray or white, underneath which are seen true English faces, exchange greetings with young gentlemen in linen coats, who, in spite of a carefully cultivated moustache or beard in the Italian style, look as much true-born Britons in aspect as they are in language. Here and there a sallow-faced Frenchman, or a fashionable-looking Frenchwoman, may be seen, and occasionally, too, a dark-eyed Italian is visible; but the great bulk of the company, if not exactly English, (for Americans abound,) is composed of persons of at least English origin. On every side the rougher tones of our island tongue overpower the soft musical language of Tuscany; to have closed my eyes on chestnut woods, on the cloudless sky, on houses unmarked by stain or mildew, on signboards with Italian inscriptions, on a group of *vetturini* lounging on the bridge, and to have judged by sounds alone, I should have pronounced myself in England.

First in importance, as well as in magnitude, of the three villages which are comprehended under the name of the Baths of Lucca, Ponte a Seraglio enjoys the distinction of being the head-quarters of the gay world of fashion. Here is the post-office, and here also the Casino, a handsome building devoted to purposes of amusement, where nightly assemblies are held during the fashionable season, in a large room ornamented with mirrors and gilding. Here, under the auspices of royalty, balls take place pretty frequently at stated intervals; but the enjoyment of dancing is by no means confined to such periods, for a piano which the room contains is constantly made to do duty for the orchestra, to whose music young ladies and gentlemen go through their varied evolutions on state ball evenings, when the Grand Duke and Grand Duchess, and the young Archdukes, deign to honor the company with their presence. Adjoining the ball-room is another large apartment, where the natives of England, Germany, France and Italy, can read the varied news of the day, each in his native language. The Casino also contains a billiard-table for such as are partial to that species of recreation; but no gaming-table is seen: for by a very praiseworthy edict of the late

Duke of Lucca, in 1846, gambling, once the opprobrium of the Baths, was strictly prohibited.

The Bagno alla Villa, the second village of the Baths in point of size, consists of two straggling lines of houses, which form an irregular street running along the base of a steep hill that forms one side of a narrow valley through which the Lima flows. Distant about a mile from the Ponte, with which it communicates by a shady road, the scenery of the Villa resembles much the first-mentioned village in general features, though somewhat more confined in character. At both, the view is closed in on every side by lofty chestnut-covered hills, at whose feet a river flows, the brawling voice of which is heard both night and day resounding in the air. While the houses of the Ponte, for the most part, however, overhang the stream, those of the Villa, retreating a short distance from its banks, interpose small gardens between. Essentially different in its general aspect, the Ponte wears a gay, flaunting, dissipated look; while the Villa* has an extremely quiet, retiring aspect, as if it shunned the pomp and flutter of the gay world. Here, indeed, come quiet families, serious families, strict in the performance of their religious duties, and families to whom the vicinity of the English church is far more attractive than that of the Casino. Gaiety, indeed, evidently

* In former times, the character of the Villa may have been somewhat different, as the Duke of Lucca had his residence in this locality.

cannot be made to flourish at the Villa, any more than roses in a sandy desert; for a pretty-looking structure, bearing the inscription of "Teatro" (Theatre) over the door, is silent and deserted, except when the Grand Duke's band, retiring there on practicing days, awakens its dormant echoes. Nor, though it be the head-quarters of the musical corps, is the quiet, serious character of the Villa destroyed by public performances; for while the Ponte a Seraglio has its band days, and the Bagni Caldi, the third number of the family group, is distinguished in a similar manner, no rakish waltz or dissipated polka ever disturbs the philosophic or religious meditations of the inhabitants of the Villa. Music, indeed, is frequently wafted on the air to the recesses of the dwellings, but music it is that could never be guilty of disturbing the mental equilibrium, by an undue vivacity of character; as any one could testify who, like me, had lived for a month within earshot of a guardhouse, where an indefatigable player on the trombone daily exhaled the sorrows of his soul in a series of the most dismal and unearthly tones imaginable.

The Bagni Caldi,* the third, and by much the smallest village of the group, has its comparative inferiority in point of size atoned for by the distinction it enjoys of containing the residence of the Grand Duke. Placed about half-way up the pre-

* Hot baths.

cipitous hill, at the base of which the principal portion of the Ponte extends, the Bagni Caldi affords its inhabitants the advantages of an extensive view and a bracing air. Still, such advantages must be considered to be dearly purchased by persons who have not, like the Grand Duke, carriages and horses constantly at their disposal; for the approach to this exalted post is by a road which, notwithstanding its serpentine course as it winds upwards on its way, taxes the breath and energies to a very considerable degree, especially on a hot summer day. On this account, probably, it happens that, while the Ponte and the Villa each possess numerous large and flourishing-looking hotels, the Bagni Caldi cannot exhibit one; in spite of the attraction of its fine Bath House, where nature, acting the benevolent apothecary's part, serves up a steaming compound of sulphur, iron, lime and magnesia, free of cost — a liberality which the dispensers of the medicated waters do not emulate.

Notwithstanding that the village of the Bagni Caldi would seem from its name to arrogate to itself some peculiar distinction on the score of the temperature of its springs, these latter possess the property of heat in common with four other sources, which are equally employed for baths. The springs of the Bagni Caldi, however, have a higher temperature than any of the rest, for whilst the warmest of these latter only reach to 112 degrees of Fahrenheit, the former rises to 136. The waters of one of the springs are used internally, and are sent to various parts of Italy, it is said authoritatively; but if such is the case, their reputation, as regards drinking purposes, judging from my own observation, must be infinitely greater abroad than it is at home; for I never saw a draught of mineral water taken by any one during my two months' residence at the Baths.

Numerous as were the English families staying at the Baths of Lucca in the summer of 1856, on every side, yet from every quarter, from hotel and lodging-house keepers down to the purveyors of horses and donkeys, I heard many lamentations of the paucity of the number of *Inglese*. There was every reason, indeed, to believe that, in comparison with the advent of the English in former years, the complaint uttered so generally in regard to their scanty numbers, was correct; for in the very height of the fashionable season, I saw many lodging-houses quite shut up, and in others, suits of apartments remained unlet. From what I heard and saw, the Baths of Lucca seemed evidently to be waning in prosperity, so far at least as the foreign element is concerned, that has ministered for many years so very largely to its wealth; for fashion, influenced by increased facilities of traveling, induces its English subjects resident in Italy to pass the hot months of the year by the shores of the lovely lakes of Switzerland. Still, however much the flow of the annual tide of English to the Baths of Lucca may diminish in amount, the English element of population will probably never fail to show itself pretty conspicuously in the place. For, whatever aspirations may exist after a summer abode by the lakes of Leman and Lucerne, these aspirations can only be indulged in, where a large family is concerned, through the medium of a well-filled purse; which is not at the command of that numerous class of English residents in Tuscany, who from economical considerations have become exiles from their native land. So Miss Henrietta, however she may long to wander amongst Alpine heights, and fill her sketch-book with views of snow-crowned mountains and chalet-dotted valleys, must perforce content herself with a summer residence by the Lima's side, and limit her artistic powers to the Devil's Bridge, or villages with red-tiled roofs, wooded heights, old church towers, and hordes of ragged beggars, whilst young Mr. George, the proprietor of a carefully cultivated and promising infantine moustache, who pants for the glory of climbing up Mont Blanc, encountering bears, or hunting chamois, must resign himself to the tamer pleasures which the Casino of the Ponte a Seraglio offers, of billiard-playing and newspaper reading in the morning, dancing, music and flirtation in the evening.

Truly, however, those English residents in Florence are little to be pitied, whom scanty means precludes from seeking a more distant place of summer recreation than the Baths of Lucca. Although compared with Alpine scenery, that of the Appenines is tame, the taste must be fastidious indeed, that would not derive a high degree of gratification from the sight of the winding valleys, hemmed in with lofty and magnificently wooded hills, with which the neighborhood of this beautiful Tuscan watering-place abounds. To such persons as are fond of riding, and can attain to a philosophical indifference in regard to roads — who will not recoil from scrambling up on horseback to peasant villages perched eagle-like on the summits of high declivities, by highways that resemble nothing so much as the dried-up rocky beds of mountain streams, a great variety of grand as well as very beautiful views may be obtained. From the village of Lugliano especially, a village crowning the hill at the foot of which the white houses of a considerable portion of Ponte a Seraglio rise, a very splendid prospect is seen, of glens and valleys, of winding rivers and wooded hills, whose undulating outlines stand out in strong relief against the deep blue sky, of villages clinging to the sides or crowning the summits of bold declivities, over which tower up in grim and solemn grandeur the naked, barren crags, herbless, leafless and lifeless, of the lofty Appenines.

Small as is the quantity of arable land amongst

these hills and glens, the unlabored earth yet affords subsistence to a population almost as dense as that which exists in the rich plains of Tuscany, judging from the number of villages that meet the view. Many are the compensating gifts of nature; and here, where the steepness of the hills offers an almost insurmountable obstacle to the cultivation of grain, a bountiful Providence has clothed their precipitous sides and lofty summits with a tree, which, while it beautifies their aspect, yields to the inhabitants of the district an abundance of nutritious food. What the potato was to the Irish peasant a few years ago, the chestnut is to the dwellers amidst these hills at this present day; and, like the former article of food, should the latter be annihilated by some fell disease, the dread Irish tragedy of 1846 would be re-enacted on a smaller scale amidst these Appenine glens. Stripes of Indian corn and patches of French beans may be seen, indeed, extending along the level ground of the narrow valleys, or growing on the summits of the hills, around the peasant villages, in small garden plots, but the combined produce of these crops, even in the most favorable season, would scarcely afford subsistence to the dense population of those districts for more than a few days.

The chestnut harvest takes place for the most part towards the end of October; but there are trees, however, of an early kind, which commence to shed their fruit some weeks before. Eagerly does the peasant watch the skies in September, for on the character of the weather in that month do his hopes of an abundant harvest in a great degree depend. Rain and sunshine following each other in quick succession, form the kind of weather that is considered to exercise the most favorable influence on the crop; for, without rain, the chestnuts will not swell, and without sunshine they will not ripen as they ought. In general, indeed, September does not disappoint the peasant's wishes in these respects; yet sometimes it proves his enemy, by bringing him the *Libeccio*, the dreaded southwest wind, laden with salt, under whose influence the chestnuts turn quite black, and drop. At such a period, general consternation prevails, Heaven is besieged with prayers to withdraw the blighting blast, and the peasant kneels at the shrine of the Madonna, and with more than his wonted fervor invokes her aid.

The proprietorship of a patch of chestnut forest is a dignity much longed for by the peasant inhabitants of these hills. Few of them, however, comparatively speaking, attain to the position of proprietors; the chestnut woods belonging, for the most part, to members of a higher class, who let them to poor laboring people, on the terms so generally prevalent in Tuscany, of receiving half the produce in the way of rent.

Although chestnuts, both boiled and roasted, are extensively eaten by these mountaineers, the principal portion of the fruit is ground like grain; and from the flour thus obtained, a kind of porridge called *pollenta*, and a cake, termed indifferently *neccio*, *migliaccio* or *castagnacio*, is made, which forms the principal diet of the people throughout the year. This cake, (*neccio*, as it is generally called by the Lucchese), is sweet and pleasant to the taste; but although considered to be exceedingly nutritious, its dyspeptic tendencies are very great, except as regards such persons as have from infancy been accustomed to its use. The manufacture of this *neccio* requires but little time or skill. Mixed with water, the *farina dolce** (as the chestnut flour is termed) forms a dough, which, when kneaded into a cake about two inches thick, is laid sandwich fashion between two small circular flat stones, on the inner side of which dried chestnut leaves are spread. Into the centre of a fire—formed probably of the wood of the chestnut tree—these two flat stones, with the intervening dough, are placed, and through the medium of this primitive stove, a cake is speedily produced; soft, dark in color, and sweet to the taste. In preparation for the manufacture of this *neccio*, large quantities of the leaves of the chestnut tree are collected in the month of September, strung all close together on a cord, and then hung up outside the house to dry. At the end of September,

* Sweet flour.

scarcely a peasant's house is to be seen, that has not one or more pendent rows of chestnut leaves garnishing its front. Other preparations for winter meals are seen also at this period of the year. Underneath the shade of the chestnut trees grow quantities of fungi, which, though bearing to an English eye a most poisonous aspect, are much made use of by the peasantry, when fresh, to form a dish, when dried, to flavor their ordinary kinds of food. Insipid, however, as these fungi are in point of taste, compared to the English mushroom, and indeed almost destitute as they are of savory qualities, they are eagerly sought for by the peasantry in the autumn months, when they appear; and though some are used in their fresh state, the most part are preserved for winter use, by being cut up in pieces and laid out to dry in baskets placed before the door.

Abundant as is the harvest which the chestnut generally yields, and cheap as is the food that it affords, a very considerable number of the population of those hills are annually driven, by the pressure of want, to seek the means of existence elsewhere. When the autumn months set in, groups of hardy peasants may be seen wending their way to Leghorn, to embark for Corsica: where they find employment during the winter, and gain sufficient money to support their families, to whom they return in the latter end of April or beginning of May. The summer past, the succeeding autumn witnesses the scene of the preceding season renewed; and so on in a similar manner year after year.

Strange to the ears of the Tuscan peasants are the tales of Corsican life that these wanderers bring home. The Lucchese women, who are accustomed from their childhood to the hardest toil, working incessantly from morn till night, daily ascending precipitous hills, carrying tremendous loads upon their heads, listen with wonder when their fathers or brothers tell how the Corsican women, for the most part, sit squatted in listless idleness on the ground; and with no less surprise, not unmingled with envy, perhaps, do the home-staying young Giovannis and Guiseppes hear how the Corsican men, scorning all kinds of drudging work, allow their fields to remain untilled, and their spades and hoes to spoil with rust, whilst shouldering their guns they hie off in company to the woods to shoot.

Not alone, however, does Corsica afford a field of employment to these poor mountaineers; scarcely a year passes by that enterprising youths do not leave their native hills to seek their fortunes in England or America, by following for the most part the trade of modelers of plaster figures. Some years ago the profession was a good one, I was told by one of these vagrant artists, who had returned home with a fortune of five thousand dollars from America. "I used often to make," he said, "from nine to ten dollars a day; but now the business is overstocked: the lads of the present day, who take to the same way of earning their bread, don't make half of that amount." This man had two brothers, modelers like himself; one had, like him also, returned enriched from America, the other had married and settled in England. Few, however, of these wandering mountaineers establish themselves in a foreign country, if they should happen to have secured by their exertions a sufficiency of means to enable them to live with the least degree of comfort in their native land. Little attractive to the stranger's eye as are the homes of the peasantry in the neighborhood of the Baths of Lucca, the natives of these hills find a charm in their dark, dirty, furnitureless, smoke-stained interiors, which the snug, clean, comfortable cottages of America or England do not in their ideas possess. With an intense yearning for country and kindred, the wandering modeler generally returns to spend his declining days under the shade of those chestnut trees, beneath which his earliest youth was passed. But sufficient as are for him the pleasures of that rough and rude existence to which he returns, and the shelter of the roof under which he first drew breath —indifferent as he is to unglazed windows and dirt-stained walls, so long as he has the means of indemnifying himself for years of toil by lounging about with a pipe in his mouth in listless idleness, far different is it with the American or English wife whom he brings with him to his native land.

"Poor creatures! it is a terrible life for such as them," said an Italian woman, speaking on the subject, to me. "I knew two; one died of a broken heart, the other, at the end of two months, left her husband, and went into service in an English family. Poor things, it wasn't to be wondered at, certainly. They had never been accustomed, like our peasant women, from their youth to climb up steep mountain tracks, or to live upon chestnut or maize. Little did they think, when they heard of the blue skies of Italy, of the kind of hard and comfortless life that the peasants amongst these mountains lead; they wanted meat to eat and tea to drink, and how were they to be had miles away from any place where such things are sold?"

Since the annexation of the Duchy of Lucca to that of Tuscany, the Baths of Lucca have become the favorite residence of the Grand Duke Leopold and his family, during the summer months. In this respect the Tuscan ruler followed the example of the Lucchese Prince, who invariably honored the Baths with his presence at a similar period of the year. Nothing can be more simple than the habits of the whole Grand Ducal family whilst ruralizing here. Difficult indeed it was to realize at times that the riding party of seven or eight, frequently to be met with, could aspire to the possession of regal dignity;

so very homely in style and dress did the whole group appear. Very stout in person, and past the prime of life, the Grand Duchess, on such occasions, was to be seen mounted on a somewhat diminutive horse, arrayed in a riding habit of some light yellow stuff, and wearing a large brown straw hat of a mushroom shape upon her head. In his plain black coat and white beaver hat, the chief member of the party, the Grand Duke Leopold, an elderly man, with a gray moustache, exhibited little of a princely air; whilst the young Archduke, in his linen tunic, and the little Archduchess, in a common Manchester print, were far from tending to increase the aristocratic aspect of the party.

If affability of demeanor in public could win affection, Leopold and his family would enjoy unbounded popularity at the Baths of Lucca; for not only do they most courteously return all salutations proffered, but they take the initiative in this respect in most instances, and the passing stranger is almost overwhelmed by the task of having to return a volley of royal inclinations. In spite, however, of this condescension on the part of the reigning family, Leopold and his rule are most thoroughly detested by the Lucchese people, in consequence of the great increase of taxation that the country has had to bear since its annexation to the Grand Duchy of Tuscany. Most opprobrious are the terms I have heard applied to him by the peasantry in conversation. "He grinds us down to the ground," says one: "He takes the piece out of our children's mouths," says another: "The old miser! he has lots of treasure by him," exclaims a third: and a fourth has gravely assured me that the Grand Duke, fearing that he will loose his throne, has sent whole sackfuls of gold to California, whither he is to follow it on the occasion of the next revolution in Tuscany. "Oh! that we had Carlo Ludovico back again," exclaimed all, with one consent: "he did not oppress us or rob us; he loved the English too, and the poor had always a kind friend in him. It was a black day for this country when it passed from the rule of Carlo Ludovico into that of Leopold of Tuscany."

This Carlo Ludovico was the last Duke of Lucca, the last bearer of the title; for, in conformity with the treaty of Vienna, he was obliged to yield up the Lucchese territory to the Grand Duke of Tuscany, on succeeding, by the death of the Empress Maria Louisa, to the Duchies of Parma and Piacenza. Though the impartial historian will be able to say little in his praise, his character resembling that of the "merry monarch" of England, yet Carlo Ludovico, like many a scapegrace in every grade of life, seems to have possessed a certain good humor and a certain affability of manner, which obtained for him a considerable degree of popularity, notwithstanding the worthlessness of his character. At least this was the case amongst the peasantry around the Baths of Lucca; and I subjoin an anecdote of Carlo Ludovico that was told me by one of his warm admirers:

"Ah! Carlo Ludovico was another sort of man from that gray-muzzled tyrant we have now over us," began my informant. "He had his faults, to be sure—who has them not?—but he was not the man to grind down the poor with taxes, or to send spies about to catch up and report every hasty or evil word that any man, or any woman either, might say against him, as does the present prince, who for our sins has been put to reign over us. A better chance has the robber, or even the murderer, of escaping on conviction from the doom of a heavy punishment, than has that man or woman who has been found guilty of saying a word against the Grand Duke or his family. Very different was it with Carlo Ludovico, even if he heard with his own ears a disparaging remark about him; and that often might readily occur, for the Duke, just from the love of a bit of frolic, as it were, was accustomed to go about in the dress of a *contadino* among the people: and to show you now what kind of a man he was, I will tell you a story about him.

"Well, one fine day, it happened that Carlo Ludovico, disguised in a countryman's dress, having gone some little distance into the country, being somewhat tired on his road home, asked a *baroccino*,* who was passing in his *baroccio*, to take him a bit of the way to Lucca. 'Willingly,' said the *baroccino*; and at the word up got the Duke beside him. Well, of course, they began to talk, and the *baroccino*, never dreaming it was any one but a mere *contadino* he had to deal with, from this and that, came to mention the name of Carlo Ludovico.

"'Well, what of him?' asked the Duke, quickly. 'What do you think of Carlo Ludovico and his government?'

"'Oh, the government is not a bad one, surely, for us country people, at least,' returned the *baroccino*, 'since it don't tax us hardly; and as for Carlo Ludovico, I have no fault to find with him, except that he lets himself be guided and governed by the ladies.'

"'But, poor man,' said the Duke, smiling, 'that is not a great crime after all, for there is many a good and wise man in the world that fares no better than Carlo Ludovico in this particular;' and the Duke went on talking quite pleasantly and good-humoredly, without the least show of anger, till coming to the gates of Lucca he got out of the *baroccio* and walked on towards his palace: not, however, without being recognized in passing by one of the guards on duty at the gate.

* The driver of a light kind of rude coutry conveyance called a baroccio.

"'You have made a fortune, I suppose, this morning?' said the guard, as he examined the *baroccino's* cart.*

"'What do you mean by that?' rejoined the *baroccino*.

"'Why, you have had a fine paying passenger this morning,' said the guard.

"'You jest,' said the *baroccino;* 'I had none but that poor *contadino*, who just now got down—of whom I did not ask a *soldo* by way of payment.'

"'Poor contadino, indeed!' said the guard, laughing; 'I tell you what, my good fellow, he is far richer than either you or I will ever be, no matter how well we may prosper in the world, for I swear, as I am a living man, that was Carlo Ludovico, the Duke, you had beside you.'

"'The Duke!' exclaimed the *baroccino*, aghast. 'Oh, *sanctissima Vergine*, what have I done? What have I said? I am a lost and a ruined man!' and calling on the saints in heaven to help him, he rushed as fast as his legs would carry him after the Duke, whom he soon overtook.

"'Pardon, your Excellency, pardon!' exclaimed the *baroccino*, throwing himself down on his knees before the Duke.

"'Pardon for what?' asked Carlo Ludovico.

* In consequence of a tax on provisions being generally levied in the towns of Italy, all vehicles entering the gates of a walled city are liable, and often subjected, to a search.

"'For what I said about your Excellency and the ladies,' returned the *baroccino*, trembling, and quite white in the face with fear.

"'Oh, if that is all you ask pardon for, it is given at once,' said the Duke, smiling; 'there are not ten men in a hundred that escape petticoat government, and why should I be angry at being told the general fate was mine. There, set your mind at rest, and go your way,' continued the Duke, and taking a couple of *scudi* out of his pocket, he gave them to the *baroccino* as payment for the drive, and went away quickly, leaving the poor man half out of his mind with joy."

With August terminated the gay season of the Baths of Lucca, for on the advent of September, balls became numbered amongst the things that were, and public band days undergo a little more tardily a similar fate. With the first week of September, all the symptoms of a general break-up of the society at the Baths were visible, and every day well laden traveling carriages might be seen starting from the doors of the numerous lodging houses of the Baths of Lucca. The lines of closed shutters, also, which the hotels began to exhibit, were also strongly expressive of the ebbing tide of population, and the *vetturino* lounging on the bridge invariably asked the passer-by if the signor or the signora, as the case might be, was in want of a carriage for Lucca.

In truth, judging from the experience of 1856, the climate strongly enjoined a change of residence as desirable. With September came thunder-storms, night after night and day after day, for a considerable period. Summer, instead of dying out, as elsewhere, by slow degrees, seemed to expire instantaneously: the air, from having been intensely warm in August, grew damp and chilly. The skies, from having been for week after week unspotted with a cloud, showed only here and there small islands of blue amidst billowy masses of leaden-colored vapor. A yellow hue began to steal over the bright green foliage of the chestnut trees, whose fruit rapidly increased in size under the favoring influences of the moisture. Depressing to the spirits as it always is to look on gloomy rain-charged clouds, in no country in the world, perhaps, can chill, damp, showery weather exercise a more subduing influence than in Italy. In England, the domestic sun that shines upon us from our hearths, the heat and light that come streaming to us from the bright coal fire, mitigate in a great degree the unhappiness of our lot in being doomed for the most part of the year to rainy, gloomy weather. But in Italy, under similar circumstances, when the sun is hid behind masses of leaden clouds, from which the rain pours down with little intermission, perhaps for not only successive days, but weeks together, the compensating influences of the English hearth are scarcely to be found. In the room which looked so pleasant in bright sunny weather, with its green *jalousies*, white muslin curtains, and smooth, uncarpeted floor, no fire-place exists most probably; or if by chance it does, the aspirer after English comforts will be half choked and blinded by the smoke, which, refusing obstinately to ascend the chimney, diffuses itself in a dense cloud through every corner of the room. The foot, as it treads on the cold, polished tiles, misses the soft warm carpet of England. Into the open terrace the rain comes beating, and the chill, damp air without, enters in currents through the many apertures of the ill-fitting doors and windows. Wise is it in English visitors to leave the Baths of Lucca ere September rains begin, for an English climate requires English comforts, such as are there unattainable.

Summer, however, though it had died out apparently in Lucca during the month of September, had a much longer life in other parts of Tuscany; for in Leghorn, where I passed the beginning of the month of October, the weather was quite summer-like in character, and enjoyable beyond description.

# CHAPTER IV.

## A PISAN CARNIVAL.

THERE are some ideas so essentially incongruous in their nature, that one involuntarily recoils from them when they are presented together to the mind: such was the grim veiled skeleton associated in days of yore in Egypt with mad revelry and luxurious feasts: such, too, would prove the allied images of a wedding procession and a hearse, or a dance performed over the graves of the mouldering dead; and but little less antagonistic than such ideas seem to the mind, is the connection of Pisa with carnival mirth and revellings, to any one who has made a personal acquaintance with that town.

For Pisa wears at this present day an air of melancholy beyond the power of words to describe; and did the same principle still prevail, which assigned in bygone years to Italian towns epithets illustrative of the several qualities for which they were renowned; as Lucca was termed "The Industrious;" Florence, "The Beautiful;" and Genoa, "The Superb;" even so the propriety of now appending the designation of "The Mournful" to the name of Pisa, would be beyond dispute.

The quiet of the country exercises a soothing influence over the feelings; there, the ear asks not for more than the sound of rippling water, or of rustling foliage, and the eye rests satisfied with such images of animated life as browsing cattle and the flight of birds supply: but the quiet of a town, and the absence there of sights and sounds indicative of the existence of human energy and activity, are depressing to the spirits in a very eminent degree. Such is the case with Pisa, whose deserted squares, untrodden courts and streets, which, with two or three exceptions, never echo to the sound of carriage-wheels and the tread of horses, imbue the mind and fancy with thoughts and images of an intensely gloomy hue. Passing along the silent streets, where a dark-robed priest or a wandering beggar alone is found, one might very readily entertain the thought that the houses, which rise up high and with solemn aspect on either side, have only ghosts and spiders for their inhabitants.

The youth of ten transformed into the greybeard of fourscore, supplies an apt illustration of the difference that exists between the Pisa of the present and the Pisa of mediæval days. A time there was when Pisa—powerful, industrious, rich, renowned—was a town in something more than name; when along the now deserted quays, between which the Arno runs, the busy tide of life poured on from morn till night; when the now silent streets resounded with the din of trade; when the grass-grown piazza re-echoed with the war-steed's tread, and from the marble palaces along the river's side issued the mail-clad warriors and the men-at-arms, whose prowess won for Pisa an extended sway and a widely known and honored name.

The mutability of human fate is well exemplified in the change which has come over Pisa during the course of years. In the Piazza dei' Cavalieri, from which the Knights of San Stefano sallied forth with plume and sword and blast of trumpet to fight the enemies of the Cross, not a sound is heard, save the step of some black-clad priest, or the strolling beggar's wail for alms, addressed to the exploring stranger. The far-famed Leaning Tower, in company with the noble Cathedral and Baptistry, rise up in lonely grandeur out of a grassy waste. One ancient palace, whose richly ornamented front testifies to its pristine dignity, has become the Caffe dell' Ussero; and in the ancient residence of the Gambacorti family—whose walls once echoed with the sound of mirth and music, whose mirrors once reflected back the forms of the fair and the highly born—clerks sit and write, discourse of tariffs, duties, and such matters as come within the province of the custom-house officials of the Grand Duke of Tuscany.

Notwithstanding the antiquity of the greater portion of the buildings of Pisa, they present in general, to an English eye, a freshness of aspect which seems inconsistent with their venerable years. In the clear air of an Italian sky, marble and stone, undefiled by smoke and unstained by damp, change little in color during the course of centuries. Unlike what occurs in our humid clime, no mildew vegetation creeps up the walls, no sooty impurities, deepening from year to year, mark with their disfiguring trail the progress of time. Yet, reasoning from a six weeks' experience of Pisa during the winter months, the absence of all external symptoms of humidity on the buildings, appears somewhat unaccountable; for during at least a month of that period mentioned, the rain fell with a violence and constancy such as I had never previously witnessed. The first sound that generally greeted my ears on waking, was the pattering of rain drops against my window, or on the flags below; and if, perhaps, in the afternoon, a cessation of a couple of hours occurred, yet at the approach of night the rain, as if it had recruited its energies by that short rest, began once more to fall with additional vehemence. For days together, the sole testimony the sun vouchsafed to the Pisans of his continued existence, was the regular alternation of light and darkness.

Under the influence of the leaden sky and the murky clouds of that wet and gloomy season, the wonted melancholy deserted aspect of Pisa became deepened in a tenfold degree. The wet pavements were trodden but by very few who were not forced to leave the shelter of their houses by some affair of pressing necessity. The north side of the Arno — the usual lounge of the idler in the afternoon — exhibited only here and there, at the favorite hour, a green umbrella, covering a shaven face surmounted with a three-cornered hat, or a melodramatic-looking Pisan gentleman shrouded in the folds of a voluminous cloak. Few and far between, too, were the beggars (usually so abounding) that were to be seen. In contrast with the silence and deadness of the streets that skirted the Arno's either edge, that river — swollen by the long-continued rain— roared madly, furiously along, bearing on its muddy surface logs of wood, bundles of hay or straw, and other memorials of the depredations it was committing in the country through which it passed. The weather was very bad, the Pisans owned, in reference to my not particulary complimentary remarks on the character of their winter clime; but while they admitted this, they hastened to assure me, with a patriotism truly commendable, that the season was *stravagante*—implying, by this term, that the weather had departed from the usual meritorious tenor of its ways: an assurance somewhat difficult to believe, when it came to my knowledge that only the year before a terrific inundation of the Arno had occurred, by which life, as well as a vast amount of property, had been destroyed.

If the weather had been the bitterest enemy of the Pisans, it could not have showed its malice more than by selecting this particular time for indulging in a *stravaganza;* as it was the period between Christmas and Lent — a period varying in length every year—which custom has for many centuries in Italy dedicated especially to pleasure. In this season of which I speak—viz., the winter of 1856—the interval between Christmas and Easter was unusually short; and instead of having, as sometimes happens, a two months' licensed season for enjoyment, the Pisans were obliged to condense their amusements into the narrow compass of five weeks — a circumstance doubtless annoying in itself, but more particularly so when it is taken into consideration that in these five weeks they had to indemnify themselves for the absence of their wonted carnival pleasures during a period of eight years.

This privation owed its origin, and also its continuance for the period mentioned, to causes of a political nature. In the winters of 1848 and 1849, the populace of the Tuscan towns were too busily engaged in making public demonstrations in favor of the republican cause, in thinking of and discussing political events, to play the merry-andrew in mask and domino. In the five succeeding years, the presence of the detested Austrians, with whom Leopold, on his restoration to power, had filled the Tuscan towns—combined with a prohibition issued against the use of masks—effectually checked all public demonstrations of carnival mirth. In 1855, however, reassured by the pacific aspect of affairs, the Grand Duke of Tuscany dismissed his troops, and this measure being followed by the revocation of the edict against masks, the Pisans, as well as the other inhabitants of the Tuscan towns, prepared to greet the next arrival of the festive season with the warmth and cordiality due to the return of a much-regretted and well-loved friend.

Under these circumstances, therefore, it may readily be imagined with what sensations of despair the Pisans looked up to their clouded skies, from which the rain fell for many weeks, with periods of but short intermission. Making the most, however, of the few hours of sunshine or of fair weather they might happen to enjoy, a motley assemblage of old and young, of rich and poor, might be seen on an occasional January afternoon, extending along the street which skirts the Arno on its northern side, shouting, laughing, talking, and cheering the oddly-dressed figures that passed before their view. At first, the masks were few in number; but, as time wore on, and as the weather towards the end of the month began to grow fine, the maskers became more numerous, until at length, in the week that preceded Lent, they increased to quite a throng. A very curious sight it was for a stranger to look down, as I did, from my window, on that crowd—to watch the eager, excited faces, to hear the shouts, and to see the antics of a people intoxicated (as it were) with joy. Nor did the amusement, often repeated as it was, seem in the least degree to pall upon the taste; on the contrary, the furor for masking, and for seeing masks, appeared daily to increase. The tradesman left his shop, the artizan his loom, the straw-platter threw her work aside, the wrinkled grand-dame put her distaff by, and all, with one accord, from every street and back lane of the town, hurried off each afternoon to take their accustomed share, either as spectators or actors, in the strange scene enacted by the river's side.

It would be difficult to say what style of dress, amongst the maskers, was the favorite or the prevailing one, so varied were the garbs that met the view. Here, a black domino might be seen, contrasting there with the motley array of a circus clown; whilst some wore gigantic masks, displaying noses of prodigious length, or faces looking four different ways; others shrouded their features from the public gaze by a simple covering of black silk, through two apertures in which gleamed forth a pair of bright, laughing eyes. Here, might be seen a cavalier, with a high cocked-hat, long flowing curls, and fashion of dress appertaining to the olden time, conducting, with an infinity of bows, a dame decked forth in a corresponding style, moving along with a suspiciously masculine stride. Now, came dancing, springing by, a bevy of masked girls dressed in white, with fluttering ribbons and flowers in their hair; and anon, a set of warriors, with polished cuirasses and visors down, drove (somewhat incongruously) slowly by. As the figures in the kaleidoscope vary with every shake, so at every moment the scene was changed. Clowns and dominos—blue, black, green, yellow, red—knights and dancing girls, prodigious noses, and miraculous heads—appeared and reappeared in new combinations each successive moment; whilst the scene was further varied by a line of carriages of every degree of dignity, from the smart equipage of a Pisan noble to the dingy vehicle called into requisition for the occasion from the neighboring stand.

Equally great as the variety of scene was the variety of sound: with the roar of the muddy river, swollen by the recent heavy rains, were blended the tramp of horses, the roll of wheels, and the tones of the human voice, from the shrill treble of the enraptured child, to the deep accents of the scarcely less delighted man; high in the air rose the masker's piercing trill, a sound seemingly impracticable for any but Italian throats or lips to give, and which, amidst the prevailing laughter, shouts and cheers, was ever distinguishable. How voices lasted as they did, when day after day their powers were taxed to such an extreme degree, appeared to me somewhat remarkable. The long continued duration of the excitement was a source to me also of some little wonder; for amongst the natives of the British isles a long protracted pastime, such as the carnival was, would, before half its course was run, have died out certainly of weariness and satiety. Here, on the contrary, to the very last moment of the carnival's existence, the evidences of popular enjoyment went on daily increasing. To the colder, graver temperament of northern climes, the huge draughts of pleasure that can be swallowed by the impulsive, excitable natures living under southern skies must prove a subject of surprise; and to some, perhaps, may assume the aspect of a privilege to be envied.

To the masquerade by day, in the public streets of Pisa, succeeded masquerades at night, in the theatre or in private houses. Not only had the rich and noble their masked balls, but the shopkeeper, and even the servant, had theirs also; and often the tardy light of a January morning dawned upon the unfinished festivities. Private theatricals were also indulged in to a considerable extent, not only by the upper, but by the middle classes of the community. Two pretty young girls whom I knew, daughters of a hotel-keeper in the town, displayed considerable proficiency in this accomplishment; and a man-servant in the house where I was staying, who enacted in the morning the housemaid's part of sweeping, dusting and cleaning, appeared in the evening, on some private stage, in the character of an actor. Another carnival amusement deserves also to be mentioned. From the hour of six o'clock in the evening, till late at night, the streets were traversed, towards the end of the festive season, with bands of masqueraders; men and women, who, disguised in fancy dress, or simple domino, rushed into their friends' houses, there to frisk about, to laugh, to utter witticisms in feigned voices for a few minutes, and then to vanish as suddenly as they had entered. One scene of this description, which fell under my notice, was about the very oddest and most curious sight I ever witnessed.

On previous occasions, the glories of the carnival came to the culminating point on the two last days of its existence; for not only was the most expensive and striking style of array reserved for this period, but a new amusement was introduced to vary the aspect of the daily scene. In former times, an amicable warfare, carried on between the several occupants of the carriages that passed each other in line, had whitened the pavement of the Lung' Arno with a carnival missile termed *confetti*, in form like comfits, but composed of lime instead of sugar.

This year, however, to the disappointment of the Pisans in general, and to the despair of the *confetti* manufacturers in particular, the customary warfare, both in lime and sugar comfits, was prohibited, under pain of heavy penalties, duly declared by means of notices posted everywhere throughout the town. That this prohibition emanated from some abstruse political motive was generally believed; but it was quite beyond the power of ordinary intellects to comprehend how, when the other carnival weapon of flowers was tacitly permitted to be used, treason and danger to the State was more likely to lurk in the interchange of *confetti* and bonbons than in a warfare carried on by volleys of violets, snowdrops or camelias.

However unreasonable the prohibition might seem to the Pisans, they were too well drilled into obedience not to conduct themselves in conformity with the Government decree. At least such was generally the case; for there were to be found a few bold spirits, belonging to the upper classes of society, who dared to act in defiance of the new-made law! Short-lived, however, was the triumph that these rebels enjoyed. One, whose spotless and well-fitting white kid gloves and boots of varnished leather formed a striking contrast with the grotesque and gigantic head he wore, and the donkey he bestrode, had not half emptied his pockets of the comfits with which they had been filled, before he was favored with some not particularly acceptable attentions on the part of the police. A similar fate awaited a party of gorgeously dressed Greeks, detected in the crime of discharging from their carriage a volley of comfits at some passing friends. Unpleasant, however, as such incidents doubtless were to the parties immediately concerned, they did not seem to cast any cloud upon the public mirth, for in default of the proscribed amunition, a smart fire of bouquets was kept up between carriage and carriage; giving rise to much excitement, and to no small danger to little boys, who scrambled amongst the feet of horses to earn a trifle by selling to the eager combatants such bouquets as, having missed their aim, had fallen upon the ground. The commodity being somewhat limited in amount, the traffic was brisk, high prices were obtained; and many a bouquet was probably sold and re-sold a dozen of times.

Amidst evidences of unabated enjoyment, the sun went down upon the last day of the carnival. Domino still saluted domino with a laugh and a shout, clowns still danced and sung, harlequin still flourished his wooden sword, Punch still sported his tremendous nose, when, as the darkness of the evening cast a veil over the scene, the whole line of the Lung' Arno became dotted over with minute points of light, emanating from wax tapers which the occupants of the carriages held in their hands; and which they as zealously strove to guard from extinction, as they endeavored to extinguish those that their neighbors held. *Senza moccolo** was the exulting cry that awaited the victims of a successful blast, and many a *senza moccolo* rose upwards on the air. Long after night had fairly set in, the gleaming lights were visible all along the river's side, while carriage still followed carriage in two lines, and tapers were extinguished, lit and re-extinguished innumerable times. It seemed as if the actors in the scene would never tire: nor was it, indeed, from any sensation of weariness that the noisy throng at length dispersed, for few were there, at least of its more youthful portion, both rich and poor, noble and plebeian, that did not dance out the last hours of the expiring festival.

With the first day of Lent, the town of Pisa resumed its ordinary aspect of dulness, solitude and dejection. In the morning, indeed, the interior of the churches offered to the eye a somewhat animated spectacle, from the number of persons of every degree who flocked thither to receive the mark of the penitential ashes on their head; and no wonder, indeed, so many should be eager to perform this act of humiliation, since, as an Italian lady told me, who had herself conformed to the requirements of the church in this particular, that not only the fol-

* Without light.

lies, but the misdeeds of carnival times, were in a great degree atoned for by this means. But after the transient effervescence attending on this ceremonial was at an end—when every professing Catholic had complied with the requisitions of his faith, Pisa sank back into its old listless and stagnant state again. The Lung' Arno, so recently the scene of an ever-varying comedy, so recently crowded with a noisy, exulting throng, now echoed only with the whining voices of the importunate beggars, who pursued the few chance passers-by with an urgent cry for alms. In place of the merry-maker's motley garb, whose brilliant colors had flashed before the eye—in place of the joyous laugh and shout that had filled the air not many hours ago—I saw the mendicant's squalid form, the cripple's distorted frame, and while the blind rolled their sightless eyes, and the maimed thrust forth their mutilated limbs, and the widow pointed to her corpse-like child, I heard repeated, with the same professional wail, by old and young, "*Dademi qualche cosa, per l'amor di Dio, signorina; un quattrino, ho tanto fame,*"* and so on, in slightly varying terms, over and over, continually.

If, to those who know Pisa but by repute, that city and its wonderful Leaning Tower are indissolubly connected in the mind; to those who have en-

* "Give me something for the love of God, lady; a farthing, I am so very hungry."

joyed, as I did, an intimate personal acquaintance with that town for several weeks, Pisa and beggars will be ideas inseparably associated together ever afterwards.

## CHAPTER V.

### FLORENTINE SCENES AND AMUSEMENTS.

THE Florentines seem quite as proud and as fond of their city as are the Parisians of theirs. Praise Florence to an inhabitant of that town, and he will smile and look quite flattered, as if what had been said was a compliment to himself; but venture even in the gentlest manner to hint at some defect, and you will see his brow contract, and find out shortly that the imputation of bad taste is fixed on you irrevocably, in his opinion.

For many ages the epithet of "The Beautiful" has been affixed to the town; and certainly, as far as its situation is concerned, no one for a moment can dispute the correctness of the term. Placed at the upper extremity of the fertile valley through which the Arno flows, it is commanded by the Appenines, whose lofty peaks, which for a considerable portion of the year are crowned with snow, tower above ranges of undulating hills of varying form, all bright with verdure, all studded over with peasant dwellings, villages, and with villas, which peer forth brightly from out a luxuriant growth of vines and olive trees. From the heights of Bellosguardo, or from the still more elevated site of Fiesole, a view is beheld which cannot fail to make an indelible impression on the memory. Below—hushed in that solemn silence, with which distance ever invests the busiest scene of human toil and life — lies Florence, crowned with its vast cathedral dome, the pride and wonder of a former age. From the amphitheatre of verdant hills, by which the city is on most sides girt, the eye turns to linger on that rich vale through which the Arno winds onward to the sea. Here, heights rising above heights; there mountains marking their outlines on the bright blue sky; with steep declivities or gentle slopes, melting down by slow gradations into a far-stretching plain of exuberant fertility — present a picture — or rather a series of pictures—from which the eye turns reluctantly away.

Though the greatness and glory of Florence have, like the renown of Pisa, passed away, it is far from exhibiting the mournful aspect which characterizes its former rival in the present day. Life does not seem to stagnate in Florence as it does in Pisa; its streets being, for the most part, neither silent nor solitary. The priest and the beggar, who appear in

Pisa on ordinary occasions to form the principal portion of the population of the town, become, in Florence, but inconsiderable items, as regards numbers, in the passing throng. While Pisa seems to brood over the remembrance of its former greatness, Florence, as if forgetful of its bygone glories, welcomes the stranger with a look of cheerfulness, and even gaiety: and that, too, in despite of the grim dark palaces, with their prison-like windows, that flank the street, and which testify to those times of insecurity and turbulence that have passed away—when Guelph and Ghibelline contended together in the streets, and when the air was rent by the cry of opposing factions.

The streets of Florence in those bygone days must have worn an aspect widely different from that they exhibit now, owing to the essential difference that exists in point of manners, of modes of life, and of customs, between the past and present. Under the deep broad cornice, projecting from the roof of the merchant noble's fortress-palace, dependants no longer lounge upon the bench of stone that runs along the basement story of the building. Through those large iron rings, which hang pendent at intervals from the wall, the bridles of waiting horses or samples of merchandise are no longer drawn; nor do they any longer serve the part of torch-holders on festive occasions. No longer do their inner courts re-echo with the heavy tread of mail-clad men, nor do their arcades resound with the hum of trade; for now no merchant comes there to confer with his brother merchant on commercial business; nor do the young and old repair thither to buy the rich products of the East or of Florentine looms—spices, gems, porcelain, perfumes, wrought ivory cabinets, brocades, and gorgeous tissues. Neither do the streets display the figure of the grim man-at-arms or of the mail-clad knight mounted on his war steed, and ever prepared for combat.

In contrast with the scene such images suggest is the one presented by the principal streets of Florence at the present day. Let us take one of them—that which runs, for instance, from the Cathedral to the Piazza del Gran Duca, and remark the objects it presents to notice. On either hand are shops of every description, into whose windows sundry passers-by gaze—some with eager interest, and some with listless curiosity. Here approach two dark-eyed Florentine ladies, dressed out for public admiration in the last extravagance of Parisian fashion; the most delicate of Tulle veils float before their faces, for they use a veil to enhance, and not to conceal, the merit of their features. Here comes the young Florentine gentleman, with delicate-colored kid gloves, French boots, glossy hat, and well-trimmed and well-arranged moustache and whiskers. In passing, he stares at the Florentine belles in a way that would be considered rude in England, but is merely received as a welcome tribute to their charms by the gratified ladies. Here comes a sallow priest, with shaven face, with long black robe descending to his feet, with buckles in his shoes, and a triangular cocked hat upon his head. Not far behind him follows a capuchin friar, clad in a dark brown cloak with falling hood, which, on an emergency, can be drawn over his shaven crown; from the cord tied round his waist, hangs a rosary, and his bare feet are shod with sandals. Moody is his face, dim his eye, and uncleanly his aspect: let us turn away from him, for he is not an agreeable object to contemplate.

Far otherwise is that well-looking, dark-eyed, sunburnt peasant woman, wearing a hat, the broad and limp rim of which goes flapping about with her every movement, and who, to judge from the basket hanging on her arm, has visited town with the object of making some purchases. Next comes into view the very impersonification of an Italian brigand, a middle-aged, dark, fierce, gloomy-looking man, enshrouded in the folds of a voluminous cloak, one end of which has been flung across his left shoulder, whilst his hat is pressed so low down on his head as nearly to conceal his frowning forehead. Does not a stiletto seem to be a natural accomplishment to that form and face, suggestive as they are of tales of blood and vengeance? But let him pass by without further notice, and fix your gaze on that strange and startling procession that is approaching: onward it comes, an assemblage of frightful-looking figures, each clad from head to foot in a loose robe of black, with eyes that stare out grimly through two apertures in the black silk hooded mask that conceals their features. Goblins they might be thought; imps of iniquity, ready for any deed of darkness. But far different, indeed, is their character, and of a very different nature, too, is the act which they are now performing from those of which their appearance is suggestive; and as they come on rapidly, bearing a litter aloft between them, the carriages and the pedestrians turn aside to make way for them; and not a man whom they pass by or meet, but raises or touches his hat reverentially to them as they speed on their charitable mission; for they are the Brothers of the Misercordia (Mercy), conveying a sick man to the hospital. All hail to ye, brothers! I also touch my hat to you, in spirit.

From the aspect presented by the streets of Florence let us turn to that presented by its pleasure-grounds, and take a view of life in the form in which it is there offered to our notice. Adjoining the magnificent palace of the Grand Duke of Tuscany are the Boboli gardens, which are thrown open on certain days to the public. Let us select Sunday for the day of our visit there, as otherwise we shall see few but nursery-maids and children. Following in the train of a joyous throng, bent upon obtaining a transient taste of rural enjoyment on this their great day of recreation, we pass by the front of the palace to a high arch, through which the gardens are entered. Along the walk which skirts the base of a precipitous hill, we follow on in the track of the greatest portion of the throng that has preceded us; and at length quitting the broad gravel way and the crowd, we turn into a side walk, where we find ourselves in a long regular arcade of overarching boughs, resembliug a continuous arbor, into which the sun, in its summer noonday might, can never penetrate further than to shed a twilight glimmer through the interior. The arcade terminates in a broad avenue, at either side of which rise up massive walls of verdure, serving as a background for numerous statues. From the summit of a steep hill, up which the avenue runs in a straight line, a fine view of the surrounding country rewards the toiling pilgrim in search of the picturesque and beautiful; but the ascent is somewhat too steep and lengthened for a warm and fine day like this, when the sun—although it has not a long journey to make to attain the horizon—still shines with warmth and power. Much pleasanter it is to descend to the very foot of the hill, where a fountain diffuses around a sense of coolness and freshness; and where arbors and shady seats offer a pleasant retreat to the tired or heated wanderer. Here, for a short time, let us sit down and enjoy the scene before us. A right pleasant seat it is, with the sound of falling water, and the song of birds, and the voices of merry children, and of men and women, blending all together and falling on the ear harmoniously, whilst the eye dwells on walls of verdure, on gleams of quivering sunlight beneath overarching boughs, on sparkling water, on vases, shrubs and flowers, and on marble statues, contrasting with the changing, shifting forms of animated life we see around us.

Pleasant, however, as are the Boboli gardens in the hot days of summer, and proud of them as are the Florentines, they are left almost entirely to the occupation of the working classes of the town on the two days of the week on which alone they are thrown open to the public. The servant in her cap, the humble tradeswoman with a red or blue handkerchief tied round her head, the artizan in his holiday dress, the soldier off duty, and the families of venders of pork, cheese, beer and maccaroni in back streets; these, and such as these—petty shopkeepers, hucksters, mechanics—in fact, persons belonging to the humbler classes of society, constitute the throng that may be seen strolling about in the Boboli gardens.

Very different is the case in regard to the Cascine, another Florentine pleasure-ground, which takes its name from an adjoining dairy farm belonging to the Grand Duke. Lying outside the walls of the town, and affording drives of considerable extent, these Cascine (the Hyde Park of Florence) are the favorite resort of the native and foreign fashionable classes of the town. On a fine summer's afternoon, mingling with the dark-eyed and dark-complexioned Italian throng, may be seen numbers of English and Americans, easy of recognition amidst the mass, not only by their air and bearing, but by their fairer skins and lighter hair; and the frequency with which faces of the Anglo-Saxon type present themselves to view, testifies to the very large colonies of that race to be found within the walls of Florence.

The Cascine consist of a narrow strip of well-wooded level land, extending parallel to the river for about a mile and a half along its northern side, and are in themselves devoid of any beauty beyond that which fine spreading forest trees, green turf, and luxuriant underwood invariably possess. But to the attractions of a general kind which they enjoy, are added some of an extraneous nature that confer on them a particular charm; for through the trees which overarch the walks and public drive, is seen the front range of hills belonging to the Apennine range—hills now sharply peaked, now gently rounded, either blending into one another in softly curving lines, or standing out bold and well-defined; hills crowned by trees and villages, and faced with olives, vines, and verdant fields, amidst which rise up thickly the red tile-roof dwellings of the peasant, and the white glistening villas of the rich or noble

Florentine; and hills which, as the sun touches the last period of his long summer-day reign, mark their dark undulating outlines on a sky irradiated with the most gorgeous gold or crimson hues.

Though at all times the Cascine are a favorite resort of the idle world, they are especially so on the days when their attractions are increased by the performance of a band; on such occasions, particularly on a *festa*, when the shops are closed and business at a stand, the walks and the broad drive, in a certain portion of the grounds, are filled respectively with pedestrians, riders, and carriages. As no Florentine of either sex seems to dream of walking, if either he or she has the means to drive, a motley collection of equipages is visible, from the smart Clarence of the Italian noble, with *chasseur** outside, down to the jingling dog-cart of the John Gilpin class of citizen, and the hack, drafted for the occasion from the neighboring stand; whilst mingling with these may be seen troops of riders, amongst whom the fair-complexioned English girl, cantering along on her handsome and well-groomed steed, occupies a conspicuous place.

The open space adjoining the spot where the band is stationed, serves as a halting-place for the throng; and while humble pedestrians press around the musicians in a circle, the occupants of carriages (the

* A *chasseur* is the name given to an attendant wearing a plumed hat and sword in the military style.

latter drawn up side by side) commence an interchange of salutations with their friends. The smart Florentine beau, with polished boots and nicely-fitting cream-colored gloves, dismounting from his horse, makes his way through the file of vehicles, and seeks out those in which he recognizes friends. Halting here and there as he passes on, he expresses his hope that he sees the Marchesa Capponi quite well—compliments the Contessa Alberti on her very becoming bonnet—begs to present the Signora Bartolotti with a bouquet he has purchased from a flower-girl—is distressed to find that Signora Bianca is still suffering from a cold—and, after lamenting to Signora Massoni that his numerous engagements prevented him from attending her last night's ball, he exchanges with her the last budget of fashionable news: as edifying in its nature as such ah article always is, the wide world over.

Thus driving, riding, talking, jesting, quizzing, flirting, time glides on; the sun disappears behind the hills, and the shades of evening fall: which, deepening fast, soon empty the Cascine of their gay motley throng. The musicians take their departure, and their audience following the example, all turn to Florence, leaving the Cascine to silence, darkness, and solitude: and yet not to darkness entirely, in that beautiful June evening; for no sooner does the night set in, than under the deep gloom of the overarching trees, are seen the minute but brilliant lamps of innumerable fireflies, rising and falling, swaying here and there, and tracing multitudinous intersecting lines of light upon the darkened air.

In Florence, several days in the year are particularly dedicated to religious display or to public rejoicing. On Ascension-day it is considered a kind of pious obligation to make merry, and many a picnic party is formed to the Cascine on that occasion. The procession that takes place on the 11th of June, through cloth-hung streets, and with flags and banners, in honor of the feast of the Corpus Domini, is characterized by great pomp and splendor. On the 15th of August, images of the Virgin are dressed up with silks, ribbons and flowers; and in this ball-room array the Madonna receives the homage of the faithful; who, still further to propitiate her favor, salute her often on such occasions with musical performances. On the 8th of September, another tribute of popular devotion awaits the Virgin; for in honor of the Nativity, altars decorated with flowers are erected in the streets, and boys and girls, in compliance with a time-honored custom, the origin of which does not seem very clear, carry about paper lanterns suspended on poles. A similarly mysterious practice is pursued during Lent also; for when half of its six weeks has elapsed, the juvenile street population of the town amuse themselves by attaching to the dress of the passer-by (in a clandestine manner, if practicable,) small pieces of paper, cut in the shape of a ladder, and named *scala*, from that circumstance.

Easter week is distinguished by many peculiar observances and ceremonies. On Maunday Thursday, I was present at the celebration of the Lavanda in the Pitti Palace, where I saw the Grand Duke go through the pantomimic action (for it was in reality nothing else) of washing the feet of twelve poor old men dressed in the garb of pilgrims; after which, I saw him again in the afternoon, as, in grand state and attended by his guard of nobles, he visited, in accordance with established rules, seven of the principal churches of the town: in whose interior, as well as in churches of less note, there is invariably one altar decorated with all the magnificence of which the resources of each particular church will admit. The example thus set by the head of the State, it is incumbent on every professing Catholic to follow; and the streets were crowded by people hastening from church to church, to get over the prescribed number of visits in a reasonable time. Though many certainly went to pray, as was evidenced by the numerous figures I saw kneeling before each decorated altar, curiosity, as with me, was evidently the motive power with the great majority of the crowd that thronged the churches; and very beautiful was the scene presented by many of their interiors to the view. The church of Santa Croce, in particular, was distinguished by a magnificence of decoration such as scarcely any description could do full justice to:—hangings of gold and silver brocade, massive candelabras of precious metals, costly flowers, and innumerable wax lights, altogether made up a scene of gorgeous splendor such as I had never previously witnessed.

The Saturday in Passion week is distinguished by a grand service in the cathedral, towards the end of which, when the choir begins to sing the "Gloria in Excelsis," a discharge of fireworks takes place from a huge kind of chariot stationed at the door. On this occurrence, guns are fired, and the bells of the city, which have been silent from the preceding Thursday, ring out a joyous peal: whilst from the same hour the church clocks, which have been constrained to observe silence for the same period of time, are restored to the exercise of their suspended faculties of sound.

But of all the days set apart for religious or public festivities in Florence, the feast day of St. John the Baptist (San Giovanni), the patron saint of the Florentines, which falls on the 24th of June, is distinguished beyond all others by splendor and variety of ceremonial observances; chariot races, horse races, music, fireworks, and illuminations, all combining to confer (as supposed) honor on the saint, and to give (most unquestionably) interest to the scene.

The preparations for these festivities commence

some time before the period fixed on for their taking place. The erection of a huge wooden scaffold on the Ponte alla Carraja, for the display of fireworks, puts a stop, first, to the transit of carriages, and finally to that of pedestrians, across it. In the Piazza Santa Maria Novella, there rises, amidst the sound of hammer and saw, a great amphitheatre of seats, for the accommodation of such persons as are desirous of witnessing the chariot races, (races of the *cocchi*, as they are termed,) which take place in this square. In other parts of Florence other seats also are erected, for the purpose of affording a view of the horse races, the scene of which lies along the central streets of the town. Long before the 24th of June, signs may be discerned of the approach of the festivities in honor of San Giovanni, the revered protector of the town.

The chariot races afford a sight characterized by beauty and absurdity in about equal proportions. The Piazza Santa Maria Novella, though irregular in form, is one of the largest and finest squares in Florence, and when in the amphitheatre of seats erected around the course, not one place was to be seen unoccupied—when from the gay state pavilion occupied by the Grand Duke and Duchess, the English ambassador, and the principal personages of the Tuscan Court, the eye, rising upwards over tier above tier of human faces, passed on still upwards to row after row of windows with crimson hangings and crowded with spectators—when all this pomp and show, this animated scene of human life, was witnessed under the influence of an unclouded sky and a bright June sun, the effect was eminently imposing and beautiful.

But what power of words can do justice to the absurdity of the races, for which all this preparation had been made; for which windows had been hung with glowing draperies, seats erected by the thousand, and at which royalty in state presided. How often through life is it forced upon the mind, that man, though attaining outwardly by grey hairs to the age of wisdom, yet never attains to the age of discretion, in reality—a fact signally exemplified in this instance; for however judicious it may be for matured mankind occasionally to accept pleasure when it comes, without entering into a strict investigation as to the dignity of its origin, yet to invest a something essentially trivial and ephemeral (as were these races) with an outward show of pomp and splendor, to expend time and money in ministering to the grandeur of an imbecility, are acts that involve a degree of intellectual development belonging only to the age of dolls, hoops, tops, and hobby-horses.

A few words will suffice to give a description of the races of the *cocchi*, by which San Giovanni is honored in Florence. To most persons, the form of the ancient Roman chariot, guided by a standing charioteer, has been made familiar through the medium of prints; of the same shape are the Florentine *cocchi;* and, saving that they are constructed with four wheels, they are fashioned in close imitation of the old Roman car. Behold, now, five of these *cocchi*, drawn by two horses each, guided by a standing charioteer attired in a classically-shaped floating tunic, differing in color from the others. Ranged together side by side in the middle of the Piazza, in the centre of that imposing-looking amphitheatre, their drivers await, in Phœbus-like attitudes, the signal for starting. It is given, and on the instant down falls the lash, and off start the horses at a gallop, dragging, apparently with difficulty, the low and lumbering cars behind them. One circle of the Piazza is made, and the Apollo in pink is first; another round, and the Mars in red has attained the foremost position, and, keeping up the advantage he has gained, at the third circuit he comes in victorious. A gun is fired, and the spectators leave their seats; for the races of the *cocchi*, which have lasted a space of about three minutes in duration, are ended.

The races of the Barberi, which take place also in honor of the feast of St. John, though widely differing in nature from the races of the *cocchi*, are equally peculiar in character. The race-course is formed by a long line of streets running through the centre of the town, from one gate to another, and the racers are riderless horses. All along the line of streets the windows are hung with crimson drapery, and soldiers, ranged in single file on either side, keep the horses in the course prescribed, and keep it also clear for the performances. Racing in the English fashion is far from being to me a pleasurable exhibition, and from what I once felt on seeing the lash descend with merciless force on the bleeding sides of panting, striving animals, I do not desire ever again to be a spectator of another English race. In point of humanity, however, the Italian races are equally obnoxious to censure; for though the feelings are spared the sight of the action of the jockey's whip and spurs, the pain inflicted is probably even less than that resulting from the artful device by which Italian horses (riderless as they be) are stimulated to action. To the eye, the small circular pieces of leather, or metal, which flap up and down on the back and sides of the Italian race-horse, might, naturally enough, be looked on in the light of merely ornamental appendages. But far otherwise is the case in reality—for every one of these small flappers has a sharp spike in its centre, that pricks the horse at every step he takes; and the faster the poor animal gallops, under the torture of these self-acting goads, the greater becomes the stimulus of pain to urge him on his course, from the added force given by every increase of speed to each flapping point. Recurring in memory to the races of the Barberi I witnessed in Florence, at the feast of St. John the Baptist, there rises up before me the vivid picture of a long line of crowded streets, of crimson-hung windows, of tiers here and there of well-filled seats, and of horses covered with flapping goads, rushing by at a rapid pace.

But another picture, infinitely more beautiful and agreeable, rises up before my view in connection with the midsummer festivities in honor of San Giovanni. Vividly do I recall that beautiful evening in June, when, standing by the river's side, I saw as it were the realization of a scene of fairy land. In the center of the Ponte alla Carraja—where a hideous wooden scaffold, a formless, unmeaning-looking thing of planks and beams, had affronted the eye by the light of day—there, in that same spot, shone forth a radiant palace, fit to be the habitation of genii. Up rose the whirring rocket into the air, marking its course across the dark vault above with a fiery trail, and perishing in a gushing shower of stars of the most glowing colors; round spun the wheels of glittering light, sending forth continuous jets of dazzling sparks, like spray from a fiery fountain; whilst along the Arno, at either side, down to the Ponte di Santat Trinità, extended close to the water's edge long lines of lamps, whose mellow lustre was reflected in the stream beneath; and the river itself, from one bank to the other, was studded over with illuminated boats, showing, like isles of light, every here and there, from its dark surface. Clearly as at noonday could one see the eager faces of the crowd around them; and the stars of heaven looked dull, and dim, and pale, by contrast with that glittering pageant.

There was no sleep that night for many. Crowds filled the streets till break of day, passing from place to place, to admire the beauty of the lamp-lit cathedral dome, the radiant glories of the tall tower of the Palazzo Vecchia, and to listen to the inspiriting strains of numerous bands, stationed here and there, throughout the city; and not till the dawn of day crept up the sky were the tones of music hushed, and the wanderings of the pleasure-seekers ended.

# CHAPTER VI.

## SOCIETY.

THE name of Italy has for the educated world a kind of magic sound. Its glory, grandeur, and might of old, joined to its more modern triumphs in the arts of the poet, painter, sculptor and musician, give it a foremost position in the sympathies of every cultivated mind. In no small degree, certainly, does England feel the spell which departed greatness, and the deathless triumphs of genius, have thrown around the country of Brutus, Cicero, Dante, Columbus, Raphael, Michel Angelo, and Galileo. By the English stranger who first treads the classic shores of Italy, the history of which is intertwined with the remembrances of his early years—whose residence is adorned perhaps by the grand creations of Italian art, who owes many a delightful hour to Rossini's or Bellini's harmonious strains—by such a one Italy and the Italians, the country and its people, will naturally be viewed through a medium of the most favorable kind. Short, however, is the duration of the bright picture painted by the imagination, when the realities of Italian life are brought before the eyes of those who respect and cherish the virtues of domestic life, and believe that existence presents some higher, nobler object of pursuit than that of pleasure.

Not more do Italy and England differ in their outward aspects than in their inward states or existence. Strongly as the bright blue summer skies, the olives, the maize, the vines of Italy contrast with the lowering clouds and less luxuriant and varied vegetation of our colder clime; the contrast that exists in all that concerns the domestic life of the two nations is far greater. From the earliest to the last moment of existence, influences, entirely different in their nature, are at work, moulding the characters and shaping the destinies of the inhabitants of Italy and England. In the different aspects presented by these two countries at the present day — England, rich, powerful, triumphant and free — Italy, poor, weak, oppressed, enslaved—in the wide distinction that thus prevails, it needs no penetration to discover which class of influences, affecting the formation of the national character in either country, is the best.

"Love, music and poetry, is the life of an Italian,"

exclaimed, one day in my presence, a young Florentine gentleman. Unfortunately for Italy, the observation was too true: Italian youths, epicureans in theory and practice, too often fritter away their time and energies in the pursuit of mere enjoyment; and too often, through the means of a vicious career of self-indulgence, their natural capacity for good is well nigh extinguished, if not wholly destroyed. Early in life the frivolous tone of Italian society exerts its enervating influence over the youthful mind. Few are the youths belonging to the upper and middle classes of society in Italy, who resolutely set themselves to achieve an honorable independence. Clinging to their kindred for support, necessity alone drives them to exercise their energies for the purpose of acquiring the means of subsistence. The idlers can be counted by tens, the workers by units. The tone of thought which ruled society in Tuscany in the days of the Medici is extinguished utterly; for industry now is looked upon as vulgar, and idleness as genteel. The lad of fifteen apes the man—apes him in the levities, and too often the vices of his career: the youth of twenty is thoroughly a man of the world, intimately acquainted with the world's worst features. Frivolities become the serious duties of his existence: he sings—he dances—he gossips—he flirts—as if life were given him for no higher aims and occupation. So long as he can find the means to buy light kid gloves, attend the opera, and pay his café bill, he lives on, contented with his position; his future troubles him not, so long as his present wears an agreeable aspect. "*Vive la bagatelle*," is his cry: "life is short, let us enjoy it whilst we may;" and, acting upon this creed, youth vanishes in a round of folly—in a whirl of excitement, that cannot but be as destructive to the moral principle as it is inimical to the development of all the higher faculties of the mind.

But whilst thus characterizing the youth of Italy as a class, it would be unfair to deny that there exist many exceptions to this rule. Doubtless, amongst the young men of Italy there are to be found many to whom patriotism supplies a motive to exertion and an object in which they worthily invest their sympathies. But whilst admitting this, it must be owned that, if credit is to be given to the words of Italians themselves, there is but a small amount of singleness of purpose, unselfishness of endeavor, and honesty of action, to be found amongst the ranks of the upper classes of their countrymen. It was a melancholy thing to me to hear the strictures passed by Italians upon themselves. Distrust seemed to me to be widely prevalent; each man appearing to suspect his neighbor of being actuated by merely selfish aims. In Rome and Naples I have heard Italians lament their unfitness as a nation for free institutions, from the low moral tone existing amongst themselves. "*Siamo troppo cativi*" (we are too wicked) for free institutions, said to me a Roman gentleman belonging to the anti-papal party; and this is the opinion of many a one in various parts of Italy. In Tuscany this feeling contributes more to the stability of the hated government of the Grand Duke than the army of Austrians he has at his command. Anarchy seems to be more dreaded than despotism; and the caprices of tyranny appear to be looked upon as more endurable than the license of a mob.

In truth, the republican drama recently enacted in Tuscany was little creditable to the inhabitants of that land. Those times were certainly not to be boasted of, when hydra-headed tyranny under the name of liberty stalked abroad: and judging from what I heard, the closing scenes of the revolution resembled in character those exhibited throughout its course.

"The concluding days of our revolution were truly disgraceful ones," observed a lady, whose husband had taken a prominent part in the proceedings of the time. "It was really pitiable to see the way in which many of our most prominent liberals deserted their ranks through the influence of gold or fear. I was in Sienna when the news of the reaction in Florence arrived. The mob in the streets began to hurrah for the Grand Duke. On hearing this, I saw the chief man of our party in the town turn pale as death, and tremble like a child. 'What must I do?' he faltered out. 'Stick true to your colors and principles,' I replied; 'I, though a woman, would scorn to do less.' Vain words! A few minutes had not passed before he was shouting for Leopold, with the Ducal colors attached to his dress. Gold, too, did its work. Few were found like my husband to refuse the proffered bribe: republican patriots became transformed into Ducal partizans in a few hours' time."

"Our present Government is certainly a bad one," said a liberal Florentine merchant to me; "but our republican rule was far worse. Liberty existed with us but in name. Florence was tyrannized over by a mob, each individual of which aspired to be king. Neither property nor life was safe, and trade was annihilated by the general feeling of insecurity that prevailed." "We were bought and sold," say the lower classes of the people. "For the sake of gold our leaders deserted their colors and us." Of a similar purport were many of the observations I heard during my residence in Tuscany.

It cannot be doubted that the defects of character, attributable to the Italians of the upper and middle classes of society, spring in a considerable degree from the despotic form of government to which they are subjected. The energies of the human mind cannot be altogether repressed; if denied vent in a useful, rational way, they will make for themselves an outlet of a widely different character. The fertilizing river, whose onward course between its banks is checked by a strong dyke, will lay waste the land around in unwholesome marshes. What the dyke is to the stream, despotic institutions are to the character. Liberty of speech and action denied, legitimate objects of ambition refused, mental activity looked upon with suspicion and discouraged, it is only a natural consequence that the innate energy of the Italian character should exhibit itself in an unworthy manner. Under other influences, it may be that the Italian sensualist, adventurer and gambler of the present day, would show himself a worthy citizen, an unselfish patriot, and a true benefactor to his country.

But, injurious as is undoubtedly the influence of Italian government on Italian character, the faulty social code of Italy is chargeable with the evil, in a still greater degree: indeed, it may be questioned if this source is not in itself the parent of all the evils under which Italy groans; for tyranny and tyrants are only the outward symptoms of a disease that has struck its roots in the homes of the land. When one man subjects many to his tyrannic sway, the many must be in fault. An army is counted but by thousands, a people by millions; and there is no power in parks of artillery, or in military tactics, to put or keep a nation down, when that nation, worthy of liberty, determines to be free. Search the annals of history, and it will reveal that the public life of a nation is in a great degree the reflex of its private one. With purity of morals will be found associated national independence, wealth and power; with corruption of morals, tyranny, weakness and poverty. If we would trace the source of oppression of millions subjected to tyranny, or writhing impotently under the oppressor's grasp, we must look into their homes and raise up the veil that hangs over private life; observe the mother, contemplate the wife, and watch the young girl as she springs up from infancy to maturity.

It is an observation justified by experience, that children ordinarily inherit their mental and moral qualities from their mother. In the biographies of great men this fact is evidenced in a very striking manner, and proves how essential to the welfare and greatness of any state is the development of the mental and moral faculties of woman. By thus ordaining that children shall resemble their mother in mental and moral constitution, Providence seems visibly to interpose in behalf of the weaker sex, and to claim for them respect, education and consideration; for practically does it say, through this means, to men, "If you desire that your sons should be clever, wise and good, develop as much as possible those qualities in woman." Unheeded, however, for the most part, does that voice speak to mankind; and throughout the east, where woman is looked upon either in the light of a toy or a slave, one sees how terribly the injuries of the inmates of the harem and the zenana have been avenged. Ignorant, oppressed and weak, the women of the east have entailed the curses of ignorance, weakness and oppression on the nations to which they belong.

To any one who mixes in the slightest degree in Italian society, or converses with the inhabitants of different grades in Italy, it will soon become very apparent that domestic life in that country partakes in its essential elements of the oriental type. Though not secluded in the interior of her house, or veiled and muffled up when she goes out to walk or drive, the Italian lady has but little real liberty of action; and in all that concerns the practical affairs and most important interests of life, she may be looked upon as a mere cipher, or a complete nonentity. Should we examine her position in the various stages of her history, as girl, wife, mother, or possibly widow, we should find her constrained and fettered to a degree that seems inconsistent with the fact of her possessing the attributes of a rational being.

Nothing exercises so baneful an effect upon the character as the destruction of self-respect. A despised race will almost invariably exhibit despicable qualities. The evidence of mistrust has a tendency to evoke the evil propensities of human nature, and errors harden often into sin and guilt, if society puts its ban upon the offender. As with the moral, so with the mental qualities. Call a man a villain or a fool, and deal with him habitually as such, and he will not unlikely prove himself deserving of the epithet you give him. In like manner, if women as a class are looked upon with contempt, and are treated as beings unfit for self-guidance and self-government, they will be found acting in accordance with their imputed characters. If an English woman is superior to an Italian woman, in mental faculties and moral qualities, the fault lies not with nature, but is traceable to that erring code of customs and opinion which treats the latter as if she were a being from whom the great gift of reason had been withheld. The hobbling gait of the Chinese woman is not a more artificial product than are the weakness, vanity, frivolity and immorality which stain the character of the women of Italy of the present day.

The contrast between the position of an English and Italian widow is a striking one. The former, recognized by English society as an independent existence, may even, though young, live where she pleases, and spend her jointure according to her taste. She may travel; she may live in town or country, as her choice suggests: no one has the power to control her, to regulate the expenditure of her income, to dictate to her what she may and may not do. But with the Italian widow the case is often widely different; and not seldom is she subjected to a thraldom of the most grievous kind.

"My life is a burden to me," said a young Florentine widow to me, despairingly one day.

"Why so?" I asked.

"Oh, Signor Carlo is so cross and unkind; he checks and thwarts me in every way," was the reply.

"And who is Signor Carlo, and what right has he to interfere with you?" I returned.

"Oh, Signor Carlo is a priest, whom my husband made a guardian over me, and entrusted with the management of my jointure and my affairs. Oh, it is really too insufferable!" she continued passionately. "Scarcely an evening passes that he does not come to make a note of my day's expenditure; and then, if he finds that I have exceeded the ordinary amount by even a couple of pauls, he knits his brows, and tells me that this must not occur again. And if he sees a nice blazing fire in the grate, he rebukes me for my extravagance. 'Signora Teresa, you must not do this, and you must not do that,' he keeps on saying, till I cry with downright vexation. Then, too, if I want a new bonnet or a new dress, I have to beg and beg innumerable times before I can get the money to purchase it. It is too bad — indeed, it is — the way he acts; treating me like a child, though a woman of upwards of thirty years of age. It is intolerable to be kept in this subjection. I would to Heaven I were an Englishwoman!"

"But why do you permit Signor Carlo to keep

all your money in his hands, and to annoy you by his constant presence and interference?"

"*Cara mia*," she rejoined, "how can I help it, since my husband willed that I should get my income solely through Signor Carlo's hands? And that is not the worst of my lot either," she continued; "that might be borne; but it is intolerable that Signor Carlo should be a spy on all my actions, keeping a constant watch on all I do."

"Why permit him? Why not tell him you will act as you choose?"

"I wish I could; but he has me completely in his power, for by my husband's will my jointure is to be transferred to a member of his family if I do not show I am a *buona vedova*,* and exhibit the most perfect discretion of conduct."

"Am I to understand that Signor Carlo is to be your judge in this particular?"

"Yes; and he is perpetually on the watch to see if I have got a lover. He thinks himself very cunning, I am sure; but sharp-eyed as he is, he has never yet discovered that Beppo comes here."

"Who is Beppo?"

"A young officer, a noble of Pisa, to whom I am engaged. Unfortunately he is too poor to marry yet, and so we must wait until he gets his next step, which will give him additional pay."

* Good widow.

"You lose your jointure, then, if you marry, I suppose?"

"Yes, certainly; or if my engagement to do so be known. It is really droll to think of the way that Beppo has to be smuggled off when Signor Carlo arrives unexpectedly."

"You will be glad when this thraldom is at an end?"

"If it were not for that prospect, I would not live," she exclaimed; "or at least not live on in the way I do. If it were not for Beppo, I should do something desperate, I am sure."

In the character of this lady I saw a striking illustration of the evil effects that flow from the restraints imposed upon her sex in Italy. Scarcely emerged from childhood, she, in obedience to her mother's orders, became the wife of a man she did not love, and who was in point of age considerably her senior. Sadly did the years of her married life pass by. Without children, without household duties (for her husband regulated all domestic affairs), without an education that would have given her resources of enjoyment in herself, she could only look to society for happiness, for the means of filling up in any way the vacuum in her existence; and from this sole resource she was excluded by the decree of a jealous husband. As daughter first, as wife subsequently — watched, guarded, mistrusted, deprived of liberty of choice and action, in despite of no mean natural endowments of heart and mind —time found her a widow of thirty years of age, in point of judgment, thought and feeling — a perfect child.

Although every widow lady in Italy may not have the misfortune to be under the rule of a Signor Carlo, it seemed to me, from what I heard, that the practice was general on the part of a dying husband to invest some one with the cȯntrol over the management of the pecuniary affairs of his widow. Indeed, in many cases this might prove a wise provision for her welfare: for from the effects of the system of tutelage under which the Italian wife has lived, she is so destitute of prudence and forethought —so much the slave of impulse, so passionately fond of dress—that with her income as a widow at her own disposal, she is capable of spending in a week, on the merest fripperies of fashion, the whole amount of her annual income. Signora Teresa was no exception to this rule: she acknowledged that she was dreadfully extravagant. The number of bonnets and dresses she possessed was absolutely startling; and nearly all the very small amount of pocket-money allowed to her by Signor Carlo was expended in the purchase of lottery tickets.

In a country where the intellectual faculties of women are rated at a very low degree, it may readily be believed that education is a matter but little attended to. Thus error tends ever to its self-perpetuation. The weak and ignorant girl merges into the weak and ignorant mother, and not feeling her deficiencies, goes on in the old beaten track; which results in daughters as weak and ignorant as she is herself. So one generation of women follows another, impressed with the belief that the chief merit of their sex is to look handsome, and their chief duty to be well dressed. The course of instruction for girls in the upper and middle classes of society in Italy is of the flimsiest character: nothing is taught of a nature calculated to develop their mental faculties. Beneath the thin varnish of accomplishments that an Italian lady possesses, the most dense ignorance of the ordinary branches of knowledge may be found. I was intimately acquainted with two young ladies in Florence, who were well educated, according to the Italian idea of that term; for they could play the piano tolerably well, speak French imperfectly, and could say "Good-morning," and "Good-night," and half a dozen more equally elaborate sentences in the English language. But with these accomplishments, of which they were extremely proud, neither of them could write without lines, or in any other than a child's large, ill-formed characters; history they were ignorant of; and the profundity of their ignorance of geography may be imagined from the fact, that neither of them knew of the existence of the celebrated Italian Lake of Como. Geographical knowledge would seem, indeed, from the results of my experience, to be classed somewhat among the unfeminine branches of learning in Italy. "Which is the farthest off, London or America?" asked a lively Florentine lady of me one day. I gave her the desired information, with a secret wonder at the ignorance the question implied; but greater grew my wonder, and severe was the test to which my gravity was put, when, after a few moments of apparent meditation, she exclaimed—"What a very large *city* America must be!"

At a very early period of my residence in Tuscany, the mockery of the miscalled system of feminine education in Italy became to me most strikingly apparent. The most favorite schools for Florentine girls are those conducted by nuns and carried on within the precincts of the convent, but there are educational establishments to be found in Florence unconnected with the religious institutions of the country. To an annual examination of the girls belonging to a school of the latter description I was invited shortly after my arrival in Florence, when I was as yet but imperfectly acquainted with the Italian language. Though doubtful of my ability to understand a scholastic examination carried on in an unfamiliar tongue, I accepted the invitation, and repaired at the time indicated to the appointed place.

Great preparations had been made for the occasion, as if to invest the coming exhibition with a character of importance and dignity. Across the end of the room, where the examination was to be held, extended a stage, gaily decorated with bright colored drapery. Upon this stage a table and some chairs were placed for the use of the examiner and the pupils, and directly in front were several rows of forms appropriated to the service of the audience. The room filled rapidly, and the benches were well furnished with occupants, when a grave, middle-aged man emerged from a mysterious side door and took his place on a seat occupying a central position on the platform. On either side of him, four or five girls, of ages varying apparently from ten to sixteen, ranged themselves in order. The ladies, of whom the company entirely consisted, kept a profound silence, as befitted the importance of the scene, and the examination began.

My doubts as to the sufficiency of my knowledge of the language were soon dispelled, for I speedily found that my endowments in this respect were most ample for all the requirements of the occasion; the questions asked being characterized by a ludicrous degree of simplicity. Difficult, indeed, it was to restrain a smile, when I heard girls, almost womanly in their appearance, required to tell how many vowels there were in the Italian language; and further, to exhibit a convincing proof of their knowledge on this point, by furnishing words in which the vowels severally occurred.

"Right, quite right," said the professor, applaudingly, as a girl mentioned *bocca*, in exemplification of the use of the letter *o;* "and now," he continued, in his consequential manner, "I write this word *bocca* (mouth) upon this slate: you see it there; and I require you to tell me what letter it is necessary to add in order to convert *bocca* into *boccia*" (bottle).

The question was too abstruse for the girl addressed to answer; but the pupil next questioned solved it triumphantly.

An examination conducted by the French master was of an equally puerile and absurd character. After requiring the French for—I, thou, she, it, etc. —requirements not always successfully complied with—he proceeded to make his pupils apply their knowledge of the personal pronouns to the conjugation in French of the phrase, "To gain one's livelihood." "I gain my livelihood," said one girl: "Thou gainest thy livelihood," said another: and so on round the circle, until "They gain their livelihood," was attained. In geography and history, not even the most superficial examination took place; and when the morning's performances came to an end, I could not help wondering at the display I had witnessed of gross incapacity on the part of the teachers, and gross ignorance on the part of the taught.

An evening exhibition that took place on the same stage, was, in its way, of a much more meritorious kind. Though the school was a large one, the same young ladies who had exhibited their attainments in the morning, and who were evidently considered the show pupils of the establishment, once more appeared upon the stage to display their dramatic and elocutionary powers. French poems were recited with fluency and considerable grace, by girls who had shown a far from intimate acquaintance with French pronouns a few hours previously. Then came a play, which was acted in a very creditable manner; and the examination concluded with some waltzing, which evidenced that the art of dancing was, above all other branches of learning, the one most thoroughly cultivated and understood.

From the reputation this school enjoyed, and the number of pupils it contained, it was evident that the system of instruction there pursued was not inferior to that adopted in any other similar kind of seminary in the town. It was easy to see, indeed, that the amount of knowledge displayed in the examination fully came up to the requirements of society; for an observation I made, relative to the ludicrous simplicity of the questions asked, seemed to give rise, in the minds of the ladies I addressed, to a sensation of surprise. It was truly not to be expected, however, that those who had been subjected to precisely the same system of tuition themselves should find anything to censure or to smile at in that morning's scene.

When such is the state of feminine education amongst the higher classes of Italian society, it can excite no wonder to discover that, in the lower ranks of female life, a state of the most dense ignorance prevails. Even girls who enjoy a very respectable position in the world remain quite ignorant of the arts of reading and writing. The popular opinion on the subject of the uselessness of such acquirements to women, was strikingly embodied in a remark made to me by the wife of a respectable Government official at the Baths of Monte Catini. Discovering that she was quite unacquainted with the mysteries of the alphabet, I asked her how it happened, that she, the daughter of a schoolmaster, had not learned to read and write? "Oh, my father said," she replied, "such knowledge was quite useless to a woman; and for all the good it did, it would be folly for me to be at the trouble to learn, and waste of time for him to be at the trouble to teach me." In towns, girls in the humbler walks of life may chance to get a slight tincture of the elements of learning; but in the country, a girl who can read a page, or write a line, is quite a phenomenon.

The idea of a girl in Italy is indissolubly connected with that of a being devoid of all moral sense, infallably preferring wrong to right, and who can only he kept from harm and evil by the most incessant watchfulness. A mother's whole maternal duties towards her daughter seem considered in Italy to be comprehended in the one act of vigilance. "My daughter has never been, since she was nine years old, for more than twenty minutes at a time, out of my sight," said an Italian countess, boastfully; and by this declaration she appeared to think that she merited to take rank in the world's esteem with the mother of the Gracchi. A girl belonging to the upper ranks of life in Italy is practically a prisoner until she marries. Into society she must not enter; neither in the morning *fete*, or in the evening dance, is she permitted to display her charms and graces. An occasional walk with father, or brother, or mother, is permitted; but she must not go outside the house unless accompanied by her nearest kindred. To be seen alone, even but a few yards from her father's door, would entail upon her the deepest disgrace and heaviest censure. Kept under a perpetual surveillance, every line she writes, and every line she receives, are subjected to rigid scrutiny.

The girl belonging to the humbler classes of society shares also, in a great degree, in the same restrictions on her liberty. The grown up daughter of a woman keeping a lodging-house in Florence could not profit by my offer to take her to see the ceremony of the *Lavanda* at the Pitti Palace, solely because she was unable to procure a proper escort to accompany her, in a ten minutes' walk through the best part of the town, to the place where I resided. A work-girl, going to her employer's house, has to provide herself with some companion; and, in emergencies, I have sometimes seen a little child do duty as duenna for the occasion. In the country, the same rule prevails; no peasant girl is ever to be seen alone: and equally in the higher as in the lower classes of society would any infringement of the social code, in this respect, be fatal to matrimonial expectations. Under these circumstances, the proceedings of unmarried English ladies excite the wonder and envy of their sex in Italy. Often have I been amused at the way in which the most commonplace exploits have been magnified into heroic actions; and not unfrequently did I find myself elevated to the dignity of a heroine, when utterly unconscious that I had in any way merited the name assigned me.

Though marriage, in some degree, enlarges the sphere of action of Italian women, the liberty it gives is of a very limited character. An Italian lady belonging to the middle classes of society, whilst lamenting to me the evil influences which resulted from the present social code of Italy, gave an instance of how it had once personally affected her in a very unpleasant manner.

"Some years ago," she said, "my husband, not

being able to leave Lucca conveniently at the time there was some trifling business to be transacted at Genoa, proposed to me that I should take my little boy, and go there to settle matters in his stead. I at once agreed to his suggestions, and went. The journey was easily and quickly performed by railroad and steamer; but the censure I brought upon myself by traveling unattended by a gentleman, was of the severest description. If I had committed some act of murder and robbery, I could scarcely have been more blamed."

Even amongst the lower classes, neither age nor matrimony gives a woman the privilege of walking about alone in a strange place, without provoking censure. For instance, when I advised a plain, elderly married female servant to visit the cathedral at Pistoja, during a two hours' unavoidable detention there on her way by railroad to Florence, she somewhat indignantly rejoined, "that to walk alone in the streets of a strange town, was an indecorum she would be sorry to be guilty of."

If it were not a sorrowful spectacle, it might well excite a smile to see the subservient public homage paid by Italian women to the conventional regulations of decorum, whilst flagrantly contravening in their daily life its essential principle. The same lady who would shrink from the impropriety of traveling five miles alone, will not scruple to prove false to a wife's highest duties. Sharing with men in an epicurean tone of thought and feeling, every womanly virtue is sacrificed at the shrine of pleasure. In the social life of Italy, vice presents itself to the sight under a veil too thin to hide from the least observant eye its offensive features. The drawing-rooms of the upper classes of the land, particularly in Tuscany, are filled with faithless wives and false husbands. So flagrant and wide-spread is the evil, that sin wears no blush, nor seeks a mask to screen it. An English lady, who had entered much into Italian society, told me that she was often shocked at the confidences which married ladies would force upon her; and when she told her husband that she must really give up acquaintance with such persons, he answered, quite truly, that to act consistently, she must then give up Italian society altogether; for Signora A—— and Signora B—— were not one whit worse than other ladies—frankness and unreserve constituting the only difference between them.

Few are the Italian girls who, on first entering as matrons into the dissipated circles of Italian society, escape its baneful influences. How, indeed, under the circumstances, could it be otherwise? The whole training of the Italian girl tends to render her a slave to impulse and a prey to temptation. Marrying, most likely at her parent's bidding, a man she does not love, and with her mind in all probability already half corrupted by the conversation she has heard in the drawing-room of her mother, she follows readily in the train of the ladies she sees around. To resist the contagion of example, to make a stand for right in the midst of a crowd of worshipers of wrong, requires strength of mind; and strength of mind springs not from the mockery of education that Italian ladies receive: learning to dance, to sing, to conjugate French verbs, and to play the piano. From empty minds, and idle hands, evil naturally ensues. To fill up the void of life, recourse is had to the excitement of rivalry, of coquetry, to indulgence in gossip and tattling. Each lady appears to try to excuse her own proceedings to her conscience and to the world, by making out that the conduct of her acquaintances is still worse. The light literature of France, which constitutes her only study, tends further to her mental and moral degradation; its pages attiring vice in the most seductive and fascinating garb. Finding their value estimated solely by the standard of good looks, dress becomes to Italian women in all classes of society an absorbing passion. The chief part of the existence of the *Marchesa* or *Contessa*, is employed in the pleasing labors of the toilette; and the maid-of-all-work will not hesitate to lay out half her miserable earnings on a light pink silk bonnet. A young peasant girl ingenuously confessed to me, that she thought perfect happiness would be her lot were she only possessed of a silk dress and gold chain like mine. In short, were woman to be judged universally by the moral and mental attributes she exhibits in Italy at the present day, the opinion might reasonably be entertained that she was a being low in the scale of intelligence, requiring perpetual tutelage, and unfit to be endowed with the prerogatives of self-guidance and self-government.

Nothing but a change in the social code of Italy can cure an evil that is a canker in the vitals of that country. As long as a girl is considered by society as a kind of chattel property, which may be disposed of by her parents to the highest bidder in the matrimonial market, female degradation will continue. The laws of nature cannot be outraged with impunity; and love, the life-stream of a woman's being, becomes, when diverted forcibly from its natural course, a dangerous quicksand, in which honor, purity, and every domestic virtue are engulphed. The refusal of liberty of choice in the selection of a husband, leads inevitably to the most evil consequences. Let society enact what laws it may in reference to the matter, the young girl feels that she has inherent rights which cannot be abrogated by its dictum. Too weak for open resistance, she seeks to contravene the projects of her parents, in regard to her future establishment, by clandestine manœuvres. Concealment induces deceit, deceit gives rise to falsehood and hypocrisy; and she stoops to despicable artifices to blind her mother to the fact that she is carrying on a correspondence with some lover. Successful or unsuccessful in her object, whether she secures a husband for herself or has to accept one at the dictation of another, the evil seed has been sown in her heart, and can scarcely fail to ripen under the baneful influences of Italian society. In the following incident will be found a striking illustration of the contest of wits in regard to matrimonial schemes, which goes on in Italy between mother and daughter.

In the summer of 1856, a widow lady and her daughter came from the city of Perugia to Leghorn, for sea-bathing. The daughter was young and singularly handsome: with the dark eyes and hair of Italy, she possessed the height and fair complexion of England—a combination rare as it was attractive. Her appearance out of doors (an event of rare occurrence) never failed to create a sensation. Admiring glances greeted the "Bella Perugiana" (as she was called) at mass, and wherever else she might be visible; young gentlemen walked up and down before the house where she resided, to catch a glimpse, if it were possible, of the young beauty. It may well be imagined that, under such circumstances, the mother found her office of duenna no sinecure. To do her justice, however, she seemed equal to the emergency; for she did not scruple to sacrifice her own convenience and ease to the discharge of her duty in this particular.

However useful servants might be, and doubtless were, in her estimation, she held them as enemies to be dreaded in her present situation; for how could she feel assured that, through the means of a bribe, they might not be induced to become a channel of communication between her daughter and some lover? The danger was too imminent to be gainsayed or denied; no vigilance on her part could prevent the occurrence of the evil she foreboded, if servants, on any pretext or business, were admitted into the apartments they occupied. Influenced by this conviction, the anxious mother resolved, with heroic self-denial, that she and her daughter should act as servants to themselves, so that the presence of strange attendants might be dispensed with altogether. Accordingly, the young beauty had to enact the housemaid's part, to make her own bed, and to clean out her own apartment. In the discharge, however, of these prescribed tasks, it soon became evident that nature had not designed the "Bella Perugiana" to enact the domestic's part, for she was constantly committing some piece of awkwardness in connection with the performance of her menial duties. Scarce a day passed by that, in hanging her towel over the sill of the back window to dry, she did not let it carelessly drop down into the small courtyard of a café immediately beneath.

As the distance, however, from the ground to the first floor apartments was but small, the evil was easily remedied, as some good-natured attendant was always at hand to throw back the dropped article to the fair hands from which it had unluckily slipped.

Thus weeks passed on: the mother had every reason to be pleased with her daughter's conduct in everything, save in the careless manner in which she still continued to perform the housemaid's business; for in spite of chidings from the one, and strong utterings of self-reproach on the other's part, such illustrations of the principles of gravitation as were referred to before, occurred frequently. At length came a day of anger to the mother and of confusion and dismay to the daughter, when the origin of the young lady's awkwardness was revealed. The dupe of an ingenious artifice, the outwitted duenna, discovered that in every dropped article which had been so kindly thrown back to the beauty from the court beneath, a missive from a lover had been enclosed; and by the same means, pen, ink, and paper, to be employed furtively (if possible), had been obtained. Under the mother's watchful eyes, a close correspondence with a forbidden lover, who had followed from Perugia, had been maintained. But vain were the daughter's wiles: the iron bars of custom and prescription were too strong for her to break; and like a bird who, after vainly flapping its wings against the wires of its cage, resigns itself to captivity, so the girl yielded to the force of circumstances: when she left Leghorn shortly afterwards, she left it as the promised bride of a wealthy nobleman. Wealth and rank! what more could any heart desire? Nothing, certainly: the essentials for happiness were fully comprehended in those terms. At least, so thought the mother; and as to the daughter, what her thoughts on the subject were, mattered not—her destiny was sealed.

From such a marriage evil must ensue: whether dazzled by the seductive charms of wealth and rank, or under the pressure of compulsion, she yielded willingly or unwillingly to her mother's views, the career of the "Bella Perugiana" is almost equally sure to be a sinful and unhappy one. Bound to a man she does not love, her heart and fancy filled with the image of her deserted suitor, with an empty mind, and time hanging heavy on her hands, an adept in deceipt and artifice — what likelihood is there that she will be able to resist the corrupting influences of the society into which she is thrown? Sad is it to follow up in thought her probable career, to see the incense of admiration, readily offered, accepted eagerly; to see mistrust, suspicion, jealousy, or hatred, perhaps, and every element of discord and unhappiness, take up their abode beneath the domestic roof — to behold the desecration of the holiest duties of existence, and every household virtue flung aside or trampled under foot with shameless audacity—husband and wife alike unfaithful to their vows—father and mother alike negligent of their parental duties—children who can neither love nor honor her who gave them birth—daughters as artful as she was herself, and to whom, in turn, she acts the duenna—sons old in vice at a youthful age, frequenters of the "casino" and the gaming table—old age ungraced with love and reverence, tormented with gnawing regrets after her faded loveliness, envy of the admiration proffered to youthful beauties, and futile attempts to efface by art the ravages that time has made in her once perfect features. Sad and painful as is this picture, who can say that under the circumstances the life of the "Bella Perugiana" is likely to be different to the one described?

Under the social code of Italy, even marriages of affection are not likely to terminate much more happily than those contracted from motives of interest and convenience. Though few in number, marriages do sometimes occur where the young lady marries the man on whom she has fixed, or rather fancies she has fixed, her affections: for generally in such cases the love professed is but a shadowy growth of the imagination; since from the secluded life she has been forced to lead, in accordance with the Italian code of propriety, her whole knowledge of the object of her choice is limited, generally, to an acquaintance with his personal appearance. At church most likely she first beheld him; and she was not too much absorbed by her devotions to remark that his eyes were fixed upon her face with an expression of admiration. She sees him following her home, to find out her name and residence; and, day after day, she notices him passing and repassing, looking upwards at the window: from which, like most Italian girls, she spends the greatest portion of her time in gazing. Flattered by these attentions, she speedily begins to think that the young gentleman who has found such charms in her is decidedly a very captivating person. She finds amiability in his smile, agreeableness in his eyes, and evidence of perfect taste in the fashion of his coat, the curl of his moustache, and the shape of his well-trimmed whiskers. The impression made upon her heart she does not fail to evidence by her smiles and glances. On this the gentleman, if in independent circumstances, demands an interview with the young lady's parents, declares his love, makes known his fortune, his family and his expectations, and if his statements are deemed satisfactory, the object of his choice is overjoyed to hail him as her affianced husband, although she has never interchanged with him a single sentence.

Thus, with the tastes, the feelings, the real character of either party mutually quite unknown, it is evident that it is a happy chance indeed which unites together dispositions in any way congenial. In ordinary cases, where no bond exists of community of thought and feeling, a few short months of wedded life suffice to weaken or destroy the love which, on either side, has been a mere creation of the fancy. The dark eyes of Gertrude loose their charm, when they are dimmed by peevishness or flash with anger; and the graceful curl of Narcisso's moustache cannot atone for ungracious words and a careless and cold demeanor. Mutual disappointment results, ere long, in mutual indifference. Devoid of that cultivation of mind which would enable her to find resources of enjoyment in herself, Gertrude tries to drown the remembrance of her domestic griefs and trials in a whirl of gaiety; while Narcisso vies with his wife in a sedulous desire to effect the same object, through a career of fashionable dissipation.

The frequency with which such results occur has given rise to a proverb that embodies with vulgar force the popular idea of the unhappy issue of love matches in Italy; but it is evident that from marriages effected in the manner described, the merits of the great principle of feminine liberty of choice have not been compromised in the slightest manner.

The celebrated Silvio Pellico has referred to this subject in very striking terms; and how fully his mind was impressed with the conviction that a reform was urgently required in the social code of

Italy, the following extract from his writings will unequivocally evidence:

"To the brief raptures of the honeymoon succeed *ennui*, and the perception that the choice was precipitate. From the regrets of one or of both the parties arise slights, offenses and daily bitter dissensions. The woman, the gentler and the more generous being of the two, becomes commonly the victim of the unhappy discord; either grieving to death, or, what is worse, losing her natural goodness of disposition, she forms attachments through which, it seems to her, she will find amends for the absence of conjugal affection, but which eventuate in nothing but remorse and shame. From such unhappy marriages proceed children who, for their first school, have the unworthy conduct of the father, or of the mother, or of both the parents; children consequently uncared for or little loved, destitute, or almost destitute, of education, without respect towards parents, without fraternal or sisterly affections, without an idea of the domestic virtues, which form the basis of the national virtues. All these things are so common that to see them we need only to look around us. No one can tell me that I exaggerate."

Words strong as these would not have been used by such an ardent lover of his country as Silvio Pellico, if the evils alluded to had not been strikingly apparent; and in no task could the Italian patriot of the present day be more profitably employed than in that of trying to extirpate the canker which is preying upon the vitals of his country. It is but a spurious patriotism that would gloss over or ignore evils that can be remedied; and since, truly as Silvio Pellico says, the domestic virtues form the basis of national virtues, Italy can never, under any form of government, become great or prosperous, until the homes from which her people issue are purified from the unholy influences pervading them at present.

The accomplishment of this object can only be obtained by elevating the social position of woman, in every stage of her career: she must be looked upon and treated as an intelligent responsible being, and not as one from whom the great gift of reason has been withheld. As a girl, she should be liberated from the galling restraints by which she is now fettered; she should be constituted the guardian of her own honor, and the influences of a cultivated mind and of moral principle fully developed, should supersede the duenna's vigilant eye, as a check upon impropriety of conduct. Her marriage would then be an act emanating from her own free will, and dictated solely by her own judgment and inclinations; and in her husband she would see the object of her love and choice, and not a constant galling memento of parental compulsion and tyranny. Under such altered circumstances, love, springing from the basis of mutual esteem, respect and confidence, would secure the sanctity of the marriage tie from profanation. Truth, honor and virtue, instilled by the mother's examples and precepts into the hearts and minds of her young offspring, would form the distinguishing features of their maturity; and by a race growing up under such auspices, the glories of the mediæval ages of Italy would be revived, or perhaps eclipsed, by the triumphs of her sons in art, science and literature.

For nature, bountiful as of yore, still sows the seeds of genius amongst the Italian people; but as in the parable of the sower, the seed now falls in stony places, where it can take no root, and by the wayside, where it is trampled down, and thus never reaches maturity. How much the elevation of woman would tend to foster and to stimulate the growth of the precious germs which now die out for want of nourishment and culture, is evidenced from the number of women distinguished by their attainments, who shed dignity on their sex in the times of Dante, Michel Angelo and Galileo. In the times which produced a Bettisia Gozzadini, the pride and ornament of the University of Bologna, of which she was created a professor; that exhibited a Domitilla Trevulzia, to whose Latin orations flocked crowds of listeners; when Isotta of Verona took a foremost place amongst the disputants in public controversies; when Novilla, the beautiful daughter of the Professor of Law at Bologna, delivered lectures to students, as the deputy of her father, in his absence; when Elena Piscopia dignified the University of Padua by the variety and profundity of her attainments; and when a silver crown, encircled with leaves of gold, was placed on the head of Laura Bassi, in testimony of the admiration felt for her genius and learning: in times illustrated by these, and other names too numerous to mention, the position, the character of Italian women must have been widely different from what it is at present; and the spirit of the past, in this respect, must be revived, ere the fame of a tarnished name can be redeemed, and Italy assume a forward place in the ranks of civilization.

## CHAPTER VII.

### THE PEASANT.

IN no country of the world, perhaps, do the signs of fertility, industry and abundance, so forcibly present themselves to the stranger's view, as in the largest portion of Tuscany. Art and nature, there going hand in hand, produce a series of rural pictures of the choicest, richest, and most attractive description. Through the combined influences of a glowing summer sun, a fertile soil, and an elaborate system of cultivation, the vales of the Arno, the Chian, the Ombrone, the Nievole, and the plain of Lucca, teem with products unknown to our less fruitful soil, and less genial clime. From the carefully garnered harvest of the olive tree, the peasant extracts the oil to feed his evening lamp in the short days of winter. The vine, until stricken by disease in recent times, afforded him an abundant supply of a grateful and strengthening beverage. In the Indian maize, which springs up vigorously in his fields, he finds a nutritious food. Fig, peach, pear, chestnut and walnut trees, drop down to him their fruits. Flowers, the hot-house nurselings or garden treasures of colder climes, offer spontaneously their rich and often highly-scented blossoms to his view. With the bramble of the wayside fence the sweet clematis twines; the small singing bird, which frequents the copse, makes its nest amongst myrtle boughs; the purple gladiolis raises its head amidst the growing grain; and, in many a grassy nook, the white petals of the gum-cistus strew the ground. With its teeming soil, and its varied produce, the primeval curse seems to sit lightly on Tuscany.

The impress of art—of industry, no less than that of a bounteous nature, is seen stamped upon the land unmistakably. Fields, where not a weed is to be discerned; farms, in which not one crooked or useless fence is visible, where the sower follows quick upon the reaper's track, and where the fresh turned up sod is fast covered over by a bright carpet of verdure; where, from dawn till dusk, the laborer is seen plying spade or hoe indefatigably: all these things, seen in various parts of Tuscany, attest that the Tuscan peasant is far from being an ungrateful recipient of the bounties of Providence. As the traveler journeys in spring or summer through this favored land, especially along the vale of the Arno, his onward course will be through scenes calculated to suggest the idea of a realized Arcadia. Far as the sight can reach on either side, farm after farm, for miles together, displays the same richness of produce, the same economy of space, the same garden-like degree of cultivation. Seen from a distance, the tile-roofed dwellings of the peasant, rising invariably at least two stories in height, though devoid of attraction as picturesque objects, seem to speak almost as strongly of comfort and prosperity as do the well-tilled fields, with their rich and varied produce, visible around them. Under the influences of the scene, bright are the pictures that fancy calls up before the traveler's eye, of the domestic life enjoyed by the Tuscan peasantry: the daily board, with its simple but abundant food; the daily toil, which exercises, but does not impair, the energies of the frame; the clean, roomy kitchen, whose walls display a goodly array of delf; the tidy housewife, with her dark hair braided smoothly beneath her snowy cap; the stalwart husband, clad in his good, homely, substantial suit; children, merry, healthy, and respectably dressed, playing in the sunshine, or clustering round the hearth; youth, happy, its joyousness lingering long, undimmed by the cares and toils of a striving, struggling life; age, cheerful, contented, the calm, peaceful twilight of a day whose brightness had been but momentarily and rarely overcast.

Unfortunately, however, between the real and the imaginary in this, as well as in many other things in the world, there exist a wide interval and a vast dissimilarity. Not more illusive is the mirage of the desert than is the picture painted in bright colors by the traveler's imagination of the condition of the Tuscan peasantry; and in both instances, a near approach destroys the delusion: the comfort, the well-being, the prosperity and contentment of the Tuscan peasant being no more real than the gleaming lakes of water, the shady trees, and the bright verdure which mocked from afar the hopes of the tired wanderer. No more striking exemplification of the truth of the old proverb that "appearances deceive," can be found than that afforded by the surface aspect of rural life in Tuscany.

To see the actual state of things with the Tuscan peasant, let us visit him in his home, selecting a fine day in early summer for this purpose. Quitting the high road, we take a narrow pathway winding through the fields in the direction of a substantial-looking two-storied house, whose red-tiled roof is seen rising above an intervening screen of foliage. Every yard of our progress, as we advance, is marked by features that cannot fail to be admired. On either hand are luxuriant crops of grain alternating with strips of lupin, vetches, peas and beans, intersected by rows of vines, whose long branches, hanging in rich festoons as they trail from tree to tree, close in the view in every direction; not a rood of ground we traverse but bears the mark of neatness, care and industry. No weeds, no crooked fences, no yawning ditches are visible—all waste of space, all waste of soil by useless vegetation, seem scrupulously avoided. Until we reach the immediate precincts of the dwelling, the rich picture is not marred by one unpleasant feature; but once there—arrived at our destination, the whole character of the scene undergoes a complete metamorphosis. The evidences of neatness, care and abundance, disappear, giving place to signs as unmistakable of dirt, slovenliness and poverty. The dwelling, which, viewed from afar, had an air of comfort and respectability, appears, on close inspection, a cheerless and utterly comfortless habitation: discolored walls, wood-work from which almost every trace of paint has vanished, windows without sashes or glass—mere large square apertures in fact, crossed at regular intervals by iron bars—present themselves to notice; and the vacant space before the entrance door is littered over with rubbish.

Inside, a still more dreary sight awaits us: stepping across the threshhold, we enter a good-sized apartment, which serves at the same time as kitchen and sitting-room for the inhabitants of the dwelling. The light that enters freely through the large unglazed casement, reveals walls begrimed with smoke and dirt, and blackened rafters. A bench here, a table there, a stool and two or three decrepit-looking rushbottomed chairs, with a few pots and pans, compose the whole amount of furniture visible. Ascending by a steep ladder with a hand-rail, serving as staircase, we gain the second story, and find the characteristic features of the scene below repeated in the foul, comfortless, and almost furnitureless rooms, which are used as sleeping apartments by the members of the household. Harmonizing well with the aspect of the interior is the appearance of the mistress of the dwelling; a dirty slattern, without shoes or stockings, clad in a coarse gingham dress, become, from the effects of dirt and age, of a kind of nondescript color; her face, arms and neck, are, through exposure to the sun, tanned to a dark brown hue, and a quantity of black, tangled, disheveled hair peers forth from beneath a red cotton handkerchief covering the back part of the head, and tied beneath the chin. The children, clustering around in scanty, tattered garments, with shocks of uncombed hair, and faces guiltless of any but a most remote acquaintance with soap and water, correspond in air and aspect with the maternal model. From a scene so little accordant with our expectations, we turn away with a sensation of mingled wonder and sadness; and, retracing our steps, marvel at the strange discrepancy that exists between the peasant's neat, trim, luxuriant fields, and his dirty, slovenly, poverty-stricken habitation.

As regards the majority of the peasantry in Tuscany, the scene described presents no exaggerated picture of the homes belonging to the mass of the rural population. Dwellings and inmates superior to the class described, may undoubtedly be found, and such I have visited myself in various parts of Tuscany; but even in the immediate neighborhood of Florence, I did not enter one peasant's dwelling, however outwardly imposing in appearance, that was not characterized within by an air of discomfort and poverty. One house, which gave me shelter for half an hour from a shower of rain, I particularly remember, as affording a striking instance of the deceptiveness of outward appearances. Almost deterred from entering by its size and aspect of gentility, I hesitated, fearing to intrude, until the sight of one of its inmates at the door convinced me that the dwellers beneath its roof belonged to the peasant class. As to size, many a gentleman in Great Britain, with two or three hundred a year, lives in a less capacious house; but as to comfort, it could not be placed upon a par with the poorest laborer's cottage I ever saw in England. In the numerous bed-rooms through which I was conducted, at my request, a low truckle bed, covered with a coarse, dark-colored, dirty quilt, constituted the only article of furniture visible. One room contained a heap of grain, another was devoted to the silk-worms' use, and adjoining the kitchen (the family sitting-room) was an apartment occupied by cows and calves. Dirt reigned supreme everywhere; ceilings, walls, floors, dresses, faces—all had a dingy, begrimed and sordid look.

Seen through the medium of experience, the existence of industry amongst the peasant class in Tuscany is quite an anomaly; for few instances can be found elsewhere of the utmost powers of the human frame being voluntarily exerted, with no higher reward in prospect than that of furnishing merely the commonest necessaries of existence. Strange is it, therefore, to find that the Tuscan peasant, who works so indefatigably in his fields from early dawn till after the sun has set, possesses no greater stimulus to exertion than that afforded by the prospect of gaining the means to afford a bare subsistence for himself and family. If industry (as it is generally held) be an ever gushing well-spring of fortune and independence, then should the Tuscan peasant eat with a silver fork, and fear the frown of no man. Scarcely is one crop gathered in, when the ground is upturned afresh with spade and hoe, and the yellow stubble of the harvest field is shortly succeeded by another, showing the tender green of the young sprouting plants of Indian corn. Not a vine is allowed to trail its branches on the ground, and every weed is extirpated by the careful laborer. As if fearing to lose a moment of his precious time, he works on with spade or hoe, even whilst answering the stranger's questions with ready courtesy. Long as are the hours of the summer day, he knows he has that to do which will keep him busy until the sun has disappeared below the horizon. But not alone does the contadino work; his labors are shared by his wife and family. That dirty, dark-eyed woman, with the baby in her arms, has an existence quite as laborious, if not more so, than that of her husband. Besides the sufferings and cares which the maternal position involves, she has to cut fodder for the cattle, to tend, to feed, and to clean them, and to take a share in outside agricultural labors. Well may her face be sunburnt and stamped with lines of premature old age, for her life is a hard and struggling one, and will continue so until the grass grows green above her head. Work, work, nothing but work, save on the day when she washes her face and combs her hair to appear at mass; husband and wife are sharers alike in a toilsome and poverty-stricken existence.

Poor in quality, and often scant in quantity is the food which sustains the lives of the Tuscan peasantry. When the landlord's share is deducted out of their small patch of wheat, the portion that remains serves but for a short time to afford a supply of white bread for family use. In the absence of this luxury, a dark, vile-looking compound of rye and other inferior kinds of grain, made into a thick, flat cake or clumsy roll, is generally eaten. Acting upon the idea that things are not in many cases at all so bad as they appear, I ventured on the experiment of trying the unattractive looking fare; but found that in this case at least, the decision of the taste fully confirmed the judgment of the eye; for, though I am very far from being dainty on the score of food, and am even obnoxious to the reproach of having eaten, with positive relish, dinners which have been indignantly denounced as insults to civilization and humanity, I must in truth confess that it would require me to be tolerably far advanced in the process of starvation, before I should feel the least inclination to repeat the experiment I made on the black bread which constitutes the Tuscan peasant's staple food.

The French or kidney bean forms a favorite article of food; the young pod is not eaten as with us, but the bean only, in its maturity. Every peasant has his patch of beans; and this vegetable seems to rank in popular estimation above the potato. Rather a strange preference it seemed to me; for though I strove to divest my mind of every insular prejudice, and to attain to an exemplary judicial state of feeling on the question, I could come to no other decision than that the merits of a dish of potatoes were incomparably superior to those of a dish of kidney beans; particularly when the latter was served up in oil, the usual and favorite condiment to everything.

Black bread, kidney beans and porridge made of Indian corn, constitute, it may be said, the fare of the Tuscan peasant. Occasionally he has in the summer or autumn season a few luxuries, such as peas, tomatoes, cherries, figs and chestnuts* to vary his unattractive food. Milk he seldom tastes, for the Italian peasant's cow is looked on as a means of rearing calves, and not of providing a nutritious beverage for himself and family; and butter, it may be said, as a general rule, is absolutely unknown. The wife of a peasant, possessing several cows, asked me one day what it was, then how it was made, and listened to my explanation with much apparent interest and curiosity. The butter I used at the Baths of Monte Catini came some thirty miles, from the dairy farms at Florence; and at Albano, a town containing several hundred inhabitants, the luxury was unprocurable; indeed, it is only in those places in Italy where the English congregate, that butter is entitled to take its place in the list of Italian produce.

From the ordinary dinner of the Tuscan peasant an English laborer would turn away with a sensation of scorn and disgust, and the more so, when he found that a cup of water was to prove its only accompaniment. Not always, however, was the peasant solely indebted for a beverage to the neighbor-

* Chestnuts form a staple article of food only in the mountain districts where they are grown.

ing well or brook, for, up to a recent period his vines, now worthless from the blight, afforded him a grateful, wholesome and strengthening drink.

With the fertile soil and the warm sun of Tuscany, joined to the indefatigable industry of the peasant class, it is quite evident that their beggarly aspect, their meagre food and their cheerless homes, must arise from some peculiar evils in their position. Devoid, generally speaking, of property in the soil, the peasantry are yet very far from standing in the same relation to their landlords as the two corresponding classes are to each other in England. The English tenant pays to the proprietor of the farm he cultivates a fixed annual sum of money; whilst the Tuscan tenant is bound to render to his landlord the half of all the produce raised upon his farm. Wheat, wine and oil are divided, share and share alike; and even in articles of the most trifling kind the halving system is applied. Of every brood of chickens the landlord can claim his half, and even eggs may come under the operation of a similar rule. The evident hardship of such terms is mitigated by the fact that the landlord contributes, in some degree, towards the expenses of the cultivation of the farm. He provides the house, supplies a moiety of the requisite seed corn, contributes in the same proportion towards the purchase of cattle and of mulberry leaves for the silk-worms. Even taking, however, these landlord contributions into consideration, the bargain on the tenant's side seems evidently a far from favorable one; and, in the absence of oppressive taxation, to this system of land tenure* must be traced the comfortless and struggling life led by the frugal and industrious *contadino.*

A secondary cause of the poverty that prevails in Tuscany may be discovered in the density of the rural population and consequent smallness of the farms. "We are too thick," they say themselves; "our holdings are too small." This is true indeed, in many instances, where a man's holding is limited, as it sometimes is, to two acres in extent; the entire produce of which would be required to afford to him and his probably numerous family a comfortable subsistence. Under such circumstances, a tenant must be poor, however equitable or even liberal are the terms on which his farm is rented. But mingled with holdings of this minute description are others evidently of a sufficient size, taken in connection with the fertility of the soil, to afford, after the payment of a reasonable rent, a comfortable subsistence to the cultivator. Yet, in the aspect of a farm so circumstanced, in the appearance of the occupier and his family, in their mode of life, in the character of their dwelling—although, in all these respects, a marked superiority over the small holding class may

* This *mezzeria,* or in French *metayer,* system of land tenure prevails throughout Tuscany.

be observed—the evidences of a hard struggling, comfortless existence are still discernible.

A system, founded on the principle of equal divisions of the produce between proprietor and cultivator, wears to the stranger the aspect of one exceedingly difficult to carry out fairly in practice; on speaking to the peasants, however, on this subject, they all assured me that the assignment of the shares was easily effected. Fraud on the tenant's part is checked by means of the landlord's steward, who keeps a vigilant eye on the tenant's proceedings, and who, from a careful inspection of the growing crops, can calculate to a nicety how many sacks of grain should await the landlord as his rightful portion. In case the anticipated amount be not forthcoming, or in case, through negligent culture, the capabilities of the soil are not developed in what may be deemed their proper degree, the defaulting tenant has to yield his place to a more honest or competent man. Changes of tenantry, however, seem to occur but rarely; for though the power of dismissal at a few months' notice rests in the landlord's hands, it often happens that one generation succeeds another in the occupation of the same house and land. Cases do of course occur from time to time, where, from exaction on the landlord's part, or fraud or negligence on the tenant's side, one occupier gives place to another in a farm; but, as a general rule, the peasant's home remains unchanged, if not for successive generations, at least for many successive years.

Amongst the tile-roofed dwellings that thickly dot the country, there may be seen every here and there one wearing an air of greater dignity than the rest, one possessing the luxury of glass windows, and making a little pretension to embellishment in the way of paint. This dwelling, on inquiry, the stranger is pretty sure to find, is the one in which the steward —*fattore*, as he is called — resides. A very important personage is this *fattore* under the land system of Tuscany. Into his hands the landlord—invariably a resident in town for at least nine months in the year — commits the management of his affairs. To the *fattore* must the tenant apply for money to help to purchase cattle, and all in the landlord's covenant to supply; and to the *fattore* must the tenant render account of every article of agricultural produce raised and sold. From the position and duties of the *fattore*, it is quite evident that, if dishonestly inclined, he has every facility to become rich at the expense of his employer; and that such a result frequently occurs may well be credited, arguing from the common weaknesses of humanity. There is a well known Tuscan saying, which embodies the popular creed and experience on this point: "*Fate mi fatore per un anno se son povero e il mio danno*," says the Italian proverb, whose meaning runs in English thus: "Make me a steward for a year, and it is my own fault if I am poor." Easy, indeed, it is to believe that, from the amount of produce, varying every year according to circumstances, and from the absence of all check over his proceedings, the steward's private stores are often enriched by sacks of grain and barrels of wine and oil belonging rightfully to his distant employer.

Notwithstanding the proverbially alleviating influences of custom, the Tuscan contadini are far from being insensible to the hardships of their lot, and very far from being reconciled to the poverty of their condition. In particular, I found the peasant women loud in their complaints and lamentations upon this subject. "We live like the beasts," they would exclaim, when, at my desire, they showed me through their comfortless dwellings; "to work hard, and to fare badly, is our lot from childhood to the grave. The hot sun scorches us in our hard field work in summer, and the cold winter's wind, as it enters through the many crevices of our wooden shutters, makes us shiver in our beds."

"Oh, would to Heavens! I had never married," was a common exclamation with them, and they would often declare that to rear up children in any kind of decency was a task that wore out their lives with trouble, anxiety and toil. "From morning to night," they said, "we slave and slave to gain a scanty supply of the commonest necessaries of life.

Ah! the hard existence which falls to the lot of a mother of a family, can be hardly told."

Though from the interior aspect of their dwellings, it is quite evident that an absence of comfort has invariably characterized the homes of the Tuscan peasantry, it cannot be disputed that their position has been much deteriorated by the vine disease, which has, for the last eight years, prevailed universally in Tuscany. The Tuscan grape was in former times famous for richness and for sweetness, and the wine it yielded was highly prized. According to the best authority, the process of wine-making was better understood, and a greater number of good wines was produced, in the Tuscan dominions, than in any other part of Italy. From France, from Spain, from the Canaries, the best species of vines have been imported by successive Grand Dukes. The *Montepulciano* wine, termed by an Italian poet *d'ogni vino il re*, ("the king of all wines,") was a product of the Tuscan State. The *Aleatico*, the *Columbano*, the *Trebbiano*, the *Vernaccia*, also enjoyed a high repute. The rocky hills of Chianti produced a fine red wine; and from Artimino came a claret that was highly famed. In those days the wine-barrels of the peasant were never dry, and every road-side tavern offered to the weary wayfarer, for a trifling coin, a refreshing and grateful drink. In those days autumn was crowned with beauty and mirth; and whilst the eye feasted on the sight of the rich pendent clusters of bright-colored fruit, the ear drank in with pleasure the joyous sounds that came floating in the air from the vineyards, where the busy vintagers plied their task.

But now, contrasted with the scenes of former years, sad is the change which the universal prevalence of the vine disease has effected in the autumnal aspect of Tuscany. No longer do rich clusters of green and purple grapes present themselves in countless numbers to the traveler's view—no longer does the air resound with the vintagers' mirthful voice and song. Though from tree to tree the vine still twines its slender stems, and by roadside fences, in fields, by cottage doors, and on terraced heights, its graceful foliage meets the view; the small, gnarled, unsightly knots of dried-up, cracked, and blackened juiceless berries, which protrude amongst the changing leaves, are a hideous mockery and corpse-like image of that beautiful and delicious fruit, which in every age has been the favorite theme of poetry and song. The wine-press of the peasant stands unused, his barrels are dry and empty; and as autumn after autumn the blighted produce of his vineyard meets his eye, his heart sinks within him in despair, although he fails not still to utter fervent prayers for the recurrence of the good old times.

Not merely, however, does the peasant mourn the loss of a pleasant beverage, in the destruction of his grape crop; this privation forms but one of others still more grievous, arising from that source. In former years, when the vine yielded an abundant and delicious fruit, the peasant could calculate, after deducting the landlord's share, on the possession of many more barrels of wine than what would be required for his own and family's use. This surplus (always the best) being sold, afforded the means of purchasing, besides many little comforts, articles of prime necessity, such as clothes. "Our wine was food, and drink, and covering to us," said a peasant, talking on the subject to me: "it quenched our thirst, and refreshed us in the summer's heat, it warmed us in the winter's cold, it gave us strength to work, it enabled us to do with far less food than we eat now, it bought us clothing for ourselves and children. With these old worn-out garments that you see, we must content ourselves, until the Almighty is pleased in his good providence to give us back our wine again."

With not less fondness than the Irishman clings to the potato, does the Tuscan peasant to the vine. Though now for several years nothing but shriveled bunches of arid, blighted berries has rewarded his care and toil, he still, spring after spring, devotes day after day of his precious time to the training and pruning of his once valuable, but now worthless, tree. Anxiously he watches the forming of the fruit and the sprouting of the leaves; and learning by experience to put no confidence in the luxuriant aspect of the vine in early summer, he waits with keen solicitude, with a kind of despairing hope, for the arrival of the time at which the first symptoms of the disease are accustomed to appear. Closer and closer does he examine his vines, as the month of June wears onward to its end; he calls to mind the date on which at the last, or previous years, he had marked the presence of the disease, and if the date passes, without the dreaded signs, his hope grows stronger: the curse, he begins to think, has been withdrawn. His spirits rise at the prospect of a recurrence of the good old times, and he dreams of tasting once again a glass of his loved wine. Vain hope, which the morrow perchance dispels. To a stranger's eye, the whitish aspect of the leaf, or a slight curling of its edges, appears but the effect of chance or accident, of dust or heat. But the peasant knows too well those fatal indications. His brow contracts, and his face becomes overshadowed with a cloud, as he notes indications which, he knows well, forebode another wineless year. As day by day leaf after leaf assumes a similar look and hue, he feels assured that the doom of his crop of grapes is sealed; though as yet the thick clusters of small green berries show not a visible symptom of disease. But not the less is the disease at work, poisoning the life-blood of the plant. As time wears on, the berries, instead of growing larger under the influence of the glowing sun, acquire a dry, shriveled, whitened look: often cracking, they burst in two; some dry up utterly; others, stunted and acid, make a faint attempt to attain a purple hue; another portion assumes a mildewed look; another turns black, or rusty-brown. With the recollection of former times still vivid in his mind—with the remembrance of the glorious clusters of bright green and purple grapes that in former vintage seasons met his view—well may the peasant turn away from his blighted vines and their worthless fruit, with feelings of disgust, despair and sorrow combined.

In the season of 1856, the vine disease did not rage quite so violently in Tuscany as it had done in the previous six or seven years: here and there occasionally, amongst the blighted produce, a few clusters of sound grapes were to be found. In some large vineyards, even, there was an attempt at making wine; but, judging from what I witnessed personally, the attempt resulted in a lamentable failure: as far, at least, as the production of a pleasant or healthy beverage was concerned; for, in addition to the really small quantity of untainted fruit that was to be found, the grapes were gathered before they were nearly ripe, in consequence of the pilfering by children of the rare dainty. And from a heterogeneous mixture of unripe grapes and of grapes both slightly and extensively affected by disease, the result may be inferred—a wine, a mere mockery of the name: pale, thin, weak, and as acrid as a sloe-juice.

One absurd theory as to the origin of the vine disease prevails extensively amongst the Tuscan peasantry; the smoke arising from the coal used in the engines being alleged to exercise a deteriorating influence on the air; and very frequently I was asked my opinion whether the railroads were really the cause. "Were there railroads in England?" I was asked invariably by the contadina in reference to this point. On my giving an affirmative reply, the question immediately succeeded—if the vines were healthy there?—a question the answer to which, as may well be supposed, tended nothing to convict or acquit the railroads of the crime alleged.

In addition to the railroad theory of the origin of the vine disease, another was started no less sage; but, unfortunately for the adherents of this latter creed, time proved its fallacy in the most irrefutable way. As before stated, from 1847 to 1856, owing to causes of a political nature, no public carnival festivities took place. Now, as it happened that with the first year of this omission the vine disease appeared, and continued to rage violently in the subsequent eight years of suspended carnivals throughout the land, an inference was drawn from this coincidence by some wise heads, that there must be a mysterious connection between the two events—that, in fact, the vine disease originated in the nonobservance of the season set apart for popular festivity from time immemorial in Tuscany. From this idea followed, as a logical consequence, the belief that with the restoration of the carnival in 1856, the vines would recover their ancient vigor; a belief unfortunately doomed to be destroyed by the autumn experiences of that year.

Little is it to be wondered at that ideas such as those described in reference to the origin of the vine disease, should prevail extensively amongst a peasantry so ignorant as is that of Tuscany almost universally. Throughout the country, schools are rare; and, in those that exist, a very infinitesimal amount of knowledge is communicated. To the teaching of the arts of reading and writing, the endeavor of the master is generally limited; and to the acquirement of these two branches of knowledge, are the aim and desire of the pupil as generally restricted. Even amongst persons occupying what may be termed a respectable position in society, and amongst persons endowed by nature with a considerable degree of intelligence and quickness of comprehension, the grossest ignorance of the rudiments of knowledge may be often found prevailing. In the country lodging-houses and hotels where I have been staying in Tuscany, it was no rare thing to find that, to the master or mistress of the dwelling, the simplest Italian book was about as intelligible as an inscription in the Cuneiform characters might prove to the world in general. Often did it fall to my lot to keep an account of expenses incurred, the correctness of which was only tested by some primitive system of self-invented mental arithmetic. At the very best, an imperfect acquaintance with the arts of reading and writing, and a mere smattering of arithmetic, constitute the utmost amount of knowledge obtainable, or obtained, by the rural population of Tuscany at the present day.

Did the peasant women of Tuscany pay more attention to their appearance; were they neater, cleaner, and tidier in their persons, they would decidedly, in regard to looks, be entitled to considerable praise; for nature has been for the most part decidedly liberal and kind to them in that respect. But, as it is, with their uncombed locks, their dirty faces, their slatternly style of dress, and their complexion spoiled by exposure to the weather, notwithstanding their large, bright, hazel eyes, their white teeth, and their thick tresses of black hair, they often present an exterior far from agreeable. The bloom of youth fades rapidly, owing to the hard life they lead, and owing also, perhaps, in some degree, to the senseless sort of out-door head-dress they wear, which leaves their faces completely exposed to a summer's scorching sun. Strange it is, that almost universally in every land and clime, in every class of society, we find the dictates of comfort and convenience completely disregarded and set aside by women, in reference to the form and fashion of their attire. In Tuscany, where the mid-day's summer sun shines with a dazzling, blinding glare—where the heat from the same source pours down with a scorching intensity—the peasant women seem to have been unable to devise a better covering for the head than a large straw hat, the limp leaf of which, instead of shading the face, for the most part hangs or flaps back quite over the crown, or a cotton handkerchief folded crossways, placed on the back part of the head, and tied by its two long ends beneath the chin. In neither case is the face protected from the heat, or the eyes shielded from the light, in the least degree; the effects of this exposure are seen in the coarse reddened skin, and in the forehead prematurely furrowed by the instinctive effort made to screen the eyes from the dazzling glare: an effort that results in the habitual contraction of the brows. In the country districts only on *festa* days, when their best attire is donned to go to mass, do the countrywomen ever resort to any means to shade their faces from the sun; and then the means employed to effect this purpose wears to a stranger's eye quite a ludicrous air, consisting, as it does, of a large fan held up perpendicularly before the eyes.

The observations made in reference to the appearance of the peasant women of Tuscany will also apply in a great degree to the exterior of the men:

very good looking specimens of humanity, for the most part, are they, with their Sunday faces and their Sunday clothes; but on working days their unwashed and poverty-stricken look detracts considerably from their natural advantages. Though in stature below the average English height, as are the women also, they are, for the most part, strongly and symmetrically formed—a circumstance that appears something of a marvel, considering the barbarous system of compression to which infancy is universally subjected in Italy, by the means of swaddling clothing. Ignorant as they are, the manners of both the men and women are characterized by a politeness that, coming from the heart, is far more winning than the cold courtesy which is the offspring of artificial rules; and very pleasantly and melodiously did their "*felice giorno*," or "*felice sera*," with which they never failed to greet me, fall upon my ears. On entering their dwellings, the inmates there would exert themselves to perform the rites of hospitality to the stranger visitor; and whilst many a regret was expressed that they had not a glass of wine to offer me, I was often presented with fruit and flowers, and in default of these, some young pea or bean pods (the contents of which it is the custom to eat raw in Italy) were put into my hands. Could I not stay a little longer? and would I not come again? were the phrases I constantly heard on my taking leave; and the burden of many an unfulfilled verbal obligation in this regard is resting on my conscience to this day.

Genuinely courteous as I ever found the peasantry, the urgent solicitations which I invariably received from them to repeat my visits to their dwellings, were the result, most probably, of a feeling stronger even than politeness acting upon their minds. Far different from the country life of England is that of Tuscany, for whilst in the former three classes of society may be found existing side by side, in the latter there is but one. In England the cottage of the peasant rises in close vicinity to the dwelling of the retired tradesman, the independent yeoman, or the residence of the peer and country gentleman; and from this arises a mingling in some degree of the upper and middle with the lower class of society. The ladies from the Hall superintend, perhaps, industrial schools, visit the cottages of the poor, send bowls of nourishing broth to pining invalids, and gifts of money or clothes to such as are in need, whilst, in a more limited degree, the retired tradesman's and the yeoman's family contribute to the comfort and well-being of the necessitous classes of the community amongst which they live. But in Tuscany a very different structure of society, a very different order of things exists. Not scattered over the surface of the country, as in England, but concentrated in towns, are to be found in Tuscany the upper and middle classes of Italian society. It is true that, occasionally, here and there, the traveler's attention is attracted by a mansion whose size and air announce it to be a rich man's property; but for at least nine, and probably ten, months in the year, that mansion, large and handsome as it is, remains uninhabited; for the rich Signor Magnane, or the Conte Baldino, loves too well (as does also his family) the town, with its society, its amusements, its parties, balls, concerts and theatres, to relish a quiet country existence. Except, therefore, during the months of July and August, when the heat renders the atmosphere of a town unhealthy and oppressive, the nobleman's or gentleman's country seat is consigned to silence and solitude. Even, too, for the time that the family may be resident at the place, no intercourse of any kind occurs between them and the peasantry in their vicinity.

The Italian lady never walks out if she can avoid it, except perhaps in some gay promenade, where she may display her costly toilet, to excite the admiration or envy of her acquaintances. Having no conception of any other kind of pleasure than that arising from excitement, no idea of any other duty than that of striving to look handsome, she spends the "*villegiatura*" season in listless indolence, sleeping away the greatest portion of the long, tedious twenty-four hours of her daily existence. The very idea of visiting a peasant's cottage and talking to the inmates, would disgust her excessively—she, with her silks and satins, her long trailing robes, to pass the threshhold of their doors — she, rich and well-born as she is, to concern herself with the interests of poor and ill-clad people — what a preposterous supposition, what an absurdity! Not that she is devoid of charity—not at all; but her idea of that virtue begins and ends with dropping a *soldo* into a beggar's hat, with conferring a *crazia* on some distorted cripple, or of contributing a *paolo* to the mendicant friar, who, with box in hand, solicits alms for the liberation of some suffering soul from purgatory.

With the same tastes for social pleasures as the class described, the prosperous merchant or tradesman never thinks of providing himself with a country house, where he may take up his residence permanently, and spend his declining days. At the most he builds, or rents, a villa (probably in the immediate vicinity of a town), to which he and his family repair for a month or six weeks, perhaps, in the hot season of the year. Thus, unlike England, where country life presents to view a blending of the different classes of society, that of Tuscany, it may be said, exhibits one class alone. Remote from the sphere of the affluent and well-born, the peasant lives and dies, and in the stylish carriage which envelops him in a cloud of dust as it dashes past him on the highway, he but very rarely catches even a momentary glimpse of those whom the labor of his hands goes to sustain.

Cut off, thus, from all intercourse with the upper classes of the land, a strange sight did it appear to the peasant and his family to behold a person in the attire of a lady entering their doors. When in addition, too, they found that the lady was a foreigner, and had come from a country which they had all heard of as a country supremely rich and grand, the marvel at, and interest in, the apparition was heightened considerably. Many were the questions I had to answer about myself and the country from which I came. "Was I married? How did the peasants live in England? Were they rich? Did the vines give good wine?" Being obliged in answer to this latter question to confess the poverty of England in regard to vines, my words were always echoed by my auditors in a tone of profound surprise. "No vines in England! was it possible? how strange! they had always thought that England was the richest and most fertile country in the world." Still greater and greater grew their wonder when they heard that not only had we no vines in England, but that we were destitute also of olives, figs and maize. At this information, whilst exchanging glances of astonishment, they would exclaim, *Sanctissima Vergine!* what a poor country it must be! how can the people there manage to support their lives?" The commiserating tone in which this remark, or others of a similar purport, was certain to be uttered, always amused me highly; and no less droll was it to see their puzzled look, when they tried to reconcile our miserable destitution of the good things of life—the absence of olives, wine and maize — with the fixed idea they entertained, that every individual of the English nation rejoiced in a commanding stature and brilliant color, in addition to a well-filled purse. Some concluded that the air must be very nourishing, though certainly the English did not look as if they lived on air; others gave up the matter as an inexplicable mystery, contenting themselves with repeating in a marveling tone that it was very strange.

In addition to the vine disease, the peasant has, during these late few years, been subjected to two other grievances of a serious kind. In consequence of the expenses to which the maintenance of the Austrian army of occupation in Tuscany gave rise, the land-tax has been increased considerably — a measure severely felt, in consequence of the low state of the peasant's exchequer, owing to the loss of his grape crop. The alteration which has recently taken place in the laws relating to military service also is one that affects the peasant very prejudicially. Under the conscription system formerly in force in Tuscany, six years was the term which the conscript had to serve; but recently the term of years has been increased to eight; and in consequence of this increase, as well as from the severe system of army discipline (borrowed from Austria), that has been lately introduced, the price of substitutes throughout Tuscany has become double, or even treble, what it was. In former times the peasant, for a few scudi, could easily find a person willing to serve in place of the son, who, just arrived at that time of life when his labor became most valuable to his family, had been seized for military bondage under the operation of the conscription laws. Now, the peasant, if in such circumstances as to render the services of his son an all-important object to retain, must, from the difficulty of procuring substitutes, pay a price for one that, if not at times beyond his means, is always beyond his power of doing, without a hard struggle, entailing sacrifices of the most painful kind. Many were the complaints and lamentations upon this subject that I heard: and not a little does this grievance serve to nourish the feelings of disaffection towards the Grand Duke and his government, which prevail generally throughout Tuscany.

In some parts of Tuscany — for instance, in the Lucchese territory — a considerable spirit of enterprise exists amongst the lower classes of the community. From amongst the dwellers in the chestnut-clad Apennine hills and glens (as has been already stated), a large number of hardy laborers go forth yearly to till the Corsican soil; others from the same district wander off to gain their bread some way or another in England or America. Even amidst the rich plains that encircle Lucca, I found it was a common thing for the younger male members of a large family to seek employment in foreign lands. One stout young lad I spoke to was on the point of starting off for France, where, on a railroad, which he said was being made three hundred miles beyond Marseilles, he hoped to be employed at wages of three francs a day. Others, from the same district, after a voluntary exile of some years, had returned from America, to take up their dwelling in their native land, with an amount of dollars that rendered them the envy of their relations and friends. To the poor Tuscan peasant the sums thus accumulated, though to English ideas moderate in amount, sound magnificently grand; for it needs but the possession of so many scudi as might make up an income of forty or fifty pounds a year, to confer on the rustic proprietor the reputation of a millionaire amongst his humble neigbors.

Much as the stranger is likely to be favorably impressed by the courteous manners and industrious habits of the Tuscan peasantry, it cannot escape the observer's notice that much of the comfortless, squalid aspect of the *contadini's* life is caused by circumstances for which they themselves are in a great degree to blame. Not only in the valleys of the Arno, where the peasant is liable to be dispossessed at a few months' notice, but in the plains of Lucca, where the tenant, so long as he pays a fixed annual rent of so many sacks of corn, enjoys a permanent tenure of house and land, the same uncleanliness is to be found prevailing in the habitations of the peasantry, as well as in their attire and persons. Small, indeed, would have been the expenditure of money required to whiten the smoke and dirt-stained walls on which I looked, and slight the amount of time which would have satisfied the claims of personal cleanliness. Though their meagre fare, their homeliness of dress, be not the *contadini's* fault, yet on themselves most certainly must rest the blame of wearing tattered clothes, and living in houses where the dust and dirt of years encrust the walls, ceilings, floors and furniture, and where vermin, fostered by the congenial atmosphere, swarm often in excess. An indifference to cleanliness, indeed, partakes of the nature of a national vice, which is equally apparent in carpets stained and disfigured by spitting, amongst the upper classes, as in the foul dwellings of the poor, and in the peasant woman's disheveled hair and unwashed face. A happy day will it be for Italy when the great merits of soap and water come to be generally recognized.

The production of silk constitutes an important part of the avocations of the Tuscan peasantry; for in almost every *contadino's* house silk-worms are reared. Few farms, however small, are devoid of mulberry trees; but as in some farms there are more, and in others less, than their cultivators have need of, an active traffic in mulberry leaves, during the spring and summer months, takes place. Some mulberry trees are forced to produce three crops of leaves in the season to feed three successive generations of silk-worms; but the trees are considered to be much weakened and injured by being so frequently docked and stripped. The hatching of the eggs of the silk-worm commences in the month of April, and is generally effected by artificial heat; the women carrying them about their persons during the day, and placing them beneath the mattresses of their beds at night. On Rogation Sunday, the peasants, both men and women, with the eggs of the silk-worms in their bosoms, go in procession to church to solicit the protection and favor of San Jolo, from whose wounds, it is believed, the silk-worms issued. As at the beginning of the process, so the conclusion of the silk harvest is terminated by a religious solemnity; for each peasant, taking from his store a few cocoons, repairs with them to his parish church, and lays them on the altar as a thank-offering to providence. These cocoons, so deposited, become the property of the priest, who sells them, either for the benefit of the poor, or to enrich his own exchequer, according as he may be charitably or selfishly inclined.

The silk crop is an uncertain one; for, even with

the greatest care, the silk-worms occasionally become diseased and die. A good deal of skill is requisite in their management, to produce a prosperous result; for at certain stages of the silk-worm's growth they become extremely susceptible to harm—the slightest touch or the most trifling noise, as I was told, being capable of affecting them prejudicially. Such crises occur during the five moulting sleeps through which they pass; after each of which they waken up, increased in size and with increased vigor of appetite. Progressively, however, as their eating capabilities are developed during their successive states of repose, the wakening up from the last sleep, called *la grossa*, arrayed in a final coat, is followed by a display of gormandizing powers astonishingly great: ravenous with hunger, they eat on incessantly for a space of eight or ten days; the supply of leaves required for their never-ceasing repast is enormously large;* and a happy moment is it for the *contadino*, when he sees the worms refuse the food that for many days they had been devouring so voraciously, and, climbing up the branches of the trees he has placed beside them, begin their work.

Very assiduously do the worms labor at their task for four or five days' time; at the end of which, having quite enveloped themselves in their silken sepulchre, they undergo a different fate, according

* A silk-worm consumes within thirty days a quantity of food about 60,000 times its own primitive weight.

to the purposes they are allotted to fulfill. Such cocoons as are destined to manufacturing uses are plunged into boiling water to kill the worm within; whilst other cocoons—which are reserved for seed, as it is termed—are strung together on a piece of thread, and hung up against a wall. From the cocoons treated in this latter way there issue, in a few days' time, large white moths of the most sluggish nature, which never quit the cloth prepared for their reception: there, having deposited their eggs, they languish and die.

Not to the present, but to the former, political institutions of Tuscany, is the garden-like cultivation of the country ascribable. When the rest of Europe exhibited nothing but poverty and barbarism, the open country belonging to each republican city of Italy had its fertility developed by an active and industrious peasantry, through the medium of a system of scientific agriculture. Though then, as now, the proprietors of the soil were inhabitants of the towns, the merchant landowners of former times contributed money far more liberally towards the cultivation of the land, than do now their impoverished successors. By them alone was the land-tax paid; at their cost were dikes and canals constructed: the former as a preservative against inundations, the latter to increase by irrigation the productive powers of the rich plains. The grand canal of Milan, which spreads the water of the Ticino over a large part of Lombardy, owes its existence to those times; and at this day in Italy,* after a lapse of five centuries, the districts formerly free, and cultivated by a free peasantry, are easily distinguishable from those where feudalism prevailed. Through those five ages, amidst all the changes that have occurred in Tuscany as well as in Lombardy, have been handed down from father to son, the knowledge and the practice of a system of agriculture, which offered in bygone times, as it does now, a model for imitation to other lands. And much, truly, is it to be desired that the time may arrive before very long, when the Tuscan peasant's home will bear in character some resemblance to his fields; that the riches, neatness and cleanliness without will find a counterpart in the scenes within; and that his toil, furnishing him with more than the mere means of life, shall surround him with some of the comforts of a civilized existence.

* Sismondi.

## CHAPTER VIII.

### MANNERS AND INCIDENTS.

TUSCANY enjoys the reputation of being the cheapest place of residence in all Italy; and, certainly, though the inhabitants of the Grand Duchy complain bitterly of the rise of prices in articles of food that has recently taken place, to the English stranger the cost of living, even under the present order of things, will appear surprisingly low. A Tuscan *scudo*, the value of which is about 4*s.* 5*d.* in English money, will, as far as lodging, food and amusements are concerned, go nearly as far in Florence in ministering to such wants as a sovereign in London. For instance, in the newest and cleanest part of Florence, in the immediate vicinity of the Piazza Maria Antonia, a bed-room and a sitting-room of moderate size on the first floor, most comfortably furnished, can be procured at the rate of twenty-seven shillings a month. For two *paoli*, eleven-pence English money, an excellent simple dinner from a cook's shop, or *trattoria*, can be obtained, consisting of a soup, two dishes of meat, and one dish of some kind of vegetable. For a couple of *paoli*, also, the doors of the opera-house fly open, where first-rate vocalists, like Mdlle. Piccolomini, are heard, and first-rate operas are performed. In short, for persons of scanty means, nowhere, perhaps, can the always unpleasant duties of economy be so agreeably practiced as in the Tuscan capital.

In England, in London especially, sixty pounds a year constitutes an income on which a family belonging to the middle classes would find it difficult to keep up an appearance of gentility; in Florence, on the contrary, an annual revenue amounting to that sum confers on the proprietor and his family the means of enjoying many of the luxuries of life. Instead of the small, mean, ill-furnished rooms, in some narrow street, in an unfashionable quarter of the town, to which the recipient of sixty pounds a year must necessarily, in London, be confined, the Florentine, with the same amount of means, can provide himself and family with large well-furnished apartments in an airy square. With an Italian family, whose circumstances were such as I have described, I was well acquainted during my residence in Florence. They occupied a suit of rooms in the Piazza Santa Croce, one of the principal piazzas in the town. Their drawing-room was a spacious, lofty apartment, not only well, but elegantly, furnished: a large mirror, in a handsome frame, decorated the wall; on a handsome pier table underneath the glass, stood a highly ornamented French clock; and the small marble tables, of which there were several in the room, were covered with vases, shells, and various articles of an ornamental kind; whilst the requirements of comfort were fully satisfied by the arm chairs and the luxurious sofa that met the view. Opening off this room was a smaller one, occupied by the family in the morning hours, and when they had no company to entertain. In the parlor, a good-sized, well-furnished room, a very excellent rosewood grand pianoforte was seen; whilst another apartment well merited the name of library, from the extensive and choice collection of ancient and modern works which the shelves of its numerous bookcases contained. The two young ladies of the family had been educated quite in a fashionable style, having had music-masters, and singing-masters, and French masters, and English masters, remaining, therewithal, intensely ignorant of everything that most concerned them as rational civilized beings to know. The out-door attire of both mother and daughters quite corresponded with the aspect of their home—dresses made in the last fashionable style, bonnets with artificial flowers, silk mantillas, and gay parasols, announced most plainly how far aloof poverty stood from their door; and yet the gilded mirror, the French timepiece, the grand pianoforte, the numerous sitting-rooms, the accomplishments, the fashionable dresses, and the artificial flowers, were the products wholly of sixty pounds a year.

In England, a villa in the immediate vicinity of any large town, is a costly luxury to procure, and one in which no citizen could venture to indulge, unless possessing a revenue of several hundred pounds a year; but far different is the case in Tuscany, for in the vicinity of Florence an excellent suit of apartments, suited to a good sized family, may be rented at the rate of 40 scudi (8*l.* 17*s.* 8*d.*) a year, and in a villa near Florence, the rent of which was no more than this sum, I passed a fortnight with some Italian friends. The situation of the house was extremely beautiful, commanding, as it did, from the eminence on which it rose, an extensive view of undulating hills and fertile plains, backed by lofty mountains. From the outer hall an inner one was entered, as spacious, high, and cool, as might be desired in a warm summer's clime. This hall gave access to bed-rooms suited to the wants of a good-sized family, also to a kitchen and two sitting-rooms; the windows of which latter opened on a terrace extending the whole length of the house, and affording a magnificent prospect.

But though an Italian family can manage to make

a show on sixty pounds a year, such could not be accomplished by an English family resident in Florence, owing to the utter difference of opinion existing between the two nations in regard to the requisites of life, and to what constitutes domestic felicity. With English people of respectability, good, substantial fare—the juicy joint, well-cooked vegetables, fresh butter, milk, and eggs, are articles of prime necessity; but poor in quality and scant in quantity is the food which suffices for the requirements of Italians belonging even to the middle classes of society.

Strange to the English eye is it to see the household life of a Florentine merchant and his family, and to mark how comfortless it is, according to the English signification of the term. The proprietor of a suit of handsome rooms in both town and country, will make his morning meal, before repairing to his place of business, on a cup of coffee without cream or milk, and a piece of sour leavened bread, devoid of any accompaniment. On his dinner table will be seen, day after day, as the principal dish, a large tureen of tasteless soup, consisting of the thin watery decoction of a small piece of beef, thickened up by maccaroni to its utmost capacity. The pie or pudding is reserved for great occasions, such as Easter, Christmas, and company days, and seldom forms a portion of the domestic meal. For supper, if milkless coffee and dry bread come not again into requisition, the day's refreshments are probably concluded with a dish of kidney-beans swimming in oil, accompanied with a glass or two of thin acid wine. Then, also, though the mistress of the household appears abroad in velvet, satin, silk, and artificial flowers, at home a nightcap very possibly constitutes the head-dress for her morning wear, accompanied by a dress which, if not very old and very faded, is certain to be composed of some material of the commonest and cheapest kind. Cold also as the winter's wind often blows from the snowy crests of the Apennines, and rainy and chilly as are generally the spring months, no fire (or at least but rarely) dispenses its genial warmth around, gladdening the eye with a cheerful blaze. It would be difficult, indeed, if not impossible, to find an English family of respectability contented with such a style of life; or one that would not willingly forego, if necessary, every feature of external show—the grand pianoforte, the gilded mirror, the showy timepiece, the velvet bonnet, and embroidered mantle—for the enjoyment of good food, good daily dress, and, above all, the good, cheerful fire in the long cold evenings of winter.

The Tuscans may well love their warm summer skies, for under those of winter their lives for the most part (at least to the English idea) are indeed dreary and uncomfortable. All along the base of the Apennines, the winter climate, for nearly perhaps three months in the year, is very little, if at all, inferior in severity to the climate of England or Ireland. Rarely is Florence unvisited by snow, and never does a season elapse without the frequent recurrence of frost; whilst overhead, dark, lowering clouds, borne downwards from the mountains, exclude the sun from view. The north and east winds blow piercingly, and even so late as the month of March, furs are a grateful luxury. In a climate such as this, it might reasonably be supposed that ample provision would be made for the enjoyment in the winter season of a genial temperature indoors, through the means of artificial heat; but, as if in defiance of all the dictates of common sense, one finds in Tuscany the dwellings of the peasantry generally, and the dwellings of the middle classes often, constructed in a manner suited solely to a climate where summer perpetually prevails; the windows of the former being devoid of glass, and the sitting-rooms of the latter being frequently destitute of fire-places or stoves. What a cheerless picture, under such circumstances, a family party in Florence presents on a winter's evening, may easily be conceived; the light from the lamp falling upon a circle of shivering mortals, whose cheeks and lips, with their pale bluish hue, attest the severity of the cold. Well may the household virtues languish in Italy, and domestic love grow cold, under the influence of that frigid temperature which prevails during the winter months indoors.

Even where fire-places exist in Italy, the English stranger soon discovers that they are generally intended far more for show than use; the principle that guided their construction seeming in general to have been, that all the heat should go up the chimney, and all the smoke should enter the room. So well are the natives acquainted with this characteristic of their fire-places, that they seem to consider the refusal of smoke to ascend the chimney, merely a logical consequence of fire being kindled on the hearth below; and the complaints which strangers utter on this subject, are considered simple and unreasonable in the extreme. "Bring up some wood, and make a fire in our room," I said to the porter of a house in Naples where I resided. The direction was obeyed; the wood was piled upon the hearth, the match box was produced, and in another moment the fire would have been kindled, had I not, suddenly recalling my previous winter's experience in Tuscany on this subject, hastily asked, "But does the chimney smoke?" At these words the man turned round, and, with a look and in a tone expressive of both wonder and amusement at the simplicity of my question, replied, "Smoke! to be sure it does."

To impute to Italians, however, an indifference to and entire disuse of artificial heat in winter, would be untrue; for, though neither open fire-places nor close stoves are patronized by them, they possess, in the great domestic institution of the *scaldino*, a means of blunting, in some degree, the sharpness of the cold. Scarcely has the power of the hot summer sun begun to wane, than the front of every crockery shop presents to view numbers of small brown earthenware jars, with high overarching handles. Holding an article of this kind filled almost to the top with charcoal embers, Italians may be often seen, both rich and poor, going through the ordinary avocations of life, on a cold winter's day, with much apparent complacence. The porter at the palace door cheers the dull tedium of his hours through the means of his *scaldino;* the crippled beggar, who entreats the passer-by, for the love of the most blessed Virgin, to give him a *quattrino*, whilst he extends one hand to receive the expected alms, holds in the other a *scaldino;* the elderly gentleman, who walks along at a slow, measured pace, has probably a *scaldino* concealed beneath the folds of his voluminous mantle; the lady, as she sits talking to her guest, caresses lovingly the warm, smooth brown surface of her *scaldino*. The *scaldino* takes its place alike in drawing-room and kitchen, and is cherished alike by mistress and by servant. One stumbles over *scaldini* on the floor, knocks down *scaldini* on the table; *scaldini* here, and there, and everywhere, exhibit themselves, from morn till night in winter, to the stranger's view inside the dwelling of a Florentine family.

The *scaldini* is not without some value, indeed, in a pleasurable point of view; and on my first arrival in Italy, being of a chilly temperament, I invested a sum equivalent to three half-pence in the purchase of a *scaldino*. Short, however, was my conformity with the national custom, for I found that indulgence to my hands or feet, in the way of extra warmth through the medium of the *scaldino*, entailed upon me severe and constant headaches; a very natural consequence of the noxious gas arising from red-hot charcoal embers, which I had been unwisely imbibing; yet though the fumes from the smouldering charcoal affected me so prejudicially, I never heard an Italian complain of the slightest inconvenience in this respect. Still, though no headache may arise from the influence of a poisonous gas to persons accustomed from childhood to the use of the *scaldino*, the native vigor of the constitution must certainly be sapped in some degree by constantly inhaling a vitiated atmosphere.

The use of the *scaldino*, and the absence or deficiency of fire-places and stoves in Italian houses, is to be attributed, doubtless, to the costliness of fuel; a good fire being a luxury beyond the power of even the middle classes of society in Italy to indulge in habitually, even in winter, without taxing their generally very limited finances in an undue degree.

The absence of a cheap, abundant fuel, like coal in England, causes much discomfort and suffering amongst all the poorer classes in Italy in the winter season; for the price of wood is such as to render the greatest economy of consumption of this article obligatory on the great bulk of the middle as well as of the entire lower class of the community. What a disagreeable economy that is to practice, no native of England can understand, who has not made a personal acquaintance with the winter climate of Italy by a residence there during the cold season of the year. So much has been written about the warm sun, the blue sky, and the balmy air of Italy, that an idea strongly pervades the English mind, that warm suns, blue skies, and balmy airs, are the almost perpetual inheritance of that fortunate country. But such an idea experience proves should be classed amongst the popular delusions enumerated by Sir Thomas Brown; for in many an Italian November day the wind blows icy cold; in many a December day the sun refuses to shine; and in many a January and February day the skies are covered with leaden clouds, from which the rain pours mercilessly down. Oh, poets and novel writers! great is the responsibility resting on your heads, for having fostered the huge illusion which so generally prevails with regard to the blessedness of an Italian winter clime. With the incessant sound of rain-drops in my ear, and the dull light from a leaden sky entering the windows of my room, my feet and fingers well nigh numb with cold, I have often longed in Italy for the glorious warmth of a fire of English coal; before which the beams of even the brightest winter Italian sun fade into mere nothingness.

Geology and morality may seem, at first sight, subjects far apart; but it is not difficult to trace an intimate connection between the mines of coal and the domestic virtues of England: for instance, if Mr. Smith, that very exemplary member of the community, who is to be found evening after evening in his easy chair at his own fireside, chatting with his wife and playing with his children—if this same Mr. Smith, the pattern husband, the model father, instead of having a good coal fire to sit beside, were to be condemned to pass the long winter evenings inhaling carbonic acid gas from a *scaldino*, in a cold, dark, fireless room, it is much to be feared that Mrs. Smith would have often to mourn an absent spouse, and that few and far between would be the rides that Master Tom would get upon the parental foot or knee. Keeping this consideration, therefore, as we should do, in view, it must be allowed that when the temperature indoors ranges at forty degrees or less, it is a difficult thing for Signor Bacilesi to sit out the long winter evenings in his cold, gloomy home, acting the Smithian part, when cafés and theatres abroad afford him, at a trifling cost, the combined enjoyments of society, amusement, warmth and light. Who, then, duly reflecting on this subject, can fail to recognize the important part which the geological conformation of Cumberland and Lancashire plays in the development of the domestic virtues in England?

Throughout Tuscany, and, indeed, I may say, throughout Italy, England and the English are very much respected by the great mass of the population. The power of England presents itself to the popular mind in Tuscany as a power of the most unlimited magnitude. The release of Rosa Madiai and her husband from prison resulted entirely, I was told, from the interposition of England in their favor, through the means of a threat uttered by the English Government on the subject. My informant assured me, gravely, that the English minister wrote to the Grand Duke, "If in six weeks' time Rosa and her husband are not free, I will send an army to release them, and knock down Florence about your ears!" Of course, such a terrific menace could not fail in producing an immediate effect.

According to the same accurate and trustworthy authority, an Englishman or Englishwoman never breaks a promise, and never defrauds. During my stay in Tuscany, I found the most unlimited confidence placed in my honesty, by persons almost strangers to me, with whom I had money transactions of any kind. In a case that came under my own knowledge, of an English lady who had defrauded a poor Florentine tradeswoman of a sum which to the latter was one of a serious amount, I had an opportunity of becoming acquainted with the deep-seated reliance on English honesty that prevailed. "How could you act so very foolishly," I said, "as to go on from month to month, and even from year to year, not only giving credit, but lending money, when it was asked?" "Yes, I feel now that I acted foolishly," was the reply; "but the lady being English, I never doubted for a moment she would repay me every farthing that she owed, according to her word." Precisely to the same purport was the remark made to me by the proprietor of one of the principal hotels in Florence, to whom I expressed my surprise that he should have permitted a swindler, a *soi-distant* Englishman, to defraud him out of the expenses of board and lodging for a lengthened time. "The gentleman always said he would pay me when he got a remittance from his London banker," was the reply; "and I, thinking him to be an Englishman, for he bore the name of one, believed implicitly what he said." "Still," I rejoined, "when you found out through the telegraph that he had no money at the bank, as he declared, I wonder you continued to give credit to his promises of eventual payment." "Well," was the reply, "if I had not believed him to be an Englishman, I would have turned him out of doors at once; but as I never knew an English gentleman to cheat or to break his word, I relied confidently on having my dues at last."

In regard to Italian female servants, I invariably found that the great desire of their hearts was to get into the service of an English lady or an English family, not so much from the increase of wages they might obtain beyond the Italian standard, as from the kinder treatment they expected to receive, and the easier life they hoped to lead, than that which fell to their lot in an Italian family. "Pray, take me as your maid," was an entreaty that I constantly heard, together with the assurance that I might fix the wages at any sum I chose. English ladies, indeed, are looked up to and spoken of, amongst Italians of the lower classes, in a manner that often amused me considerably; by the women, especially, whose depressed social condition leads almost universally to the most extreme cowardliness of mind.

Constantly, when performing the most simple actions in the world, I have found my achievements regarded as belonging to the heroic class; for instance, when bathing, I advanced into the sea until the water reached up to my waist—when during a thunder storm, I stood near the window to watch the lightning flashes—when I crossed a narrow street between, perhaps, two very slowly moving lines of carriages—I was looked upon as having done something truly wonderful. Many were the tales I heard of English ladies' deeds of daring; how this one had undertaken a journey by herself—how that one had not scrupled to ride or walk for several miles alone—and how another, who had lost her way one evening in a chestnut wood, instead of going well nigh crazy with fright, (as an Italian girl under similar circumstances would be certain to do,) treated the affair as a good joke, by bursting out into a merry laugh on being wakened up the ensuing morning by some members of her family, who, going in search, had found her sleeping quietly beneath a tree. The extreme pusillanimity of Italian women gives, in their opinion, quite a marvelous character to the simplest deeds; and this failing—unchecked in childhood—grows sometimes to an excess that must often detract much from the happiness of their lives.

"*Ho paura,*" (I am afraid,) is the commonest expression one hears in Italy from feminine lips. I was acquainted with a young girl of seventeen, who stayed in bed three days to recover from the effects of some silly hobgoblin fears; and a middle-aged servant of mine remained in a dead swoon for upwards of an hour, in consequence of seeing a large eel unexpectedly: it is, indeed, rare to find amongst rich or poor, an Italian woman who will not scream, or jump, or start, on the slightest provocation imaginable.

Although the English are generally liked and respected throughout Tuscany, they are very far from being favorites with the upper classes of that land. Whilst to the Tuscan peasant, to the tradesman, or to the merchant, the term *Inglese* stands as the impersonification of honor, probity, courage, wealth, and generosity, to the Tuscan gentleman or noble that same word is the synonym for every phase of disagreeableness: a result attributable in a great degree to the pride and shyness which characterize, in general, English manners; for to the polished Italian, brought up to respect the established forms of politeness beyond most other things, and gifted with a volubility of speech that knows no check, English silence and reserve very naturally wear the aspect of studied rudeness or want of courtesy.

To the estrangement resulting from this source is added that which proceeds from uncongeniality of tastes and characters. Excluded from the real business of life, without public duties of any kind to engage his mind, and with no profitable avocations to occupy his time, the Tuscan nobleman, or gentleman of independent fortune, seeks refuge from the approaches of ennui by a headlong plunge into the whirling gulf of pleasure and dissipation. A career of such a kind, whose only aim is self-indulgence, whilst it destroys the sense of right, infallibly imparts a tone of frivolity to the character. The English nobleman or gentleman, brought up under influences widely different, with many opportunities of useful occupation, and a consciousness of public duties as landholder or magistrate, and with the means of honorably satisfying his love of excitement in the wide field of political life that is thrown open to his ambition, acquires a certain seriousness of thought and solidity of character, which but ill harmonize with the tone of Italian society; where the advent of a new *prima donna* holds the same place in interest as the advent of a new Prime Minister does in England, and where the graces of a pirouette and the merits of a roulade are discussed with the same amount of earnestness and animation that might be employed in English society in criticising the acts and words of English public characters and statesmen.

Another cause may also be discovered for that dislike which is entertained by the upper classes of Tuscany towards the English generally. With an innate fondness for display, a national taste that manifests itself throughout every rank of society in Italy, the Tuscan nobleman or gentleman, having a fortune of moderate amount or a scanty revenue, finds himself eclipsed in his own land, in external pomp and show, by that wealthy Anglo-Saxon race whom a love of change, of art, of sunshine, or other motives have impelled towards the shores of Italy. The *princepe* or *marchese*, whose ancestors played a distinguished part in Floretine history, and whose fortress-palaces adorn the Tuscan capital, must be galled and mortified by the consideration that, in equipages, in style of living, in splendor of entertainments, they cannot compete with Mr. Brown or Mr. Smith, whose gentility dates not, perhaps, beyond the quarter or half-quarter of a century. But still more powerful than any of the causes of estrangement enumerated is that which has its growth in the different codes of morals that bear sway respectively in Italian and English society. "The English talk scandal about us," say the Italians: and, probably, this charge is not without foundation; for no pure-minded Englishwoman, or right-thinking Englishman, can frequent Italian society without finding much to condemn.

To one custom, prevalent not only in Tuscany but throughout Italy, no length of residence abroad can ever reconcile the English stranger. In the British isles the practice of bargaining is looked upon as a very plebeian transaction, and in the lowest order of shops alone, and amongst the lower classes of the people chiefly, is the practice of bargaining general. With us, no shopkeeper, who aimed at securing the custom of respectable persons, would offer to abate one farthing in the prices first demanded for his goods; and even the most thrifty lady would scarcely venture to compromise her gentility so far as to attempt to higgle over the purchase of a yard of calico or a pound of tea. Far different in this respect is the custom in Italy; for the Italian shopkeeper, whether he lives in a fashionable street or in a back lane, whether he vends satins or maccaroni, almost invariably demands for his commodities a higher price than he will take, or indeed calculates to receive; since his customers, whether rich or poor, on their part quite as universally stipulate for an abatement in the cost of the article they wish to buy. The difficulty to English strangers of shopping, under such circumstances, may easily be conceived; unfamiliar with the art of bargaining as they usually are, as well as being ignorant of the just value of the article they may desire to purchase. Of course, however, for those fortunate individuals on whom economical considerations need exercise no restraint, shopping in Italy is an occupation that involves as little trouble as does shopping in England; but to those natives of the British isles who do not find it convenient to pay a third, or perhaps one-half, more than the fair value of every article, Italian shopping is a grievance, and a burdensome affliction. Disagreeable to me, however, as was always the avocation, I often derived considerable amusement in listening to such negotiations, and witnessing the manner in which they were carried on between the vendor and the purchaser.

A lady asks the price of a ribbon she admires—"Three paoli the braccio," is the reply.

"Three paoli!" rejoins the lady in a contemptuous tone, giving the ribbon a slight toss aside; "how dear! how enormously dear!"

"Dear! no, not at all," returns the shopkeeper, blandly; "rather it is cheap, remarkably cheap, if you consider the color and quality of the goods."

The lady takes up the ribbon again, looks at it, and after a moment's consideration says she will give two paoli the braccio for it.

The man shakes his head, with something of an indignant air. Two paoli the braccio for such a ribbon! quite impossible to give it for such a price as that; but to accommodate the signora as far as practicable, he will say twenty crazie* the braccio for it.

"Still much too dear," is the rejoinder; "the ribbon is not really worth more than twelve crazie; but as the color suits me, I will give seventeen crazie a braccio for it."

"I am very sorry, but I cannot sell it at that price."

A short silence follows; the lady looks at the ribbon with an approving eye, the shopman waits for some new proposal; but none being forthcoming, he suggests, at length, an accommodation of the difference; for eighteen crazie the braccio the ribbon shall be hers.

* There are eight crazie in a paoli.

The proposition being acceded to, the negotiation comes happily to an end.

Not always, however, does the transaction terminate so speedily. On two or three successive days I have known negotiations renewed, before a satisfactory settlement of the price could be attained. On one of these occasions, a straw bonnet, of the value of about seven shillings in English money, was the article under discussion. On the third day, the negotiations had so far advanced to a favorable termination, that a difference of about two pence three farthings alone prevented the sale from taking place; and on the fourth day, I have no doubt the difference was finally adjusted, and the sale effected by the sacrifice of a few farthings on either side.

The process of shopping, under the Italian system, would be much simplified to the stranger, if any certain rule could be given as to the proportion that the real value of an article bears to its nominal one. But though, unhappily, Italian shopkeepers all agree to ask far more for their goods than they are worth, they by no means show the same accord in adopting one uniform rate of overcharge. Each shop has its different sliding scale: as the stranger will find from painful experience; whilst in one, an article may be procured for half the price first asked, in another an abatement of only a third or a fourth part of the original price will be made. Amidst the intricacies and perplexities of such a system, the stranger stands but little chance of obtaining any article at a price at all approximating to the one it ought in equity to bear.

"*Quanto vuol darmi?*" ("How much will you give me?") is a phrase much in use amongst tradesmen, on an objection being made to the price demanded for their wares; and when I have left a shop, rather than conduct negotiations for sale on the established higgling principle, my proceeding was looked upon, I could easily see, as something quite eccentric and absurd: so firmly is it established in the Italian mind that every one who wants to buy, and every one who desires to sell, should each endeavor strenuously, on their respective parts, the one to make the most, the other to pay the least he can, whether the matter involve the value of a few pence or many pounds.

Yet, universally as the Hebrew principle of trade prevails throughout Italy, and biassed as minds become in favor of customs sanctioned by prescription, I have met with Italian tradesmen sufficiently rational and enlightened to condemn the principle of overcharging as dishonest and injurious.

"But what can I do?" said a Florentine mercer to me one day, in reference to some observations of mine; "though I admire the English system of dealing as being an essentially good and honest one, the practice of it on my part would certainly banish from my shop every Italian customer I have; for no

Italian lady would purchase from me the most trifling article, unless I made some abatement in the price declared; however reasonable and fair that price might be. Under such circumstances, therefore, not only to make any profit, but even to save myself from actual loss, I must ask in the first instance a high price for my goods, in order to allow for the abatement that every customer will inevitably demand. Fixed prices are best, I freely admit, and I wish heartily that they were the established rule in this land; but for a solitary individual like myself to oppose a universal custom, and to set up a system of English dealing here, would soon result in ruin and bankruptcy."

To the reasonableness of such observations I could not but assent; recalling the keenness with which the process of bargaining on the part of intending purchasers had often, under my own eye, been carried on. Not only in this, but in many other respects, Italy affords a striking example of the way in which evils act and re-act upon each other, so as almost hopelessly to perpetuate their rule.

The universality of beggary in Italy detracts much from the pleasure of a stranger's residence in that land; and though the Neapolitan dominions, perhaps, possess an unhappy pre-eminence in that particular, the curse of mendicancy prevails to a most lamentable extent in Tuscany. From the rich plains through which the Arno winds, there issue a ragged, squalid tribe, who sustain their miserable lives on charity. In Pisa, the beggars would almost seem to constitute the most numerous class of the population; and, in the other towns of Tuscany, mendicancy exhibits itself on a scale of scarcely less magnitude. Under the bright blue summer sky, and in a land where plenty apparently reigns, nowhere could I escape from sights and sounds of misery; everywhere was heard the monotonous cry, lisped by the young, mumbled by the old, and chorused forth by ragged wretches of both sexes and of every age—"*Datemi qualche cosa! ho fame, ho tanto fame! Datemi una piccola moneta, per l'amore della sanctissima Vergine!*" *

Extensively, however, as poverty does really prevail in Tuscany, and numerous as are the fit objects of charity that one sees, the tribe of beggars is often largely swelled by additions from a class of individuals who are mendicants more from choice than necessity; having other means of sustaining life than those derived from alms. This class of unprofessional beggars abounds especially in country districts; and so deficient, for the most part, are the lower orders of the peasantry in a consciousness of anything inherently degrading in the mendicant's trade, that petitions for aid will come from persons evincing in their looks and dress an air of respecta-

* "Give me something! I am hungry; I am so very hungry! Give me a trifle, for the love of the Blessed Virgin!"

bility. Almost before the power of speech is attained, the bright-eyed, round-cheeked child of the *contadino* will stretch out its little hand to the passing stranger for some trifling coin; and the peasant woman whose husband cultivates a small plot of land, will more than hint how extremely acceptable would be the donation of a cast-off petticoat or gown. Very probably, not a little of the favor with which the beggar's trade is regarded in Tuscany originates in the circumstance, that mendicancy and religion are exhibited constantly to the people's view in intimate union. The brown-robed friar, with wallet on his back, who begs from door to door—here, for a piece of bread, there, for a contribution of chestnuts or of meal; the Brother of Mercy, who goes his rounds with begging-box in hand; the friar, who takes his stand in the public streets, to solicit alms for the relief of suffering souls in purgatory: acting as they all do under the sanction of the Church, not unnaturally tend to invest with a kind of dignity the mendicant's trade in the public estimation. Be this, however, the cause or not, one thing is certain, that amongst the lower classes of Tuscany no feeling of pride, independence and self-respect will restrain the utterance of petitions for aid, even on the part of many whose circumstances are such as to place them far above the ordinary mendicant class.

By universal assent, Tuscany, with one single exception, ranks high above all the other Italian States in regard to elegance of expression and purity of pronunciatian of the Italian tongue. Rome alone, the exception referred to, can contest the palm of superiority with Tuscany in this particular; and though, according to the well-known saying "*la lingua Toscana in bocca Romana*," be the best, the inhabitants of Tuscany, and more especially the citizens of Sienna, pique themselves on the possession of the exclusive power of speaking the Italian language with perfect purity. On such a point, a foreigner can necessarily be no judge, for many a minute shade of difference in the pronunciation of an unfamiliar word escapes the untutored ear; but one thing is certain, that the merest novice in the Italian language will soon discover that, as a general rule, the Florentines, throughout the middle and lower classes of the population, take certain liberties with their language that neither good taste nor dictionary authority can in the least degree justify. For instance, they very frequently convert the letter "c," when it begins a word, into an "h" in sound, so as to make *hasa* out of *casa* (house), *havallo* out of *cavallo* (horse), and so on through a great number of words of the same kind. With this particular fault, which is one pretty much confined to Florence and its immediate vicinity, the Tuscan pronunciation of Italian was pleasing to my ear above that of any other part of Italy, the Roman not excepted. It is a truly pleasant thing to hear Italian spoken in a voice possessing the charms of softness and sweetness — qualities, however, which, strange to say in a land of vocalists, are seldom found in the *speaking* voices of Italian men, and still far more rarely in those of Italian women. I have often been pained to an indescribable degree, in Italian society, by the shrill, sharp voices of the ladies whom I heard around me. One young lady in particular, with whom circumstances brought me unfortunately into frequent contact, used, by every word she uttered, to cause me the same suffering as I have endured from the grinding of a saw, the scratch of a slate pencil, or the scream of a steam whistle; and I have often felt tempted to beg that she would chant or operatize her sentences; for, curious to say, like many other Italian ladies I knew who possessed speaking voices of a similar description, she sang with taste, power and sweetness.

In the British Isles, music is a passion with the few, an amusement, or object of mere liking, to the many; but in Italy, music seems to speak to the heart and soul of every inhabitant of that country. In Florence, rich and poor are alike adorers of the opera. The London artizan, intent on pleasure, hurries off to a third-rate theatre, to luxuriate in the comicalities of some broad farce, or to seek excitement in the exhibition of melodramatic horrors: blue lights, green lights, and red lights, are his delight; he loves to see fairies flying in the air; dragons with fiery tails, and magicians with magnificent turbans and splendid beards. Beyond a popular song or two, the tune of which the itinerant barrel organ has made familiar to his ear, he knows little of music; his own attainments in that art being probably limited to humming or whistling "God save the Queen," or some negro melody.

The Florentine artizan, though not inferior in natural intelligence, yet certainly inferior in point of education, seeks for enjoyment in pleasures of a more elevated kind. Passing by with indifference the gigantic placards which announce the performance of some wonderful horse, or the hundredth representation, amidst universal applause, of some laughter-exciting play, he hies with his small savings to the opera-house, to listen to the *prima donna's* harmonious strains. Not a note escapes his ear; he listens with every faculty; prepared to applaud or to condemn each vocalist, where praise or blame is due. He can trace the silver thread of harmony through passages where the clue seems lost to a less gifted and cultivated ear, and each note he hears makes a distinct impression on his memory. He feels no fatigue, he knows no tedium, though he listens to the same opera, sung by the same vocalists, for the twentieth time; and the strains thus heard he carries back in mind with him to cheer the weariness of his labor hours. From the carpenter's shop

I have heard the finest airs of the "Sonnambula" rise up melodiously in the air; the work-girl, with a power and sweetness of voice which I could not but envy, has sung me the best pieces from the "Traviata" in a truly admirable style; and I knew a maid-servant who could go unerringly through at least twenty operas, from beginning to end. "Music! how I adore music!" is the universal cry in Italy, amongst old and young, rich and poor. According to the principle of the Scandinavian mythology, which made the happiness of heaven for the righteous consist in an endless repetition of the pleasures they had most enjoyed on earth—even as the followers of Odin were to drink mead out of the over-flowing goblets, and to chop off each other's heads, and limbs, and arms to the end of time—so a paradise constructed for Italians on the same plan would necessitate an inexhaustible supply of first-rate operas and *artistes* with vocal powers equally divine.

At Easter time, either a little before or after that festival, the streets of Florence exhibit a sight which cannot fail in some degree to excite the stranger's curiosity and surprise. Dressed in robes of white, composed of some light material, such as muslin or lace, over-skirts of satin or silk, with large white veils enveloping their heads, young girls may be seen proceeding along the public streets, either singly or in groups, accompanied by a lady of matronly aspect. The attire, so suggestive of matrimonial proceedings, instantly led me to the conclusion that the young girls whom I saw were either going to, or returning from, the wedding of a friend or relation; but, on inquiry, I found that the dress which had excited my interest and curiosity was significant, not of matrimony, but of religion; it being adopted by such young girls as, for the first time in their lives, were admitted to receive the Communion.

English philanthropy takes under its especial protection the blind, the deaf, the dumb, the maimed, and the diseased in mind and body; for these subsrciptions are raised, donations given, and legacies bequeathed by charitable persons. But Italian, and particularly Tuscan philanthropy, would seem, for the most part, to take a different direction; for, judging from the amount of funds set apart in Florence for various charitable purposes, the want of sight, of speech, the failure of health, the loss of limbs, of hearing, and of reason, are each accounted a calamity of less weight than that which afflicts the maiden destined to see her youth go by, and grey hairs arrive, unprovided with a husband. English benevolence contemplates with indifference the woes of spinsterism, but Italian benevolence rushes to its aid with a zeal truly commendable: enhancing the effect of feminine graces, and increasing their power to subdue the manly heart, by the substantial charms of money. In Tuscany, as well as throughout all Italy, the bestowal of marriage portions has ever been one of the most favorite charities; and in Florence alone the sums thus distributed annually amount to between three and four thousand pounds. The Society of St. John the Baptist, the patron saint of Florence, was founded chiefly for the purpose of endowing girls in humble circumstances with marriage portions; and to the same purpose is annually applied a certain portion of the funds of the brotherhood of the Misericordia. Another charitable society takes upon itself to provide every fatherless Florentine girl with a matrimonial dowry of fifty scudi (about eleven pounds English money). To entitle themselves, however, to receive such donations, girls must pay great attention to their religious duties: attend mass frequently, take the Communion at proper times, go to confession regularly, and, above all things, present themselves at the catechetical examination, called *dottrina*, held by the priests in the several parish churches after morning service on Sunday. The girl who absents herself from the *dottrina* without a sufficient cause to justify her absence, has a mark attached to her name on every occasion of such truancy; which marks accumulating to the number of three or more, invalidate her claim to the reception of the next installment of the marriage portion, which otherwise would be hers. According to the age of the recipient, within a certain limit, the portion varies; for from eighteen years of age up to thirty-five, the young maiden's dower (which she is alone, however, entitled to receive on her marriage day,) undergoes generally a triennial increase; but the limit of five and thirty being reached without a husband being obtained, the hapless maid is doomed to mourn over the destruction of all her matrimonial hopes, from her exclusion henceforth from the benefits of the charitable endowment through which she trusted to win her way to marriage. Poor, hapless maid of thirty-five, if such there be in Florence! Who cannot sympathize with her sorrows, as she sees that dreaded day and hour approach when she loses every right to claim the seventeen years' accumulating heap of silver scudi, the due reward of years of sedulous attendance at mass, confession, and the *dottrina!*

Sad, however, as the old maid's fate is deemed in Italian popular estimation, it may well be questioned whether the Tuscan spinster's lot, in the lower classes of life at least, is not in reality frequently a far happier one than that of many by whom the marriage portion has been rightfully claimed. If not actually maltreated—as from several cases that came under my own observation I have cause to know she not unfrequently is—the Tuscan wife, in the lower classes of society, occupies the position of a mere servant in the husband's view; and on a *festa*, when her work is done, while her husband goes forth to enjoy himself, she must stay at home.

"It would be a fine sight, indeed, for my husband to take me off with him on a pleasure walk or jaunt," said an extremely respectable woman to me one day. "What a joke the neighbors would have about it! how they would shout out, when they saw us going arm-in-arm, lovingly together, or driving together side by side, that sugar was cheap, honey was plenty, and a hundred such like impertinences! No, no! we Italian wives must just stay at home, cook, dust, and clean; and if we would lead peaceable lives, bear a frown or an angry word with quietness and patience."

In addition to remarks of such a nature, an expression that became quite familiar to my ears during my residence in Tuscany, was little indicative of feminine conjugal felicity amongst the lower orders of society in that country. "Would to heaven I had never married!" or, "If I had been wise, I had never married," was a plaint that, time after time, I have heard repeated by wives, in tones of the most unquestionable sincerity.

Twenty-three o'clock is the favorite hour with the Italians at every time of the year, but more particularly the summer season; this twenty-three o'clock, which the hour before sunset is called, being used by them for purposes of recreation and amusement. At twenty-three o'clock the merchant leaves his counting-house, the clerk his desk, the student his books, the officer his barracks and the idle gentleman his lounging-chair, and go forth with one accord to saunter along some fashionable promenade, there to smoke, to chat, and interchange news and salutations with passing friends. With ladies, this hour is also a favorite one; for whilst the married ladies, equipping themselves in their most captivating array, also go forth to swell the sauntering throng, the unmarried, to whom a similar privilege is denied, station themselves at the front windows of their respective residences, deriving no small enjoyment from the occupation of seeing and the consciousness of being seen.

Considering window-gazing from an English point of view, it would seem a sufficiently dull and uninteresting feminine recreation; but viewed through an Italian medium, it becomes a highly exciting feminine employment. No young lady who takes her station at a front window on an afternoon but may readily entertain the idea of captivating by her charms the heart of some passing stranger; innumerable instances being known to her of a husband having been obtained by a glance shot down from the altitude even of a second story. It was highly amusing to hear from the lips of one of these romantically-wooed maidens the history of the courtship, from the moment when she first observed that she was the object of the stranger's attention, on through many successive afternoons, blessed by the interchange of mutual admiring glances, until the arrival of that happy hour when the enamored youth made known his name and his position, and in explicit terms demanded her hand in marriage. So recognized is window-gazing in Italy as a favorite feminine occupation, that few windows of houses of any pretension to gentility, in the principal streets of Italian towns, have their inner lower ledges unprovided with cushions, for the especial use and benefit of the leaner's elbow.

The strictness of Italian rules of decorum, even with reference to unmarried girls in the humblest classes of society, was once illustrated to me in a very forcible and somewhat amusing manner. In the interior of a public conveyance, in which I was traveling to a small provincial Italian town, I had for *vis-a-vis* a girl of nineteen, belonging to the peasant class; a fact evidenced at once by the peculiar costume she wore. Besides the latter and myself, a lady friend of mine, and a priest, occupied the interior of the conveyance. The girl, on my entering into conversation with her, took particular care to inform me that she had been waiting for several days for a good opportunity, like that which had at last presented itself, of returning home in safe company. Arrived at the town in which her family lived, the driver of the conveyance asked her to alight; as the ascent to the lane where her parents resided was very steep, and she could walk with ease the distance in three minutes. At this request the girl exhibited the utmost amount of indignation, and declared it was one to which it was quite impossible for her to accede, without being guilty of the greatest impropriety. Walk alone to her own house! that would be a fine thing, indeed, for her to do: what would her mother, what would the neighbors say, to see her return in this discreditable way? How could he ask any respectable girl to commit such an impropriety? Evidently considering that such objections were very reasonable, the driver gave up the point, and the girl was deposited safely at the parental door.

The towns of San Miniata, Colle, Volterra, and Fiesole, in Tuscany, all enjoy prerogatives of a peculiar kind. In each one of these small towns is what is called a Libro d'oro (golden book), in the pages of which it is only necessary to have the name inscribed, to change the proprietor of that designation from a plebeian, perhaps of the lowest rank, into a member of the nobility. Of course, as may well be supposed, this transformation is not effected on purely disinterested principles of philanthropy; but it must be admitted, considering that, in addition to a title, an inscription in the pages of the Libro d'oro confers upon the proprietor of the name inscribed the right also to appear at court, that the terms upon which the valuable privilege is granted are very moderate. For about thirty pounds the title of chevalier, the lowest order of nobility, may be obtained.

For double that sum the dignity of baron can be reached. A count or marquis's degree costs something more; but an aspirant to nobility need not despair of arriving even at the highest of these grades, at the expense of a hundred pounds.

The inhabitants of Fiesole turned the privilege their city enjoyed to a highly praiseworthy use. Perched on the top of a steep hill, along the precipitous sides of which no road practicable for carriages had been made, they found themselves, though only about five miles distant from Florence, in a great degree insulated from the world. A remedy for this state of things at last entered the head of an ingenious citizen. Distinguished as was the ancient Etruscan city in point of historical dignity, still it had become, through the agencies of time, a poverty-stricken place. From a population, the majority of which found it a difficult task to earn their daily bread, the funds essential for the construction of even a mile and a half of road could not possibly be obtained. But if the inhabitants of Fiesole had themselves no money to expend in public works, they had, by a liberal exercise of the privileges conferred on them by their Golden Book, the means of raising the necessary supplies for the object in view. A suggestion to this effect being made and approved of, the scheme proposed was carried out with much energy and activity. "Titles to sell! who will buy? who will buy?" was their cry, and in answer to that cry came numerous demands for patents of nobility. Marquises, counts, and barons were created by the score; and not a few Englishmen became ennobled through the medium of a well-filled purse. Money flowed copiously into the exchequer of the impoverished city, and sufficient was raised to make the road by which the stranger now ascends the hill of Fiesole to visit the ruins of this old Etruscan city.

The term *frutta* (fruit) is much more comprehensive in the Italian than its corresponding term in the English language, for under the word *frutta* are comprised young peas and beans; which, like the class of products with which they range, are often eaten uncooked. In an Italian house where I was staying, my invariable refusal to partake of these so-called *frutta* exciting some surprise, I explained that I had not been habituated to eat them raw; whereupon, in deference to my prejudices, the peas were subjected to a culinary process the succeeding day; but I found to my distress that the flavor of the dish was destroyed, in the opinion of most of the members of the family, since it was scarcely touched by any one but me.

To spill oil, and to break a looking-glass, are both considered in Italy to be evil auguries, and death is inevitably foreboded by the hooting of an owl near a sick man's window. The hair is considered to be acted upon by lunar influence; for, according to the popular creed, no one who values an abundance of hair should submit his or her head to the hair-cutter's operations whilst the moon is on the wane.

A few years ago an occurrence took place in Tuscany, which caused the most unbounded merriment to the lively Florentines. A young student at the University of Pisa fell under the suspicion of being heretically inclined, and whilst his education was still uncompleted, he sickened, and, after a short illness, died. Having on his death-bed refused the offices of the priests, and thus tacitly declared his disbelief in the tenets of the Church to which he nominally belonged, a reverend teacher in the seminary considered that circumstances justified recurrence to a stratagem, which, more than any words, might impress upon the minds of the deceased's companions the dreadful consequences that the rejection of the Catholic faith involved. A rumor emanating from this source, to the effect that the devil would surely come to claim the dead student's soul, excited a vague feeling of fear in the mind of a young man who had determined, from affection to the deceased, to keep watch over the dead body of his friend during the night preceding its burial. Actuated by this sensation of dread, and having a presentiment of the appearance of some evil spirit during his lonely watch, the young man carefully loaded a brace of pistols, armed with which he proceeded to his post. Alone with the corpse—that cast-off garment of humanity, whose pallid, unchanging features and cold impassability never fail to evoke in the gazer's heart a feeling of awe—and with vague apprehensions of being brought into contact with beings from another world, one may fancy the thrill of horror that ran through his veins, when at midnight he heard a rattle as of chains, and saw a hideous figure approach, with horns sprouting from his head, and a long tail sweeping the ground.

But, however appalled the young man might have been at the apparition, his courage and presence of mind did not desert him; for, seizing a pistol, he fired, and with so true an aim that the spectre fell, and, with a very earthly shriek of suffering, lay prostrate on the floor. "The devil is dead! the devil is dead!" shouted the young man triumphantly; and forthwith rushed off to proclaim to his companions that mankind had been freed from their great enemy by his hand. "The devil is dead! the devil is dead!" resounded through the walls of the university. But, unfortunately for humanity, it was soon discovered that the supposed devil was a very undeniable sample of the human species, who had been dressed up in character for the occasion to perform the devil's part. "All Florence rung with this incident," said the Italian lady who told me this tale. "'The devil is dead! the devil is dead!' was in every one's lips, and the joke was not let drop for a considerable time."

At a period when the whole monetary system of

Europe was in a most unsettled state, and when monarchs — either to defraud their creditors, or to force their debtors to pay more than they had received, or the tax-payers more than was due — continually varied the title and weight of the coins of their respective kingdoms, the republic of Florence was honorably distinguished by possessing a golden florin, whose weight and value remained unaltered as long as the republic itself endured. Unhappily for the traveler, this florin exists no longer; for cumbrous, heavy and inconvenient to a degree are the large silver coins denominated *scudi*, which bearers of letters of credit and circular notes receive in exchange from their Tuscan or Florentine bankers. A gold coin, denominated a *zecchino*, is indeed declared to form a portion of the monetary system of Tuscany at this present day; but its existence must be a mere matter of faith with most strangers, as it was with me; for it certainly does not enter into the ordinary transactions of purchase and sale, and during the whole period I was in Tuscany, I never saw this coin. The Grand Duke and Grand Ducal family alone, indeed, I was informed, enjoy the privilege of filling their purses with gold: and what a privilege this is, no one can fully appreciate, who has not retired from the counting-house of a Tuscan banker, groaning beneath the weight of silver *scudi*.

The reign of cheapness is attested in Tuscany by

the issue of coins representing a value exceedingly small. For instance, the *paolo*—worth a little more than five-pence, English money—is divided into eight *crazie;* and as every *crazia* undergoes a subdivision into five *quattrini,* a Tuscan *quattrino* represents a value considerably below that of the smallest coin of England. In former times, the *quattrino* was divisible again into four *denari;* but the *denaro,* though it still holds its place in the tables of Tuscan currency, has only now a nominal existence. Another small coin, called a *soldo,* containing three *quattrini,* is current in many parts of Tuscany, and often causes the stranger infinite perplexity and bewilderment in small shopping transactions; for, as a *soldo* contains three *quattrini,* and a *crazia* five, and as payment for an article is often necessarily made in a coin differing from that one in which the price was asked, to ascertain the due amount of *crazie* requisite to discharge a debt contracted in *soldi,* or *vice versa,* as the case may be, involves a somewhat elaborate arithmetical calculation. "I hope to learn your language, but I do not expect I shall ever understand your money," said an English lady to a shop-keeper of Pisa: and I have known several persons who, even after a residence of many months in Tuscany, have never attained to a thorough mastery over the *crazie, soldi* and *quattrini* difficulty.

In no part of Italy is the foreigner more worried with police regulations than in Tuscany. From the moment natives of other States enter the Grand Duchy, they are under the constant surveillance of officials, as well as under the disagreeable necessity of contributing to the Grand Ducal revenues.* This proceeding of the Tuscan Government towards foreigners is not only ungenerous, but ungrateful; considering the vast benefit which Florence derives from the large sums of money annually expended there by tourists and resident visitors. The permission to remain even for two or three days in the Tuscan capital involves an expenditure of eight *paoli*, and should the stay be prolonged beyond that period, a license—called a *carta di soggiorno*—must be taken out, at a cost of twelve *paoli*. Even with this *carta di soggiorno*, the strangers who may wish to reside for some time in Tuscany are far from being at the end of their pecuniary contributions to the police authorities; for in general, at the end of every two months, a new *carta di soggiorno* must be procured, involving a fresh expenditure. Nor is this even the whole grievance of the matter; for, although a *carta di soggiorno*, taken out in any town in Tuscany, gives to the holder the right of a two months' unmolested residence in the place where it was granted, the virtue of this license is limited in a great degree to the immediate locality of its issue; for though, armed with this document, the stranger may travel through

* This regulation applies to Italians as well as to natives of France and England, or other countries.

Tuscany unmolested by fresh official transactions, yet, if a stay be made in any one place for a longer period than ten days, the purse must again be opened to pay for another *carta di soggiorno.* Sometimes, though very rarely, the expectant victim may escape this exaction, through some negligence or oversight on the part of the police. At the Baths of Monte Catini, where I stayed for several weeks, I found to my satisfaction that my tax-paying liabilities seemed to have escaped the attention or perception of the local authorities; but in a succeeding place to which I went in Tuscany, I did not experience similar good fortune.

The custom-house regulations of Tuscany also sometimes prove an annoyance of a serious kind. The examination in the frontier *Dogana* of the State being passed, the stranger who fancies that, as far as the Grand Duchy is concerned, all luggage troubles are at an end, will find, by subsequent experience, that this idea is incorrect, since the entrance into a town of any note in Tuscany entails the liability of having the interiors of trunks, portmanteaus and carpet-bags explored anew. The walls of the mediæval republican cities of Italy afford a most tempting facility for levying taxes upon their inhabitants—a facility which is taken advantage of by the authorities, who, through the medium of officials stationed at each gate, exact the payment of a duty on every imported article of food. As not only the principal cities of Tuscany, such as Florence, Pisa, Sienna, Lucca, etc., are girt with walls, but towns of meaner note — such as Prata and Pistoia, containing scarce 12,000 inhabitants — are similarly enclosed, the infinite examinations to which the Tuscan tourist's baggage is liable may be imagined. Not generally, however, it must be said, is the traveler subjected to annoyance from this source; for with many officials, the innocence of the baggage, in regard to offenses connected with the revenue laws, is taken on trust of the proprietor's word. Still, in many instances, a different course is pursued; for though the expectation can never of course exist that such articles as butter, eggs, milk or cheese will be discovered secreted in a lady's or gentleman's box or bag, there are to be found officials who will insist upon availing themselves of their right of search, in case the fee that they have demanded as the price for its non-exercise be refused.

But the culminating point of vexations of this description in Tuscany is attained at Leghorn, where not only articles entering, but articles issuing from the town are subject to taxation; the latter additional affliction arising from the circumstance that Leghorn, as a free port, enjoys the privilege of receiving all foreign merchandise free of duty within its walls. The officials at the gates have thus a double duty to perform, for whilst they have to guard against the furtive entrance of articles of food within the town, they have to exert themselves still more sedulously to prevent the clandestine exit of Manchester prints, French gloves, and, in fact, all kinds of merchandise. No inhabitant of that portion of Leghorn which extends beyond the walls can buy the most trifling article in the town, without being obliged, in bringing it home, to have recourse to some stratagem to evade the payment of heavy dues. The lady who has bought a bonnet from some fashionable milliner, conveys the new purchase home upon her head; and each dress that issues from the workwoman's hands is conveyed to its destination on the person of the proprietor. Gloves, laces, ribbons, boots and shoes are stowed away in secret pockets, and many a crinoline has been made to lend its aid to hide the smuggling transactions of its wearer. There is no place in the world, perhaps, where the contraband trade is so vigorously prosecuted, so ardently carried on, as at the gates of Leghorn. Lady and gentleman, artisan and servant, all smuggle: all alike try to evade the revenue laws, and to elude the vigilance of custom-house officials; and I confess that on two or three occasions during my residence at Leghorn, I followed in this respect the example set me by the inhabitants of the town.

The system of espionage which prevails under the government of the Grand Duke affects most prejudicially the domestic happiness of the natives of Tuscany, for through its influence, mistrust and suspicion are infused into the social intercourse of relatives as well as of friends. Even women are sometimes haunted by a dread of treachery on the part of their nearest kindred; and a strict injunction to secrecy often followed remarks of a political character that were made to me. On one occasion a daughter asked me to refrain from mentioning her observations to her father, and was still more urgent in her entreatise that I should pursue a similar course in reference to her sister; alleging in justification of her request, that although she did not believe the latter was a Government spy, she yet could never divest herself of a certain feeling of insecurity on the subject. This was an extreme case, no doubt, but still it affected me painfully; for no state of existence can be more deplorable than that in which the Scripture denunciation seems in any degree to be fulfilled: "A man's foes shall be they of his own household."

The ceremony of blessing the houses is to the stranger one of the most peculiar religious observances of Passion week in Italy; and, as this rite may be novel to others as it was to me, I shall detail the mode in which it was performed before my view.

One afternoon in Easter week, as I was reading in my sitting-room, my studies were suddenly interrupted by the entrance of the maid-servant, who, calling out in a loud voice, "il prete" (the priest), threw the door wide open to give admission to the visitor. Somewhat startled by this announcement, I glanced towards the door, just as a tall young priest, wearing a white cassock, entered the room. Keeping my seat — for I saw at once the visit was not to me — I watched the priest as, preceded by the servant, he advanced at a slow and measured pace into the room; and whilst he recited in a low tone some sentences from an open book he held in his hand, there followed in his train a boy attired in white, who sprinkled the floor as he proceeded, by swinging to and fro a small vessel containing water. Progressing in this order, the strange procession defiled before my view, until reaching the door of my bed-room, which was flung open by the servant, they disappeared within. A minute or more elapsed, during which I continued to hear the priest's low, mumbling tones, and then the procession reappeared, to defile again before my view in the same order and with the same ceremonial as previously.

Amongst the different ways of traveling in Italy, that by *vetturino* (as it is termed) implies a mode utterly different from any practiced in England; for whilst an hotel bill is ever an inevitable accompaniment of journeys performed within the precincts of the British Isles, we may travel, if we choose, through the whole extent of Italy, from north to south, with only an occasional glimpse of one of those unpleasant documents. Notwithstanding, however, this happy exemption from a great grievance appertaining to an erratic life, the traveler by *vetturino* cannot make his way, save through the medium of a well-filled purse; for his immunity from the sight of hotel bills is only secured by the payment of the cost of board and lodging on the road to the proprietor of the carriage in which he travels. The essential difference, therefore, between this mode of traveling and any adopted in England, consists in the payment of the whole expenses of the route to one person, who undertakes, for a certain stipulated sum, to convey the traveler free of all extra cost to his destination. No *vetturino* carriage will, however, go beyond a certain distance from its starting-point; at least, as a general rule, there are two stations between which it plies exclusively. For instance, the Neapolitan *vetturino* carriage goes no further than Rome; the Roman conveyance stops at Florence; and from thence Genoa or Venice is only attainable under this system by a Florentine vehicle, or by one performing its return journey to either of those towns.

*Vetturini* carriages vary much in size and character; some are small and thoroughly uncomfortable, whilst others afford ample and even luxurious accommodation, to the party of four inside and two outside they are in general constructed to carry; and when every one of these six seats are occupied, this mode of traveling is the cheapest that can be adopted in Italy. Though a *vetturino* carriage is usually hired for the journey by a family or a party of friends, yet in cases where the number rendered desirable by economical considerations cannot be mustered by the parties themselves, the proprietor of the carriage will generally be able to fill up the vacant seats; a registry being kept in his bureau of persons who have signified their wish to travel, about a certain period, by a particular route, to some specified town.

The party being made up, and the price arranged, the next step in the business is the signature of a contract, which sets forth, in the most precise terms, the amount of *scudi* to be paid per head, the number of days to be occupied by the journey, the number of horses to be furnished, the hours for starting and for resting, the halting-places for the night, and the three daily meals that are to be supplied. This done, half of the stipulated price is paid, and in case of any alleged breach of faith, the payment of the remaining moiety may be withheld until the case has been submitted to legal adjudication.

In an age of which the characteristic feature is rapidity of movement, it seems like going back to the last century to creep along in *vetturino* fashion; for, as the horses are never changed throughout the journey, a distance of more than five and thirty miles a day is seldom accomplished. To the ordinary race of eager, impetuous, restless travelers, whom the British Isles annually send forth to traverse the Continent, this snail-like rate of progress would certainly prove most intolerably wearisome; but to quiet temperaments, the *vetturino* mode of traveling is not devoid of charm. Doubtless, in the uncertain climate, and under the cloudy skies of England, the railroad system of locomotion is to be preferred; but in Italy, where, except in the winter months, the landscape is steeped in light by a sun that, day after day, pours down its rays from a vault of the clearest blue, a tincture of the *dolce far niente* in traveling, as well as in ordinary life, commends itself to the sympathies of impressionable natures in a considerable degree. Many a pleasant scene returns to me connected with my journey by *vetturino* from Naples to Rome; scenes in which orange gardens, vine-encircled fields and mountains, bathed in the warm tints of a southern clime, blend with remembrances of ruined castles and dilapidated old towns.

But if the slow rate of progress incident to the *vetturino* system of traveling in Italy transports the stranger back in fancy to a bygone century, the same effect is still more powerfully produced by the danger existing in that country of a personal encounter with highwaymen. A hundred years ago, no English country gentleman, who left home for London, felt any assurance of reaching his destination without being plundered on the road by robbers; and he never passed across a lonely heath, without casting many an anxious glance around, to see if masked and mounted highwaymen were drawing near. The stories told by stage-coach travelers to each other, related chiefly to this theme, and so many tales of highway robbery were to be found recorded in the columns of the public journals, that such accounts could scarcely aspire to the distinction of taking rank above the mere commonplace incidents of the times.

But whilst with us the phase of social life marked by the presence of highwaymen has passed away, far different is the case in Italy, for there the traveler is exposed to the same risks our grandfathers or great grandfathers incurred. Fostered by the misrule which prevails throughout the greatest portion of the peninsula, brigandage is rife not only in the Papal and Neapolitan dominions, but even in the better governed State of Tuscany. During my residence at Florence, a diligence guarded by soldiers was waylaid near Arezzo by a band of twelve brigands, who, after a sharp conflict, fled, leaving four of their number dead upon the ground. But though incidents of this description are by no means rare in Tuscany, they fade into insignificance in number and interest compared with those the Papal States afford; and to judge from recorded facts, the brigands living under Papal rule are at the head of their profession in Italy, in point of fierceness and audacity.

A very daring feat was performed by them in the immediate vicinity of Velletri, only a few weeks before I passed through that town on my journey from Naples to Rome. An Italian gentleman, residing in Velletri, drove out in his carriage one autumn day, for the purpose of visiting an estate he possessed in the immediate vicinity of the town; but before he had reached his destination, and whilst he was within a mile of the town, his progress was arrested by a band of armed brigands. Being quite unprepared for such an encounter, neither the gentleman nor his servant dared to resist the order they received to accompany their captors, who led them speedily to a cave. On arriving there, the gentleman was provided with a seat, and pen, ink and paper being produced, he was ordered to write forthwith to a personal friend of his residing in Velletri.

With a heavy heart, resulting from unpleasant forebodings in regard to the nature of the communication he would be obliged to make, the gentleman commenced the note, in the terms dictated to him by the robber at his side; but before more than a few words had been written, he dropped his pen, with an exclamation of horror and dismay, on finding himself ordered to intimate that certain death awaited him at sunset, if a sum of eighteen hundred *scudi* was not transmitted to his captors before that time.

"It is impossible," protested the prisoner. "In such a town as Velletri, a sum so large as that cannot be collected before sunset."

After some discussion on the point, in which remonstrances on one side were met by threats on the other, the brigands agreed to abate their demand to twelve hundred *scudi;* and the gentleman, finding he had no alternative but to choose between death or submission, wrote in the most urgent terms to beseech his friend to make every exertion to collect the amount required in the specified time. The letter finished, it was given to the servant, who was despatched to town, with the intimation that the slightest symptom of treachery on his part would infallibly be expiated by his master's instant death.

The day wore slowly, anxiously onward to the prisoner in the cave, his mind being harrassed with the doubt as to the possibility of the sum required being raised in time to save him from his threatened fate; and as he saw the sun approaching the horizon without any visible sign of the returning messenger, hope died within his breast. At length, just as the fatal moment was at hand, an intimation being given him to prepare for death, the servant was descried hastening to the spot; and as he brought the stipulated sum, the brigands, true to their promise, liberated their prisoner, and then fled to the mountains, to secure the unmolested enjoyment of their prize.

Another still more melodramatic incident occurred in the Papal States not long ago, the heroine of which was a young lady of noble birth, residing for her education in a convent situated in the immediate vicinity of the town of Bologna. An orphan, and destined to inherit a large property on the attainment of her majority, this young lady was a particular object of solicitude to the nuns under whose guardianship she was placed; and relying on the high walls which surrounded the convent grounds, they entertained as little apprehension in reference to her safety as they did in respect to their own. The confidence, however, which they felt in the security of their position was destined one day to be rudely destroyed; for a nun, while walking in the garden, was suddenly confronted with a masked and armed bandit, who, seizing her by the arm, while he pointed a pistol at her head, swore that he would kill her if she did not immediately point out the heiress, or deliver her up to him. The threat was effectual; for the nun, in an agony of terror that destroyed all presence of mind as well as all power of utterance, pointed to the girl, who happened to be visible on the terrace; and the intended victim, ere she was aware of the danger that threatened her, was seized and carried off before the eyes of the shrieking and terror-stricken sisterhood.

Rejoining his comrades outside the convent walls, the brigand mounted a fleet horse, and galloped off to the mountains with his prize.

This audacious act produced the most intense excitement at Bologna, but before any step had been taken to liberate the girl, the brigands, into whose power she had fallen, sent an intimation that they were willing to restore her for a certain sum. The amount, however, which they demanded by way of ransom was so large, that its payment would involve the surrender of more than half the young lady's fortune; it was therefore agreed that an attempt should be made to recover her by force. On this determination being made known, many students at the University of Bologna offered their services to effect the object in view; and, under the leadership of a young man who evidenced the most ardent interest in the captive's fate, the chivalrous troop succeeded in rescuing the young lady from the brigands' den. The conclusion of the tale was quite in keeping with the romantic character of the incidents detailed, for the heiress subsequently married the leader of the student band; and it is to be hoped that they now enjoy as great an amount of bliss as in general awaits the hero and heroine of fiction.

The famous Claude Duval of robber literature seems to have his counterpart in Italy at this present day; for, though I am not aware that there is any instance on record of an Italian brigand allowing a lady to ransom herself by dancing a *coranto* with him on the road, yet a very Claude-like spirit of courtesy was displayed by a troop of bandits, who, waylaying and stopping a diligence on the northern frontier of Tuscany, in the spring of 1856, not only entreated the ladies to dismiss all fear, and politely assisted them to alight, but gave *bonbons* to a child to still his cries of terror at the sight of the many masks. The same spirit of courtesy characterized their subsequent dealings with the passengers, for, satisfied with 20,000 franks of Government money they found in the diligence—and for which, probably, from information received, they had come in search—they left untouched the baggage of the travelers, and, without depriving one of them of purse, watch, or ring, took their departure in the most courteous manner, saluting the travelers with many bows, whilst uttering expressions of regret at having caused them alarm or inconvenience. Chivalrous brigands like these, however, are rare in Italy, for brutal fierceness and audacity are in general the distinguishing features of the Italian highwayman.

But notwithstanding the danger of encounters with brigands, tourists abound in Italy; and stimulated by the old Vyking spirit of love of enterprise and change apparently inherent in the Anglo-Saxon race, the Americans vie in number with English travelers; and vie with them also in the broadcast style in which they scatter their money over the land. Let the English *milord* take heed, for he has a rival in the field who contests with him the first place in the love and respect of guides, waiters, and hotel keepers.

"Ah! signorina," said a cicerone to me one day, "it is a very pleasant thing, I allow, to have dealings with your country people, but I prefer to serve the Americans; for while the English give like kings, the Americans bestow like emperors."

A course of foreign travel is theoretically considered to exercise a beneficial influence on the mind through the information it supplies, as well as through the new and enlarged views of life it offers to the stranger's notice. Rational, however, as such a theory seems, experience proves it to be far from generally true; for though in some instances the predicted benefit may be found, yet there are very many of the swarm of English tourists to be met abroad, who return to their own country no wiser than when they left it, except in so far as the mere guidebook lore of Murray is concerned. The results of foreign travel on the mind and character, depend entirely upon the spirit in which it is prosecuted, and those who journey from place to place, as many do, with no object but amusement, are not likely to derive much benefit from their wanderings. As an illustration of this class of tourists, I shall detail a conversation I had with a young English gentleman I met in Italy.

"You will doubtless visit Venice on your way to Switzerland?" I observed, on hearing him express his intention to go to Geneva.

"I don't think I shall," he drawled out, languidly, in answer; "it wouldn't pay, I fancy; for I am told that the opera-house there is not open at present."

The idea of Venice being only attractive to the stranger in a musical point of view, struck me as being so exquisitely ridiculous, that I had a great difficulty in maintaining a polite degree of gravity, as I rejoined:

"You are, I conclude, extremely fond of music?"

"I can't say I am," was the reply; "for I don't well know the music of one opera from another; but for all that, an opera house affords me a pleasant enough lounge, and helps me *to get through the time* when I am traveling."

Another means resorted to by this young gentleman "to get through the time," was by smoking incessantly; and I fairly shrink from the labor of calculating the number of cigars he must have consumed in pursuance of this object, ere, on the completion of his travels, he returned to enlighten the London world with the result of his foreign experiences.

# CHAPTER IX.

## RELIGION.

IF the influence exerted over the heart corresponds in strength with the impression made upon the eye, the Roman Catholic Church of Italy has reason to exult in the great power it enjoys. From the first to the last hour of residence in Italy, mementoes of the Roman Catholic faith continually meet the stranger's sight. Go where we may throughout that land, the church is the most prominent object in the view. Not less, assuredly, is this the case in Tuscany, than in the other States comprised within the one common term of Italy. In Pisa, one-half of the population of that desolate place would almost seem, to the stranger's eye, to be composed of priests. In Florence, though the number of that body does not appear to be so great in proportion to the rest of the inhabitants, one cannot walk a dozen yards without encountering a black-robed figure, whose shaven face is overshadowed by the luxuriant brim of a clerical three-cornered hat. With scarcely less frequency, too, does the eye discern the shaven crown, the cord-girt waist, and the sandaled feet of the brown-clad Capuchin monk. Here and there, also, the attention is very probably arrested by the sight of a burly friar, or member of some religious order, clothed in a dress of spotless white; whilst from time to time the Sister of Charity, with her snowy coif surmounted by a large straw hat, comes into view. On every hand churches with open doors silently invite the sinner to prayer, and church bells cease not to issue their noisy summons to the same effect, with an unwearying assiduity quite painful to the ear.

Throughout the country generally, the externals of religion offer themselves to the stranger's notice in a no less conspicuous manner. Within a niche formed in the road-side wall, a picture or image of the Virgin attracts, every here and there, at very short intervals, the traveler's notice. In the midst of every small cluster of rural dwellings, the village church is seen; and in secluded spots, and bypaths worn almost solely by the peasant's feet, small oratories are found. In quiet lanes and narrow tracks, as well as by public thoroughfares, large crosses are upreared, to which the emblems of the Passion, carved in wood, are not unfrequently attached, and thus the unlettered peasant has daily before his eyes a pictured Gospel, wherein he daily reads the history of that great sacrifice which was offered up for human sin. Rude, and sometimes ludicrous, are these representations; but the details of rustic artists' work are unmistakable—the crown of thorns, the seamless coat, the scourge, the cup that held the vinegar, the sponge, and the reed to which it was fixed, the nails that pierced hands and feet, the hammer which drove in the nails, the pincers that took them out, the hand that struck, the sword that smote, and the severed ear of the High Priest's servant, the ladder by which the body of the Saviour was taken down, and the cock whose loud clarion pierced to the depths of the erring apostle's soul—all these, and other signs of the same description, are constantly displayed on the road-side cross.

With the external emblems of faith thus abundantly displayed, it becomes an interesting point to ascertain if the Roman Catholic Church exercises a real sway over the hearts and minds of the inhabitants of Italy. The aged tree will put forth leaves when time has wasted its trunk to a mere shell; and the temple, with its marble front, may still outwardly make an imposing show, whilst inside it is mouldering to decay. How stands the question, then, with the Roman Catholic Church of Italy? Are the hollow tree and the ruined temple types of its position at the present hour in that country?

Though the answer might not differ with regard

to the position of the church throughout the whole of Italy, yet restricting the question to Tuscany, it is only due to truth to say that, from what fell under my observation during a ten months' residence, it seemed to me that even the warmest opponents of the Church of Rome could not in fairness but admit that, far from being a mouldering fragment of the past, the church, though old, is still a vigorous living plant, well rooted in the hearts of the great bulk of the population of that country.

The evidences which point to this conclusion force themselves plentifully on the stranger's eye. Before the altar at which the priest says mass—whether in the grand cathedral adorned with precious marbles, costly pictures, and glittering with gold, or in the plain, unpretending whitewashed interior of the village church — a throng of kneeling worshipers is always seen. Though some, perhaps, may be diverted from their devotions by the unwonted sight of a stranger in their midst, yet these are few compared with those whose bended heads, unwandering eyes, and earnest looks attest the reality and fervency of their faith. But whilst such is the scene invariably displayed on every *festa* day — when, amidst tinkling bells and swinging censors, the richly robed priest offers up the sacrifice of the mass—not less strikingly, on ordinary occasions, does the city church give evidence of strong devotional feelings on the part of the humbler classes of the land.

Between dawn and night, the heavy leather curtain that hangs before the entrance of every sanctuary is often raised to give admission to the devotional visitant. Strikingly impressive to the eye are the kneeling forms which one sees scattered here and there over the vast pavement of the grand columned aisles of Santa Croce, or bending low at some side altar before the Madonna's venerated picture. The servant, on her way from market, with basket in hand, the tradesman's wife, with handkerchief-covered head, the mechanic, the artizan in his work-stained dress, the beggar in his tattered garb—each and all come, with earnest and reverential mien, to offer up their prayers. In country districts, a bunch of freshly-gathered flowers is generally seen in a niche in the roadside wall before the image of the Madonna, attesting the peasant's pious zeal; and still more forcibly is the same spirit shown when, on the occasion of some church festival, he presses forward to take part in the procession—to follow in the train of chanting priests in a holy garb of black, carrying the wax-taper, or bearing aloft the ponderous image or sacred banner.

But, whilst the Roman Catholic Church seems to possess the respect and love of the lower classes of Tuscany, its power amongst the upper ranks of society appears to be feeble and circumscribed. Judging not only from what I saw, but from what I heard, infidelity prevails in the upper circles of society to a considerable extent. To enter a fashionable church at Florence, at a fashionable hour, is to witness a display of vanity, of show, and irreligiousness, and to behold a sanctuary, built for communion with God, degraded to a theatre, a lounge, a haunt of idleness. The Florentine lady, dressed out to the last extreme of the prevailing mode, comes not to pray, so much as to exhibit her graces to the eyes of admirers. Within the folds of the young lady's handkerchief may not unlikely be found a letter destined to be transferred clandestinely, if opportunity offers, to the hand of the favored lover. The gentlemen, on their part, display, in the most unambiguous manner, how little religion has to do with their appearance in the sacred place. They stand together in groups of two or three, and turning from the altar and the officiating priest, gaze with effrontery on every lady's face; they talk together in loud whispers, smile, nod their heads, and even indulge occasionally in a silent laugh. Hypocrites they are not, certainly, for they do not try to cloak, by any affectation of devotion, the purposes of mere amusement, for which they came; they make no pretense to pray: to bow their head during the elevation of the Host is the only religious act they perform. Truly, a visit to a fashionable church at Florence, at a fashionable hour, and a visit to a more humble, religious edifice, frequented by the lower classes of the community, afford as great a contrast as can be well conceived.

"There was not one of all the leaders of our party who was not an infidel," said the wife of a gentleman who had taken a prominent part in the republican movement in Tuscany; and this testimony to the prevalence of infidelity was corroborated from other quarters. Young men who hope to gain a government appointment, which is dependent in a great degree on the favorable report of a minister of the church, adopt a stratagem to save themselves from going to confession at the period obligatory on every Catholic for this rite to be performed. A short time before Easter, every house is visited by a priest, not only to bless it, and sprinkle each room with holy water, but to write down the name of every grown up individual therein, on each of whom it is obligatory to appear in the confessional; and a ticket is given to each one who confesses, testifying to the religious duty having been performed. A short time after Easter, the priest makes his round again, to take back the tickets that have been given, in order thus to ascertain if the ordinances of the church have in every instance been obeyed. A register is kept of those who can produce no tickets, and the black mark affixed to their names effectually bars them from the chance of obtaining the smallest government appointment; as, before such appointment is conferred, reference is invariably made to the minister of the parish in which the applicant for office resides, to know if the religious duties of such applicant have been properly fulfilled. To avoid, therefore, the pains and penalties that follow on the priest's unfavorable report, and, at the same time, to escape from the abhorred obligations of the confessional, young men are in the habit of buying up the services of not over-scrupulous consciences, who, fulfilling the obligatory rite in the names of their employers, receive a ticket, which is duly delivered up at the required time. An Italian Catholic assured me that this confessional agency business was a thriving trade in Florence, and that in many instances one young man would, under the names of his different employers, visit in the course of a few days a dozen confessionals in Florence; and of course receive a dozen tickets purporting that Giovanni, or Giuseppe, or Gaetano, or Tomaso, etc., as the case might be, had duly confessed his sins.

But though amongst the mass of the population in Tuscany, the evidences of a warm faith in the tenets of their church may be discerned, their respect and affection for the ministers of that church by no means seem to correspond. On the part of many who were extremely strict in the performance of their religious duties, who held implicitly every tenet of the Roman Catholic faith, I have found a feeling towards the priesthood very far indeed from a reverential one. At the Baths of Monte Catini, the mistress of the hotel where I was staying, a rigid Catholic, told me she avoided as much as she possibly could the admission of the *cose nere* (black things) into her house; and she gave me reasons for doing so, which were anything but complimentary to the ministers of her church. I have heard avarice, stinginess and immorality imputed to them, by persons entirely free from all Protestant tendencies. The very bitterest enemy of them I knew was a zealous Catholic woman, who had masses constantly performed for the benefit of a deceased uncle's soul, who wore a medallion of the Virgin next her heart, kept a bone of St. Anthony in her purse, and had a memento of some other saint suspended round her neck.

Ready credence is given by the *gente bassa* (lower classes) to every tale of a miraculous nature they may hear. According to them, heaven still communes directly with humanity in various ways; the angel or the saint comes down from Paradise to whisper into the slumberer's ears; glances into the land of spirits are obtained at times, by mortals spiritually pure; the Virgin smiles upon her devout worshipers through the painted canvas that bears her name; and the touch of the sacred relic restores vigor to the paralyzed limb, hearing to the deaf, and sight to the blind. As a sample of one of this class of modern miracles, the following tale may not be uninteresting, narrated in the manner it was told me by an Italian girl:

"In a convent in Florence, called the Santa Rosa, there lives a nun, a very holy nun, by whose means last year many a one dying of that terrible cholera* was cured. The convent belongs to one of those orders which shuts itself out most entirely from the world; and the nun about whom I am going to tell you, passed her days almost wholly in her cell, where she told over her beads, and repeated litanies to the Virgin continually. She lived quite like a saint; and surely she could not have been far from one either, when a real saint came down from heaven to speak to her, as you will hear. Well, quite away from the world as this nun lived, she could not help hearing about the cholera when it came to the town; and how, week after week, it was carrying off hundreds to their graves. Death, you may be certain, was no terror to her, for where should she go except to the angels in Paradise? But she, knowing that many a one, cut off in an hour perhaps by the cholera, was ill-prepared to die, and had no time to make peace with God, grieved very much at the news she heard, and she prayed very fervently for hours together that the scourge might be withdrawn.

"One night, after she had especially supplicated the saints' and the blessed Virgin's aid, she awoke

* The cholera raged in Tuscany during the summer and autumn of 1855.

up suddenly from her sleep, and saw before her a form like that an angel might have, all radiant as the sun. Trembling greatly, but filled with joy, she bowed her head with reverence; and then came words to her ear that told her it was St. Dominick who was her visitor. After which, the saint informed her that he had been sent down from heaven, in answer to her prayers, with the power of conferring on the water of a particular well in the neighborhood the power to cure all such as might be attacked with cholera. Having said these words, St. Dominick disappeared, leaving the nun filled with joy and thanksgiving; but when morning came, she, thinking what a poor sinful creature she was, and of the unlikelihood from this cause, that any saint should be sent from Paradise to talk with her, began strongly to doubt the reality of the vision she saw; and at last, persuading herself that she had been deluded by a dream, she determined not to breathe a word upon the matter to her sister nuns; particularly now that she recalled to mind that the well referred to in the midnight vision had long been dry.

"On the succeeding night, however, all doubts as to the reality of the vision she had seen were removed; for once more appeared the radiant light, and the form of the glorified saint, and once more he spoke to her, repeating what he had said before about the powers conferred upon the water of a particular well to cure; and reproving her for her incredulity, he told her to loose no time in making known the good tidings to the world. Then, in obedience to the holy saint, the nun on the next morning communicated to her sisters and to her confessor what had occurred; and on hearing the intelligence, the confessor going off to see the well, found it, not dry as it had been for years and years before, but filled up with water to the brim—a certain proof of the truth of all that the nun had told. The news of the miracle that had been wrought spreading far and near, the people, not only of the town, but from the country, came flocking to the well with bottles to be filled; and the blessed water did indeed work many miraculous cures."

The special intervention of the Virgin in cases of danger and sickness, is thoroughly believed to be a circumstance of almost daily occurrence. In the church of the Annunciata in Florence, is a fresco of the Annunciation, painted by angels (according to popular belief), and possessing also, according to the same authority, miraculous powers to heal. Confidence in the supernatural gifts popularly ascribed to this picture must in all probability have recently received a great increase, as the Virgin, in this piece of angelic workmanship, has lately been crowned with a glittering diadem, costing 8,000*l.* This picture is only exposed on extraordinary occasions; such, for instance, as the Feast of the Annunciation, or during a period when death may happen to be menacing the life of any of the members of the Grand Ducal family: in whose behoof it is supposed the uncovered face has power to expel from the suffering frame the fell poison of disease. According to the authority of the sacristan of the church, a very recent manifestation of the miraculous healing gifts of the picture had occurred; a young archduke, whose life was despaired of by the faculty, being restored to health by the unveiling of the Virgin's face for a space of three days' time!

In the church attached to the monastery of Monte Nero, situated in the neighborhood of Leghorn, may be seen a celebrated picture of the Virgin, which has been an object of veneration to the inhabitants of the surrounding district for more than five hundred years. The history attached to this picture is a somewhat curious one; for, according to the concurrent testimony of different writers on the subject, this picture, setting off on a long voyage in the year 1345, sailed by itself from the island of Negropont to the shores of Tuscany; where, found by a shepherd at a place called Ardenza, in the immediate vicinity of Monte Nero, it was, by the direction of the Virgin, carried to the spot where it may now be seen.

Dimmed and darkened, by the effect of time and the smoke of tapers, to a degree that renders the Virgin's features almost undistinguishable to the distant gaze—this picture, enshrined in costly marbles, and occupying an elevated position above the high altar of the church, calls forth in the humble Catholic feelings of the most unlimited reverence. More especially also is this the case with those whose lives are passed amongst the perils of the deep—a circumstance attributable, doubtless, to the maritime peregrinations of the picture, according to the traditionary tale. To the mariner from those coasts, that dull, dim painting awakes the liveliest feelings of reverence and devotion in his breast: before it he breathes his most fervent vows; and amidst the roar of raging winds and waves, and every danger to which he may be exposed—the protection of the holy "Lady of Storms" * is ardently invoked. The menaced danger escaped, the sailor returning to his native coast, speeds to the Monte Nero church, and there suspends a votive offering to the Virgin, as a tribute of his gratitude to her who in the hour of danger had saved him (as he believes) from death.

It is a curious sight to see those sailors' offerings, mingled as they are with others contributed by the neighboring peasantry. A bunch of cable ends hangs in close vicinity to various articles of feminine attire; old coats and muskets range together, and a great stock of crutches cover a considerable portion

* An epithet applied to the representation of the Virgin in the picture.

of the wall. Pictures, however, form the principal portion of the offerings to be seen, and the sides of three or four small rooms opening off the church are covered with small pictorial representations of the most tragic scenes. Here is a picture of a ship ready, apparently, to be swallowed up by the devouring waves; which picture, according to an inscription underneath, was presented as a votive offering to the Virgin by Angelo Biondi, who on the 4th of September, 1843, was saved by the favor of the Virgin from impending death. This painting, the type of innumerable others of a similar kind, contains, in the corner, the representation of the Virgin and Child appearing amidst the clouds.

Another class of pictures (if such rude daubs deserve that term) are devoted to delineations of perils escaped by dwellers on land. The dwelling on fire, with the alarmed inmates descending from the third story by a rope, is matched in artistic merit by a composition representing a man in the act of tumbling from the roof of a high house. Very desperate, indeed, seems the position of the poor wretch, over whose head the wheel of a carriage is about to pass; but it scarcely yields in tragic power to the representation of a scene where a hapless individual is being tossed up into the air by an infuriated bull. Surrounded by weeping relatives, the sick, extended upon their beds, appear as if about to take their departure from this world; and past hope of cure most certainly it would seem are those (and not a few are thus depicted) from whose mouths there flows a gushing torrent of blood. But time would fail to enumerate all the various instances in which life (according to the evidence of these records) has been preserved through the Virgin's gracious aid. These few examples are enough to evidence the prevailing popular belief in the daily occurrence of miraculous events.

To no doctrine of the Church of Rome do Italians seem to cling so fondly as to that which inculcates a particular devotion to the Virgin. To her, do sorrow-laden hearts repair for consolation in the hour of their distress; to her, vows are offered up in times of danger and sickness; and through her, penitents hope to gain pardon for their transgressions. The sinner whom the thought of divine justice confounds, turns from the presence of a justly offended God to kneel before the shrine of a being whose image rises before his mind as the incarnation of kindness and mercy. In the Virgin's name the beggar solicits alms, and the blind, the halt, the sick, and the maimed invoke compassion for their infirmities. The first prayer the child is taught to lisp, and the last upon the dying man's lip, is one to Mary. The shrine before which the lamp is burning in the city street, or the image set up on high above the peasant's door, is that of the Madonna; her picture graces every church, and before it bow down the young and old, the pure in heart and the sin-stained soul: differing in all beside, they yet agree in this, to do homage to the Virgin. On no subject does the preacher love to expatiate so much as on her virtues and her glory; fondly he dilates upon and depicts in vivid words the sorrows of the bereaved and heart-stricken mother on the mount of Calvary: he paints her oppressed with grief unspeakable, watching beside the cross to which was nailed the form of her cherished Son, listening to the low groans of suffering that escaped his lips, and marking the slow waning of the powers of life, amidst the intensest agony. In another strain, and in a perhaps still more forcible and enthusiastic one, the preacher passes on from a review of the Virgin's sorrows to a description of the glorious privileges which now are hers, exalted by the Saviour's love to a power and dignity far beyond that of the saintly and angelic throng; and with fluent eloquence he describes the pleasure that she takes in exercising her influence, and the high prerogatives with which she is endowed for the relief and benefit of suffering, sinful man: interceding for the erring but contrite soul, shielding youth and innocence from harm; protecting the fatherless and the forsaken; pouring balm into the bruised and grief-stricken soul; and suspending the hand of Death, when his arm is raised to strike the fatal blow.

In the praise of Mary, language seems to have exhausted every conceivable epithet of veneration, eulogy, and fondness: — "Mother of piety," "of clemency," "of holy love," "of consolation;" "Supreme Queen of Heaven;" "Star of the morning;" "Queen of saints," "of angels," "of sinners;" "Immaculate lily of purity;" "Glass of sanctity," "of truth," "of holiness;" "Most blessed," "most adorable," "most glorious Virgin;" such are a few of the many terms applied by the devout member of the Roman Church to the mother of the Redeemer. Everywhere one sees in Italy signs and evidences of the most unlimited devotion to the Virgin.

In the summer and autumn of 1855, the cholera raged violently in Tuscany, and the victims of this terrible disease were numerous amongst every class of the community: young and old, rich and poor, were alike stricken. When the cold of winter came to arrest the progress of the malady, great fears were entertained that the check would be but temporary, and that on the arrival of the warm weather in the succeeding year, the scourge would be revived; but the winter ended; spring, summer, autumn came in due succession, and no cholera appeared. The boon of this exemption from the dreaded scourge was then immediately ascribed to the "Blessed Virgin," and solemn services of praise and thanksgiving were ordered by the Church to be celebrated in her honor throughout all Tuscany.

Of two of these services I was an accidental witness, being a resident in the vicinity of the places, at the period there fixed on for the thanksgiving service to be performed. The religious rites which I had thus an opportunity of seeing, were celebrated successively at the Baths of Lucca, and at Monte Nero, near Leghorn. At the Baths of Lucca, the service assumed quite the aspect of a festival, and lasted several days; during which period the principal church was visited by many hundreds of the country people from the neighboring districts, to perform their devotions before a large painted wooden image of the Virgin, dressed for the occasion in a black velvet gown, and wearing on her breast the similitude of a heart transfixed with small silver daggers on either side, the symbol of "Our Lady of Sorrows."

The concluding portion of the ceremonial took place on a Sunday afternoon; and in the church, which was densely crowded, after a fervent preacher had poured forth from the pulpit, in the rich, melodious language of Tuscany, a rhapsody in the Virgin's praise, many were the candidates for office who pressed forward to take a part in the procession that had been ordained. In a short time there issued from the church a number of stalwart peasants, bearing aloft upon their shoulders, on a wooden platform to which poles were attached, the sacred image of the Virgin under an overarching canopy.

The image was borne triumphantly through the village, amidst two long files of peasant women, girls, and men; the latter dressed in a long loose robe of black, the former wearing veils upon their heads, and all with waxen tapers in their hands; whilst priests, attired in their festival robes, chanted prayers and psalms. The ceremony was a striking one to a Protestant, and an edifying one, doubtless, to every zealous Catholic, from the air of earnestness and devotion that characterized the appearance of all the participators in the performance of the pageant.

Although members of various monastic orders abound in Tuscany, it would seem, judging from the paucity of inhabitants in many of the large religious edifices erected for their use, that, in comparison with former times, conventual institutions are on the decline. Near Florence, the extensive monastic building called La Certosa, belonging to the Carthusian friars, is occupied now by only twenty-four. At Monte Catini there is a convent of imposing size, giving shelter now to only one nun, the solitary survivor of a sisterhood whom death has called away. Poor lone old woman! what a forlorn existence must be that of hers, without companions to cheer her solitude—without a being save her confessor, with whom she can interchange a thought or word! Fancy represents her wandering with feeble steps through the long passages and deserted cells, whose echoes are never awakened by any footstep but her own, recalling the faces and voices of those who have passed away in slow succession from her side, and whose mortal forms are resting below the sod, where before long her own may lie. How heavily the burden of life must weigh upon her soul! Without human ties, without aught but religious exercises to fill up her time—feeble, infirm, half blind—how fervently must death be hailed as a deliverer, a benefactor, a friend—longed for and asked for in earnest petitions addressed to the Throne on high!

Fancy draws yet another, and perhaps a truer picture of the solitary old nun. I see her sitting in the sunshine with bent-down head, hands folded in one another, and eyes half closed; not sleeping, but looking like one who sleeps, with no thought or feeling save that of a consciousness of the grateful warmth: torpid, listless: the present a blank, the past brought up before her view only now and again by the faint flickering flashes of an expiring memory: a human vegetable: a once reasoning, thinking creature, transformed by years of idleness and solitude, combined with the effect of age, into a mere curious mechanism of flesh and bone.

All monastic institutions very naturally tend to the deterioration of the intellect, the enfeeblement of the mental faculties. Solitude is, indeed, sometimes a great teacher; purifying the heart and elevating the mind; but solitude, to effect such ends, must address itself to natures of a superior order: to capacities above the range of those that fall to the lot of the ordinary class of mankind. To those who can find "sermons in stones," whose intelligence is sharpened by education, and who have capacities to follow up long trains of thought, and the ability to investigate into great moral truths—yet who, too weak to resist temptation, find themselves dragged into sin and its attendant sorrow by communion with the world—seclusion is a real, undeniable good, an unequivocal benefit. But to ordinary intellects, solitude is fraught with baneful consequences; since for such limited intelligences a deficiency of ideas must necessarily be supplied by a variety of sensations, or else the human being declines into something akin to a mere vegetable. To the common herd of men and women, the discipline of life is necessary; hopes and fears, joys and sorrows, successes and defeats, affections, friendships, rivalries, and all the changes and chances of ordinary existence are required by them to sharpen perception and to supply nourishment to thought and imagination. Vain is it to contend against Nature and Providence; the material and spiritual portions of our being, blended together by its Creator, cannot on earth be sundered with impunity: the attempt to become wholly spiritual, either turns man into a fevered visionary, a fanatic, or else (as is too commonly the case) degrades him to a mere brute-like, unreasoning creature. In the countenances of the majority of the many monks and friars that came under my notice in Italy, I saw most unequivocally evidenced the evils that result from the isolation of man from his fellows. Here and there, indeed, amongst that class, I noticed a face through which the mind shone forth; but such were few compared with those in whose dull, moody looks and lustreless eyes I read the signs of a torpid or a well-nigh blighted intellect.

Though conventual life, with its loneliness, its isolation, its paralyzation of the affections, is even more opposed to the nature of woman than to that of man, and still more likely therefore to result in baneful consequences to heart and mind; there are yet circumstances in the position of most of the religious sisterhoods of Italy, which neutralize the evil in a great degree, and give them, intellectually and morally, eminent advantages over most of their cowled and cord-girt brethren; for many orders of nuns enjoy the privilege of converting their convents, in a great degree, into educational establishments. Numerous schools of this description exist in Italy, and not a few in Florence, where young girls, under the guardianship and instruction of nuns, are duly initiated into all that is thought necessary for girls to learn. The fashionable mother, harrassed by the requirements of the supposed maternal duty of keeping a constant watch over the movements of her young unmarried daughter, gladly makes over the task to the pious sisterhood, whose high-walled precincts bid defiance to the approach of lovers. The otherwise lonely and monotonous existence of the nuns is thus enlivened by many sources of pleasure and interest; and towards their young pupils they become naturally bound by many ties of affection and sympathy. Nor surely by this, and by the diversion of her thoughts for some hours of every day from merely spiritual things, does the nun's nature become less holy, or she herself less deserving of mercy or salvation, than if from morn till night she sang hymns and repeated prayers continually.

But even within the walls of these conventual seminaries there exist women, to whom the occupation of teaching does not suffice to fill up the void which the severance of domestic ties has caused in their being. "Many nuns seem very happy and contented," said girls to me who had been educated in convents; "but there are some who never smile or say a word, and who always wear a sad, pining expression of countenance." A pining nun! what painful ideas does such a term evoke: how unspeakably mournful must be the existence of one who, consigned by family influences to a life for which she had no natural avocation, or who, abandoned by the enthusiasm which had impelled her to the act of worldly abnegation, finds herself bound by irrevocable vows to a lot which every moment becomes to her more wearisomely monotonous and dreary! How vividly in the darkness of night, or in her many solitary daylight hours, must rise up before her inward sight bright pictures of the world from which she is severed so entirely! Father, mother, sisters, brothers, assembled around the domestic hearth, their faces bright with smiles, with gladness and enjoyment; strolls in company with friends and relatives under the overarching trees in the summer time, and seats by cooling fountains; vows breathed forth of love and admiration; the kind husband, the merry children—ideas like these must often rise before the vision of the pining sister. Each bird that wings its flight from tree to tree in the convent garden, each breath of wind that plays amongst the rustling foliage, each filmy wreath of cloud that flits across the bright blue sky, symbols of freedom as they are, must all increase her longing, her craving, her intense desire for liberty.

An Italian lady told me of an incident that occurred in reference to this subject which came under her own personal knowledge—an incident of the same kind that has given the name of the Fair Maid of Roncesvalles a place in song and story. A girl in the higher ranks of life was betrothed to a young officer, who, being sent off on a somewhat distant military expedition, had not very long left the side of his destined bride, when the intelligence reached her ears that he had fallen in an engagement with the enemy. Despair seizing her at this news, she declared that for her the world henceforth had lost every charm, and precipitately retired to a convent; where, as soon as conventual regulations would permit, she took the veil and vows. But far too hasty, she soon found out, had been the act to which despair had urged her; for shortly after she became numbered amongst the sisterhood, some relative, with thoughtless cruelty, conveyed to her the information that he whom she mourned as dead was alive. The effect of this intelligence upon the mind of the young nun was such as to drive her well nigh mad. From feeling her suffering spirit soothed by the seclusion in which she lived, by constant communion with the powers on high, the offices of religion became distasteful — the convent with its silence, its repose, a prison—her cell, a dungeon and a tomb. Wildly did she solicit freedom from those with whom she was immured. The pale sisters heard with horror and surprise the words which issued from her lips. "Freedom, freedom! give me freedom—without freedom I cannot live," was the cry that, from morning to night, resounded in their ears. What was it to her that she was told there was wickedness in that cry—that by such a demand, by the exhibition of such a rebellious spirit, she was committing a terrible sin in the sight of God—that she was but dooming herself to sorrow in this life, and to everlasting suffering in the next. To such remonstrances she would not listen, much less heed.

Finding prayers and entreaties vain, and being refused permission to communicate with her family on the subject of her release, she resolved in her frenzy to endeavor to obtain the boon she sought, through the agency of hate and fear; and to make herself so dreaded, so detested, that, for their own sakes, the nuns would be glad to expel her from their walls. Poor girl! as well might the imprisoned bird try to gain its liberty by beating against the strong bars of its cage, as for her to win her way to freedom by such means. She might rend, she might break, she might tear up the nuns' favorite flowers, she might insult and maltreat them, and hurl imprecations in their ears; but all she gained by every act of this kind, was close confinement in a darkened cell. At length, one day, having fortunately found access to writing materials, she wrote a note—a short, frenzied note to her father, beseeching him to visit her; and then, trusting to Providence to befriend her, she clandestinely threw this note down from a high window of the convent that looked out on the high road; having previously written on the cover of her note an entreaty that the person into whose hands it might fall would send it on to its destination with the utmost speed.

Little to be depended on as the success of such an expedient must necessarily be, the father got his daughter's letter, and in compliance with her entreaty hastened to her side; when, worked upon by her frantic prayers, by the sight he witnessed of her distracted mind, he promised to do what he could towards the furtherance of her desires. From his position, his rank, the father had no difficulty in communicating on the subject with the Pope; and having represented strongly the circumstances of the case — the impulses of despair that had driven the girl to take the religious vows, her subsequent discovery of the falseness of the news by which she had been impelled to the renunciation of a secular life, the reaction of feeling that had since then set in, her regrets, her cravings for liberty — all these points strongly urged on the father's part, availed so far as to obtain for the rebellious nun — not indeed a revocation of the vows of celibacy, but a permission to change her residence from the convent to her father's house.

The convent in which this incident occurred, was in the neighborhood of Terracino, from which place my informant came; and many a tale of sorrow might perhaps be told, could one lift the veil that hangs before the lives of the inmates of such outwardly peaceful sanctuaries. It would be wrong, however, to imagine that discontent, unhappiness, and regret, as an invariable rule, lurk under the religious garb. I have seen faces beneath the shade of the white, spotless lawn, which looked to me the very type of purity and peace; of a quiet conscience, a mind that knew no shadow of regret, and a heart weaned truly from the vanities of this world.

But, whatever be the number of purified hearts and spiritualized minds that may be found within the precincts of convent and monastery — though every nun might be a saint, and every monk and friar the same — the existence of such institutions must still be a source of deep regret to all who think and feel that the very essence of Christianity is active charity. Amidst the turmoils of a stormy age, when the strong hand of power smote down the weak, the convent and the monastery had many claims to reverence and regard; for in them alone the helpless of either sex could find a refuge from wrong and violence: in them, too, was the torch of knowledge kept alive during the long night of ignorance that darkened over the land. But with the change of times, with the substitution of the rule of law for that of brutal might, and the diffusion of knowledge everywhere, monastic establishments as sanctuaries for youth and age, or as calm retreats for the scholar and sage, have become utterly useless. On widely different grounds from those on which they rested in former times, must they therefore now put forth their claims upon our sympathies. Acts of charity and love, to extend a helping hand to distressed and suffering fellow-creatures, being the Christian's appointed duty, in conformity with the teaching of the Gospel, the solitary recluse in his narrow cell, shut out from all communion with his kind, excluded from all opportunity of doing them good, fails in the performance of the fundamental obligations of his creed: and failing thus, however heavenward his thoughts may flow, deserves more blame than praise. Like the servant who hid his talent in the ground, he has turned to no profitable account one single gift of God with which he was endowed. What answer can he give when called to the great account? What hungry has he fed? what naked has he clothed? what poor has he relieved? what sick has he visited? what sorrowful has he comforted? That he loved his soul more ardently than his body he can show; but he cannot bring forth a single proof as evidence that he has cared for any one save himself.

But let justice be done. To deny our sympathy to all the religious orders enrolled beneath the banners of the Roman Catholic Church would be unfair; since at least one is to be found, the members of which devote their lives to the fulfillment of the great requirement of Christianity. It is pleasant to turn from the inert inmate of the convent cell to her who is truly termed, as her acts can prove, a Sister of Charity. From bed to bed on which the sick lie stretched, she glides with quiet step on her errand of love and mercy. Hers is the self-appointed task to watch beside the couch of pain, to cool the fevered brow, to present the ever-welcome cup to the parched lips, to adjust the pillows for the aching head, to soothe the perturbed and terror-stricken soul, and to close the glazed eyes of death. Patient, enduring, untiring and unflagging in her zeal, she is ready at every hour, by day or night, to respond to the call of suffering. Through noisome streets, through pestilential lanes, the abodes of poverty and vice, she takes her way; she climbs the ladder to the attic where the sufferer lies, or descending to the cellar's damp-stained walls, she takes her seat on the oozy floor, beside the bed of straw on which lies stretched the victim of starvation or disease. She braves contagion fearlessly, and undauntedly, in the discharge of her mission; she enters the haunts of crime, the prison cell, and the beggar's lair; the hospital wards also know well the voice, the form of the Sister of Charity. Surely no one can act more fully the heroic part, or deserve more richly the applause of man, than she who, uninfluenced by hopes of fame, of a place in history or verse, consecrates the flower of her youth, the prime of her life, to the relief of suffering humanity; and we, who reverence and applaud a Fry and Nightingale, should not withhold our meed of praise from those whose acts are in harmony with the deeds which have conferred honor and renown on the names of our two noble countrywomen.

## CHAPTER X.

### COMPAGNIA DELLA MISERICORDIA.*

OF the many unfamiliar objects which arrested my attention in the streets of Florence, none excited so forcibly my feelings of curiosity and surprise as the sight of the members of the Brotherhood of the Misericordia. Certainly the garb adopted by this fraternity when on duty is one more likely to suggest the idea of deeds of wickedness than acts of virtue; and when they are first beheld, clothed in a long monastic dress — a mass of black from head to foot — their heads entirely enshrouded in close-fitting hoods, and their eyes glaring out through two small apertures in the black calico veil which hangs down loosely before their faces — they present a sight calculated to startle any individual afflicted with sensitive

* Brotherhood of Mercy.

nerves. Hideous, however, as is the dress, it yet has the merit of fulfilling the object for which it was designed, as it shrouds completely the individual by whom it is worn. Under the folds of that black dress, and beneath the *cappa*, as the united mask and hood are termed, a wife could not possibly recognize her husband, a sister her brother, or a mother her son, so perfect is the disguise.

The Society of the Misericordia is a time-honored institution in Tuscany, and tradition dates its origin in Florence from an early period of the thirteenth century. According to the authority I now follow on the subject, this institution owed its origin to the humanity of a certain Pietro Borsi, a common porter, who, with others of his profession, frequented the Piazza San Giovanni for the purpose of hiring out their services to the merchants of the town. Briskly, however, as commercial transactions were carried on in Florence at that time, the number of porters was so much in excess of the number for whom employment could be found, that the different members of this fraternity had daily many unoccupied hours on their hands. Seeing this, and thinking it a pity that so much time should be wasted unprofitably, it was proposed by Pietro Borsi, and assented to by the rest, that a certain number of their body should in turn take upon themselves the duty of performing charitable offices towards such sick and wounded of their fellow citizens as might be in circumstances requiring aid. The scheme prospered under the direction of Borsi, and the porters went through the different districts of the city, carrying the sick and wounded on hand-litters to such places as the sufferers might wish to be transported.

The benevolent association thus set on foot by the porters, soon included members of other callings in its ranks, and it was further consolidated and extended in consequence of the great plague that ravaged Florence in 1348. During those frightful times, when the Angel of Death was knocking at every door — when corpses strewed the streets, and the busy, cheerful hum of life gave place to sighs, groans, and the wailings of suffering and despair — the Brothers of the Misericordia discharged their onerous and perilous duties with a zeal and assiduity that won for them the protection of the authorities of the town. For many years the society flourished, and the wealth with which it became endowed from various sources, reached to a considerable amount; but under the influence of a misdirected religious zeal, the society was dissolved by a decree of the Republic in 1425, in order that its funds might go to increase the revenues of the Ospitalieri, a fraternity instituted to supply the wandering pilgrim with food and lodging on his road to the Holy Sepulchre. The extinction of the society, however, was a loss very sensibly felt in Florence, on account of the accidents and sudden deaths that frequently occurred; and the services of the Misericordia soon commenced to be very highly appreciated in the city, when events of daily occurrence proved the advantages that had arisen, and the evils that had been avoided, through the existence of an organized charity to look after the sick amongst the destitute classes of the community, and to secure the decent interment of the dead.

An incident which happened in the year 1475, was the means of restoring to Florence its highly-valued fraternity. As a spirited and benevolent citizen was one day walking through the town, he saw, lying in the middle of a street, the corpse of some poor friendless, destitute outcast of humanity. Seized with indignation at this sight, the worthy Florentine, raising up the corpse, placed it upon his shoulders, and, laden thus, hurried off with his strange burden to the Pallazzo della Signoria, where, presenting himself, he demanded to speak with the Gonfaloniere, the chief magistrate of Florence. The demand was granted, and the Gonfaloniere having appeared, his visitor lost no time in entering upon the object of his mission. Pointing to the ghastly burden he had borne, and recounting from whence it had been taken, he described in strong and vivid language the evil consequences that had arisen from the suppression of the Brethren of the Misericordia. The representations of the zealous citizen, enforced as they were by the mute but forcible pleadings of the dead, had an eminently successful issue; the suppressed society was speedily re-established on its former footing, and before very long, the influence of its example spread to the neighboring cities. In the many pestilences which ravaged the soil of Tuscany, during a space of four centuries, suffering humanity was comforted and relieved by the indefatigable zeal of the members of the *Compagnia della Misericordia.*

Various are the works of charity to which the Florentine fraternity dedicate their time and revenues. At any hour at which their services may be wanted, they transport patients to the hospital: and to the sick amongst the destitute poor they furnish aid in money, linen, medicine and attendance. The poor mother in her hour of suffering, whilst herself a particular object of the society's care, is indebted to them for the clothes with which she covers her new born infant; the convalescent owes to them the soups, and wine, and nourishing food, by which his strength and energies of mind and body are re-established. The case, in which rests the fractured leg or arm of the poor laborer, or needy artizan, is the donation of the fraternity; bandages for wounds, leeches, cupping-glasses, baths and medical appliances of every kind, all are supplied, as circumstances require, by this truly useful and active charity.

Through the means of an excellent organization, the services of the fraternity are available at any moment. The members of the society, consisting of all classes of the community, are divided into sections, numbering about forty in each section; and to every section is assigned in turn a certain period, in which each member of its ranks must hold himself in readiness—according to his vows, taken generally for a limited period—to obey the call of duty. At the sound of the loud tolling of the great bell, the brother of the Misericordia, whose appointed period of service has arrived, must hasten to the place of rendezvous of his fraternity: it matters not at what hour, whether in broad mid-day or in the dead of night, at morning's dawn or evening's dusk, he must instantly obey the summons. The warm bed must be left in the cold night of winter, and the scorching heat of the mid-day sun must be encountered in the height of summer; the rich man must start up from the dinner-table around which his guests are seated, the shopman must leave his counter, the shoemaker must put down his awl, the tailor his needle—each and all must, in accordance with the obligations entailed upon them by their vows, hasten off without delay to perform various offices of charity for distressed and calamity-stricken fellow creatures. Now the bell summons to convey a fever-struck patient to the hospital; then it rings out for the same purpose in behalf of some bricklayer or mason who may have suffered grievous injuries by falling down from a high scaffold; at one time it is for the resuscitation of some half-drowned creature; at another, for succoring the inmates of a house on fire; and more commonly it is for transporting a corpse to its last resting-place in some neighboring church or cemetery. Various are the functions to be performed and the duties to be discharged, for which the bell of the great tower, that once called the citizens to arms, now sends out by day or night its mandatory summons to the members of the Misericordia.

The manner in which the fraternity discharge the offices of charity towards the sick is deserving of particular description. As soon as that member of the society to whose turn it comes to fulfill the office of director—as soon as this head watch (*capo guardia*, as he is called), receives, a certificate from a medical man that a certain person, laboring under disease, should be removed to the hospital—the customary signal is made, and at the sound of the summoning stroke, such members of the fraternity as are at the time liable to be called out for duty hasten to their church, the appointed place of meeting.

This church, situated in the Piazza del Duomo—formerly the Piazza San Giovanni—is almost as ancient as the community to which it belongs. It is said to stand on the margin of the gulf which was dug to receive the numerous victims of the pestilence of 1348. On the altar, a few tapers burn night and day, continually, whilst six members of the order keep watch in the sanctuary. On the walls are hung the dresses of the community, as well as the torches which are made use of at night and in funeral solemnities; and along the floor are ranged biers and litters for conveying the sick and dead to their respective destinations. Hitherto, this church, whose pavement is never trod by any foot but that of a member of the fraternity, the summoned brothers of the Misericordia repair, to receive and execute the orders given to them by their *capo guardia.*

Enveloped in the black vestments of their order, the members of the Misericordia issue from their church, marching two by two, preceded by what may be termed a marshal (*bidello*), and by four brothers bearing a litter on their shoulders. This litter is adapted with great forethought to every exigency of the service in which it is used. On a framework of wood, spanned by girths from side to side, lie the ordinary appurtenances of a bed; the mattress is always as soft a one as can be found; the sheets are ever clean and white; the blanket either heavy or light, according to the requirements of the season; and the pillow, by an ingenious contrivance, can be made to take the particular slant desired. A light low arching canopy, composed of fine iron wire, over which is extended a quilt, or, if occasion needs, a waterproof covering, serves as a protection against the weather for the occupant of the bed. To the lower part of the litter torches are fastened, in case night should overtake the brotherhood whilst discharging the offices of charity to the sick without the city walls; for, to a circuit of three miles, measured from the centre of the town, extend the self-imposed duties of the fraternity. Besides the torches, the lower part of the litter contains a box, in which is to be found everything that the sick might desire or need during transportation to the hospital—water, wine, lemon, sugar, vinegar, hartshorn—all are in readiness for service when required. Provision is even made for the performance of the last rites of the Roman Catholic Church in case any occupant of the litter may be placed in a position to require them: for in the same box with the restoratives is found the Holy Oil, with which the dying may be anointed.

Arrived at their destination, the litter is deposited on the ground, and the brothers, entering the sick chamber, prepare to effect the removal of the patient in a most tender and considerate manner; by means of a long, thin, smooth piece of bone, four strong strips of linen are quickly and easily inserted below the sick man's body, at short intervals, from underneath his shoulders downwards. At a sign from the *capo guardia*, the brothers, who each hold an end of the several strips, raise up the patient sufficiently high to allow a quilt, which is held ready by other members of the society, to be extended beneath. The sick man is gently lowered again, so as to rest upon the quilt, and conveyed in it slowly and carefully to the litter wherein he is deposited; the greatest care being taken that he should be placed in a position of the utmost possible ease. The bedclothes adjusted, and the protecting covering properly fixed, the object of the fraternity's solicitude is borne upon the shoulders of the brethren to the hospital; two of the number walking, one at either side of the litter, on the watch to see if the sick man has need of anything on the way.

The transportation, however, of the sick to hospitals forms but a small part of the self-imposed obligations undertaken towards that class by the brethren of the Misericordia. To every district of the city is assigned a certain number of individuals belonging to the order, who, taking their name from the functions they fulfill, are termed Convisitatori. Acting singly, each on his own judgment and responsibility, the Convisitatore is bound to see that all the sick people committed to his care are well provided with everything they may stand in need of, in regard to linen, nourishment, baths and medicine. To him, also, is committed the duty of furnishing the sick with nightly attendance, if such should be requisite; and it is on his attestation to the fact, joined to the certificate of a doctor to the same effect, that a nightly watcher from the ranks of the society is supplied.

Thus, not only do the fraternity transport the sick to hospitals, and look after the wants of that helpless class in their own homes, but they leave their comfortable, perhaps luxurious abodes, to watch during the night in cheerless dwellings, by the bedside of the suffering poor. This service is discharged by one member of the company, on ordinary occasions; but by two, if the disease be of an aggravated character, and danger to life is feared. In case it may be a woman who requires assistance of this kind, the night watcher also is a female, (for several individuals of that sex are included in the ranks of the Misericordia); but if the sick woman be dangerously ill, a brother of the order comes to the sister's aid. Nor are the benevolent operations of the society entirely restricted to the destitute poor, as far as nightly attendance is concerned; for not unfrequently in the dwellings of the upper classes the pillows of the sick are adjusted by the hands of members of the Misericordia: and in all such cases, however humble the renderer, and however rich the recipient of such services may be, the nightly watcher is not permitted to receive the smallest thing, either food, or drink, or money, from the family served, under the penalty of a sudden and ignominious expulsion from the ranks of the society to which he or she belongs. In order to ascertain if the sick are tended with due care and zeal, inspectors and sub-inspectors go out nightly from the ranks of the society to visit those dwellings of the poor to which the night watcher has been sent.

Amongst the various benevolent acts of the fraternity deserving of special notice, are the offices of charity they perform towards imprisoned criminals. Theirs is the self-appointed task of visiting the goals, and of seeing that every regulation connected with the salubrity of these abodes is duly attended to. The food provided for the prisoners comes under their inspection, and not unfrequently clothes and linen are supplied by them to those who, by a long, weary term of exile from the world, are expiating past crimes or misdemeanors. Under the sanction of the Government authorities, they also take measures to provide that class of criminals with the means of profitable employment; and, deducting only the prime cost of the various articles supplied, they leave to the worker the full value of his work. On certain occasions, such as the great religious festivals of the Church at Christmas, Easter, Quinquagesima, Pentecost, and Ascension Day, the inmates of the prison are provided with a feast at the expense of the fraternity. The conveyance of this feast forms also a portion of the duty of the brotherhood; and at the periods above mentioned, a troop of black-robed brethren may be seen issuing from the head-quarters of the company, walking two and two, each couple bearing between them a large basket filled with provisions of excellent description, covered over with branches of myrtle and laurel. Arrived at the prison-door, the baskets are deposited on the ground and speedily emptied of their contents; each brother taking a dish and carrying it with his own hands to the prisoner's cell. Who can doubt the good effects exerted on the prisoner's mind by each and every benevolent act of which he is the object, on the part of this charitable association? The hearts of the most abased of human kind still vibrate to the touch of kindness and sympathy: gratitude is a powerful moral agent, a purifier of the mind, a softener of the heart. Could the inner life of the inmates of a Florentine prison be unfolded to the view, it is more than probable we should find that many a virtuous resolve, or many a kindly feeling, has owed its origin to the little myrtle-covered dish presented by the hand of a Brother of the Misericordia.

The interment of the dead forms a very important part of the functions of the society; and the company charges itself especially with the duty of carrying to the grave the corpse of any poor friendless stranger whom death has struck down in some humble lodging or tavern. But though such unfortunates commend themselves particularly to the sympathies of the society, the burial charities of the brotherhood are far from being restricted to this class; for funeral rites are performed by them for those that die in their own homes and amongst their kindred, in every instance in which the family of the deceased is too poor to provide the means of decent interment for their dead. For such, as well as for other occasions on which the services of the fraternity are needed, the bell rings out its summoning peal; and at that sound, the members whose period of active duty has arrived, hasten to obey the call, generally issued for this particular purpose at half an hour before sunset; and, marching in files of two and two, they bear the bier with its lifeless burden to the place of sepulcher, after having previously assisted at the performance of the customary funeral rites in the church.

On the occasion of the death of any distinguished member of the order, the society assembles in great numbers to accompany the departed brother to his grave. During my residence in Florence I was witness of a funeral of the society conducted on a scale of imposing magnitude; the Misericordia having to lament the loss of one of its members in the person of the Bishop of Fiesole, who had been suddenly stricken down in the midst of health by a stroke of apoplexy. From the house where the dead bishop had lain in state, dressed out in his episcopal robes, the lifeless body was removed by the black-hooded brethren, and, elevated upon a bier, was borne by them to its last resting-place at Fiesole. The procession was a very imposing sight, seen from the elevation of the steps in front of the cathedral, before which passed the funeral array. In vivid contrast with the shifting, stirring crowd, and the many forms of animated life with which the piazza of the cathedral was densely filled, was the motionless figure of the dead ecclesiastic, as with face uncovered, and decked out with all the insignia of his mortal dignities, he was borne aloft, extended on a bier, upon the shoulders of a certain number of the fraternity. The rigid features of the deceased ecclesiastic, and his recumbent form, dressed out in all the pomp of ecclesiastical vestments, the chanting priests, the flaring of countless torches, and the long train of black-hooded brethren that filed along through the midst of the bustling throng, formed, altogether, a picture of a very impressive character.

A charity of an essentially Italian character remains yet to be enumerated amongst the philanthropic acts of the Compagnia della Misericordia. It is provocative of a smile to find that young portionless girls are reckoned amongst the class of unfortunates requiring assistance from the funds of the charitable society. The hapless case of the undowered maiden who, for want of the heart-subjugating power of money to forge the nuptial bonds, is doomed to a life of single blessedness, appeals strongly, it would seem, to the sympathies of the Misericordia; for, on one particular day in every year, marriage portions are distributed, with edifying solemnity, to various girls belonging to the lower classes of the community. It is to be hoped that the money* thus bestowed really benefits the recipients, and that the commodities purchased by such means do credit, in some instances, to the purchaser's sense and discrimination; but, as Italian girls generally select their lovers on a principle far different from that which actuated the Vicar of Wakefield's wife in the choice of her wedding-gown, this hope is of a very doubtful realization.

The source from which the Misericordia derives the greatest portion of their revenues is from begging: *la questua*, as it is termed. This *questua* is made once a week by ten brothers of the order, who, dividing the town between them into so many parts, take each his way through his allotted district to seek for alms. Attired in the black dress of the fraternity, and shrouded in its impenetrable disguise, the *questuante* may be seen at an early hour of the day pursuing his mission through the streets of Florence, with a begging-box in his hand. In ghostly silence he carries on his work, the only mode of solicitation used being the presentation of his begging-box to the passer-by, accompanied by the appealing gaze of eyes, that peer through two small apertures in the black mask he wears. Into every shop the

* The amount of the girl's portion, though not received by her until the wedding-day, is known beforehand.

*questuante* has free access; for him the doors of public offices and monasteries unclose; into his box drop the silver of the rich and the copper of the poor: the *quattrini* of the working-man mingle with the *paoli* of the noble. Where the palace rears its proud front on high, or where the dark, damp cellar gives shelter from the midnight air to poor wretches of either sex and of every age, in streets where wealth parades its silken robes, or in noisome lanes where poverty shows its rags, the black-shrouded form of the begging brother of the Misericordia may be seen. Seldom does the begging-box remain unfilled, for rarely does either avarice or poverty refuse to the *questuante* the small coin he seeks. On the evening of the day on which the *questua* is made, the ten *questuante* meet together in the rooms of the director of the society, and, each box being opened and its contents examined, the amount obtained is duly registered and transferred to the general funds of the community.

Besides the regular weekly *questua*, there are other collections made occasionally, for particular purposes; at one time, money is required for the sufferers in some public or private calamity; at another, it is wanted to give relief to the poor family on whom some great calamity has fallen unexpectedly: now, the collection is taken for prisoners; and, again, for procuring masses to be said for the benefit of some suffering soul in purgatory.

In addition to the contributions raised by the means described, the funds of the society are sustained by a small annual tax imposed upon the members of the fraternity. This tax, varying within certain limits at the pleasure of the contributor, can never be less than one paolo (5½*d.*), or exceed five of that coin. On the holiday of their patron saint, or during the course of the eight following days, the pecuniary obligations of the members of the Misericordia are annually discharged.

I have entered into the foregoing account of the history and proceedings of this charitable society, not only from the intrinsic interest of the subject, but on account of the estimation in which the Compagnia della Misericordia is held in Tuscany. Before a procession of the black-robed brethren, the crowd respectfully open and give way, whilst every hat, from the noble's to the beggar's, is reverentially raised as they go by; and as each man bares his head, he knows not but that he uncovers in the presence of the Grand Duke himself, or some of his family: for not unfrequently the highest in the land has donned the garb of the Misericordia for a stated period, either from a motive of a penitential kind, or from one of a purely philanthropic nature.

But if to make atonement for evil done and for wrongs committed, be the motive which chiefly swells the ranks of the Misericordia in Tuscany—if in general the impelling impulse to take the vows be remorse of conscience—who would not prefer the acts of self-mortification of the Misericordia penitent, to those of any contrite sinner shut up in the seclusion of monastic walls? Far beyond the merits of sighs, and tears, and fastings, and penitential psalms, surely are the lone midnight watchings by the sufferer's bed, the cup presented for the parched lips to drink, the pillow adjusted for the aching head, the visit to the prisoner's cell, the gift by which the pangs of cold and hunger are relieved, the prompt answer to the summoning peal which calls, perhaps, from the chamber of mirth and feasting to the cheerless home of poverty or death. A truly noble institution is the Misericordia, one that reflects credit on the nation amongst whom it is found.

# CHAPTER XI.

## GALILEO AND MICHAEL ANGELO.

BY the remembrances which its name invokes, Florence powerfully commends itself to the sympathies of every cultivated mind. Distinguished in war, in power, in industry, and, above all, in literature and art, Florence shines out in the prevailing darkness of the mediæval times with a lustre peculiarly brilliant. The woollen stuffs, the gold and silk brocades, the produce of Florentine looms, were prized, renowned, and sought for throughout the western world; and to Florence especially belongs the merit of making the merchant's an honored name, and of raising the industrial arts to dignity and esteem. Of all the republics of Italy to which the Middle Ages gave birth, Florence was the one in which the love of liberty was the strongest, the cultivation of the intellect the greatest, and the laws the best framed and the best administered. Noted for the genius of its citizens, and the intelligence of its people, to Florence belongs the glory of having given to the world, during the Middle Ages, a greater number of illustrious men than all the rest of Italy was able to send forth. Whilst the darkness of barbarism still hung densely over the British Isles, while knowledge there could find no resting-place save in the monastic cell, and art and artists there were terms almost unknown, the poet, painter, sculptor and scholar, daily met together, as honored, cherished guests at the rich and noble Florentine's board.

But amongst the many sons of Florence who shed honor on that republic in bygone days, there are none who have left behind them names so well deserving of our respect and homage as Galileo and Michael Angelo: the first, astronomer and philosopher combined — the teacher of great truths to an incredulous world; the latter, an artist whose works in painting, sculpture and architecture occupy a foremost position in the domain of art.

Florence is full of the memorials of her two great sons; and in Pisa, where Galileo lived for several years as teacher of philosophy in the university there, his memory is indissolubly associated with the far-famed Cathedral and Leaning Tower of that city. Their very stones are eloquent to us of him, for with both these structures are connected incidents of no small moment in his history.

To the philosophic mind, trifles are often fraught with teachings of wisdom. The swinging of a large bronze lamp suspended from the roof of the Cathedral at Pisa was apparently an incident of the most trivial description, but to Galileo that sight evoked a train of thought which resulted in the discovery of the theory of the pendulum. Hanging yet where it hung in the days of that great man, that lamp can never be looked on without interest: perhaps, too, this interest is heightened by the accessories of the surrounding scene. For very beautiful is the interior of the Cathedral of Pisa, seen, as I have seen it, when the bright beams of a midday sun, streaming through richly colored windows, illuminated the nave with its rows of splendid columns, lit up the richly carved and gilt panels of the roof, the age-dimmed pictures, and the decorated altars. But still more beautiful was it in the evening hour, when the long aisles seemed to lengthen out, and the lofty columns to grow more lofty in the twilight gloom; when here and there, from the distant chapel, the taper shot forth its small starry gleam, and all details of arches, columns, altars, pictures, sculptures and carving lost to view, the soul was inly touched by the solemn influences of vastness, silence and solitude.

Still more suggestive of Galileo than the Cathedral is the far-famed Leaning Tower adjoining it; for here it was that he proved by a simple experiment that the doctrines of Aristotle, which he had been appointed to teach in the university of Pisa, were fundamentally wrong. Denounced by his brother professors as an ignorant pretender in the school of philosophy, as the defamer of an illustrious and unerring sage and the disseminator of untruths, Galileo eagerly called out, "Bring my doctrines to the test of experiment, and by this prove whether Aristotle's theory or mine in regard to the law of falling bodies, is true." The challenge was accepted, and the Leaning Tower of Pisa was selected as the place where the demonstration was to be made.

Let us bring up the past before our view, and see assembled round that wonderful Leaning Tower, grave professors and solemn sages, who have come, confident of triumphing in the approaching discomfiture of an ignorant pretender in the paths of science and philosophy. Around them cluster an eager crowd, looking with curiosity at that obscure young man; who, though alone and friendless, the object of reproach and scorn, yet strong in the power of truth, stands up before them with sparkling eye and undaunted bearing.

The experiment is to be made by means of two balls, one of which is twice as heavy as the other. If Aristotle be right in his theory of the velocity of falling bodies, the heavy ball, when dropped from the summit of the tower, should reach the ground in exactly half the time taken by the lighter ball to pass through the same space, both being dropped at the same time. If Galileo be right, the two balls should not differ one instant in the rate of their respective descents. Nothing can be simpler than the experiment, and nothing more clearly and easily ascertainable than its result.

The moment comes when the issue is to be determined, and at a given signal, down drop the balls from the tower: they strike upon the earth in the same moment of time. A proud moment was it for that young sage, and exulting was the look he cast on the discomfited philosophers. Again and again the experiment was repeated, with the same uniform results; and from that day Aristotle lost the sway that he had exercised for centuries over the human mind.

But the pioneer of knowledge, the discoverer of truths, needs a brave heart to sustain him in his battle against error and ignorance in this world; and no one more than Galileo required the endowments of a daring spirit and unflinching mind. Through his whole life he had to contend with determined incredulity, and with ignorance that pertinaciously refused to be enlightened. "Oh, my dear Kepler," writes Galileo to his friend, "how I wish we could have one hearty laugh together. Here at Padua is the principal professor of philosophy, whom I have repeatedly and urgently requested to look at the moon and planets through my glass, which he pertinaciously refuses to do!" Unhappily for Galileo's lot in life, the Paduan philosopher was only a fair sample of the pseudo-scientific sages of his day.

But bravely as Galileo bore himself, for the greatest part of his long life, in a continuous contest with error and bigoted ignorance, he was in his old age guilty of an act of cowardice that has left a deep stain upon his memory. Who does not grieve at the thought of that old man on his bended knees, before the Cardinals of the Roman Church, swearing that he abjured, cursed and detested as erroneous and heretical, the doctrine he had held and taught, that the earth moved round the sun; whilst in his heart he knew that the words he spoke with his hand on the Holy Gospel were utterly untrue? for, on rising up from his humiliating act and attitude, he turned and said to some one near, "*E pur se muove*,"—"For all this, it moves." Still, recalling to mind the dreadful torture of the rack, to which the aged philosopher was subjected ere he publicly abjured his belief in the great and eternal truths he had proclaimed, we must not judge him hardly for this deed.

Florence warmly cherishes the name and memory of the great astronomer, and exhibits to this day many memorials of him. Attached to the Museum is a temple erected by the present Grand Duke to Galileo, and here may be seen the telescope which revealed to him the satellites of Jupitèr. The Observatory where most of his observations on the moon were made, still exists; and the stranger is shown the residence where, blind, infirm, and weighed down by years and humiliation, his vexed and suffering spirit passed away.

But Florence possesses a still more touching memento of her great son than any of those described. In the church of Santa Croce, the stranger's step is arrested by the tomb that bears Galileo's name; and insensible is the heart that does not do homage to the illustrious dead — a teacher of truths which can never die, and who by years of obloquy and persecution, by imprisonment, torture, and a shattered frame, paid a heavy penalty for the distinction he enjoyed of being the greatest genius of his age.

But, however we may be disposed to compassionate the sufferings of Galileo, and great men like him, our pity for the hardships and trials of their lots in life is probably in most instances misplaced. Outwardly unfortunate as his career may be, the man of genius bears that within his mind which probably far more than compensates him for the hardships he endures. The lonely study, wherein the midnight lamp burns on through the changing year, is the scene, perhaps, at times of joy more intense, of triumph more perfect than any which the world—through the means of wealth, rank, power and distinction—can offer to the common herd of men. Glorious must be the moment when the long sought-for truth flashes vividly across the deeply meditating mind, and the "Eureka" of every inquiring sage on whom the day-star of discovery dawns, must be fraught with the most exquisite happiness. And though such moments in the lifetime of even the most gifted student must be rare, there is for him a constant source of enjoyment in the exulting sense of power which accompanies the exercise of the higher faculties of his mind. Withal then, exposed as the great astronomer was through his long life, to calumny and reproach—though a torture-forced recantation of the truth escaped his aged lips—yet in the grand triumphs of his intellect, in the proud consciousness that was his, of having given forth truths which the world would not let die, the life and lot of Galileo stand forth before our gaze as deserving not of pity, but of envy.

In Santa Croce, also, lie the mortal remains of Michael Angelo. His tomb is one of the first that meets the eye on entering the church; and it is said that before his death he chose that particular spot of sepulture for himself, for the whimsical reason that when the doors were open he might, even in his grave, as he said, be able to see the Cathedral's towering dome; of which his admiration was so great that he took it as a model for the construction of the cupola of St. Peter's. A fine and noble nature was that of Michael Angelo. Amidst an age of general moral corruption and laxity of principle, his life, by its unsullied purity and its unblemished integrity, stands out in brilliant contrast with the lives of most of his cotemporaries, and challenges our respect and admiration. An ardent patriot, he threw aside his brush and chisel to join the ranks of those who strove to save the independence of his native soil; and on the battlements of Florence he proved that Italy's greatest architect, painter and sculptor, had qualities that might well confer on him the title of being one of her greatest heroes also.

The memorials of Michael Angelo in Florence are numerous; for in its churches, its palaces, and its public squares, we are brought face to face with the mighty creations of his genius. And yet, with all their excellencies so universally acknowledged, and with all the homage now paid to that mind which gave them birth, Michael Angelo, in his early days, had to contend against that detraction and envy which denounced his noble works as things of little worth. An amusing incident is recorded, in connection with this subject, of the means he took to heap confusion on his adversaries, by proving that their disparaging criticisms were founded on prejudice, and not on truth or justice.

In the seclusion of his studio, with a secrecy he

took care no one should penetrate, Michael Angelo sculptured the marble group of a Faun and Bacchus. The work being completed, he broke off the right hand a little above the wrist, and laying it carefully aside, he conveyed the mutilated figure to a hole previously excavated in the ground, and there buried it. After the lapse of some little time, judging that the damp earth would then have conferred upon his work a decidedly venerable appearance, he ordered workmen to make certain alterations in the grounds; which would, he knew, lead necessarily to the discovery of the buried piece of statuary. The event answered his expectations: the mutilated statue was found; and as Michael Angelo took care that this great discovery should be at once noised abroad through the city, his bitterest critics rushed to the spot; and on the earth being cleared from about the figures of the Faun and Bacchus, they speedily pronounced the group to be an antique of the finest description; warmly congratulating themselves on the fact that of this masterpiece of antiquity only one hand was missing. Amongst the group that surrounded the statue, eagerly engaged in enlarging on the beauties of the work, stood Michael Angelo, who gave but a very faint assent to the general encomiums it called forth; and on being pointedly asked his opinion on the subject, he replied, in a careless, disparaging way, it was a pretty thing enough. "Oh, doubtless you can make as good a statue yourself," was the reply, uttered in a satirical tone: and Michael Angelo, continuing the conversation in a strain which led on his adversaries to say all that he could wish, suddenly startled them by the question—"What will you say if I made this?" To the idea thus suggested, smiles of incredulity and derisive laughter were the response; in the midst of which, begging their patience for a little while, Michael Angelo went to his house, and speedily brought back with him, as evidence of the truth of his words, the hand which he had broken off; and it was found, to the confusion and discomfiture of his antagonists, to correspond exactly with the mutilated arm of the newly-discovered Bacchus.

This memorial of the triumph of Michael Angelo occupies a conspicuous position in the Gallery of the Uffizi at Florence; the seam which marks the place where the arm was fractured being very distinctly visible.

Michael Angelo himself was far from being niggardly of praise of the artistic productions of his immediate predecessors or cotemporaries. "*Meglio di te non posso*," (better than thee I cannot make,) he exclaimed, in reference to the great cathedral dome of Brunelleschi in Florence. In a similar spirit he stopped before the statue of St. Mark by Donato, and exclaimed, in allusion to its life-like expression, "Mark, why don't you speak to me?" Of the bronze gates, the masterpiece of Ghiberti, he said—"They are so beautiful, that they are worthy of being the gates of Paradise." On seeing the medals of Cæsari, he declared, "Art has reached its last hour, for beyond this it cannot go;" and on looking at Bigarini's fine statues in terracotta, he exclaimed, "Woe to the antique statues, if these should become marble!"

In the same house where Michael Angelo lived in Florence, some descendants of his family still live at the present day; much of the furniture remains in its original position, unchanged, and many personal relics of the great sculptor and painter are there to be found. His sword, his crutch-handled walking-sticks, his slippers, and the table at which he used to write, challenge the stranger's notice; whilst some of his vigorous sketches adorn the walls of the various apartments, which have been fitted up in a style to do honor to his memory. Right is it, indeed, that in Florence, his native town, and for whose independence he vainly fought, every memento of him should be preserved and venerated.

"I commend my soul to God, my body to the earth, and my property to my nearest of kin," were the terms of his last will and testament, dictated by him on his death-bed. He breathed his last in Rome, on February 17th, 1563, within a fortnight of entering on his ninetieth year; and his remains were, at his express desire, conveyed to Florence, where they were buried, with every circumstance of pomp and solemnity, in the church of Santa Croce.

## CHAPTER XII.

### THE LATE REVOLUTION.

ALTHOUGH the events which took place in Paris on the 24th of February, 1848, exercised an immense influence on Italy as well as on other European States, the revolutionary era commenced in the Peninsula considerably before that time. At Rome, in the year 1846, when Pius the Ninth was at the height of his popularity, amidst the shouts which resounded of "Viva Pio IX," there was voices heard to say, "Abbasso il Pontefice!"* Under the triumphal arches that were raised to the reforming Pope, the progress of the carriages belonging to prelates forming part of his cortége, was impeded, or stopped; and returning from St. Peter's, he was often followed by bands of students from the university, demanding, with loud voices, their political rights.

* "Down with the Pontiff."

At this period, Florence began to show symptoms of the same spirit of disquiet that prevailed at Rome. Public demonstrations were made which had for their avowed object the acquisition of a civic guard and the liberty of the press. In the middle of January the people of Leghorn, with Guerrazzi for their leader, rose in arms. The rebellion was repressed; and in the fortress of Porto Ferrajo the imprisoned chief had ample leisure for meditation over his defeated plans.

In 1847 fresh disturbances occurred. The whole of Italy was agitated in every part; throughout the Peninsula there were symptoms that a storm of no ordinary violence was about to break forth. Day by day the clouds grew darker overhead; and popular tumults, like premonitory gusts, gave evidence that a great conflict between the opposing forces of power and numbers was nigh at hand. Bologna and Ferrara demanded and obtained a civic guard. The same demand was echoed at Rome with clamorous cries; and by a papal decree issued on the 5th of July, the privilege of forming a national guard was conferred not only on Rome, but on every city in the States of the Church. Tumults commenced at Naples; Sicily and Calabria were stirred with the first throes of popular discontent; and Genoa also. From north to south, Italy was a smouldering volcano.

The eventful year of 1848 was ushered in by a

revolution at Palermo. Sicily declared itself independent; and Ferdinand II found the fairest portion of his dominions wrenched away violently from his grasp. Naples rose up in arms to demand a constitution, which was granted through the influence of fear. The commencement of February was signalized by commotions at Turin; and, following the prevailing example, Tuscany extorted from its intimidated ruler, on the 18th of February, the concession of political rights.

The revolution of the 24th of February, in Paris, acted on the impulsive Italians as a strong blast on a glowing flame. Milan, after five days' desperate fighting, threw off the Austrian yoke. Charles II, Duke of Lucca, found himself constrained to fly from his dominions to save his life. Venice, on the 22d of March, declared itself a republic; and in a few months afterwards, in the ancient capital of the Cæsars, amidst the joyous shouts of thousands, a similar form of government was proclaimed.

Yielding to the spirit of the times, the Grand Duke of Tuscany ceded to his subjects a constitution, which was, for the most part, founded on the model of that of France. This concession was followed by an amnesty, in right of which Guerrazzi issued forth from the fortress of Porto Ferrajo to play his part in the great political drama; in the first act of which he had lost his liberty and periled his life. Of unbounded ambition, of distinguished talents, orator and author, he was a man certain to occupy the foremost place upon the public stage, in troubled times. His release was hailed with acclamation, and his return to Florence was greeted as a triumph to the liberal cause. The current of popular enthusiasm in his favor ran high and strong. Three separate constituencies chose him for their representative, when, under the new constitution, the election for the Chamber of Deputies began. Amongst his colleagues, there was no one but Montanelli who seemed in a position to dispute with him the post of chief.

In the month of September, the people of Leghorn once more rose up in arms; this time with the view of casting off the supremacy of Tuscany, and of raising their town to the dignity of an independent State. A serious conflict seemed at hand; for, with the view of reducing his rebellious subjects to submission, the Grand Duke repaired to the camp of Pisa, where was assembled a numerous portion of the national guard. But after some days of warlike preparation on either side, the opposing parties showed a disposition to avert the effusion of blood by coming to terms; the insurgents abating their high pretensions, demanded that Montanelli should be appointed to the post of Governor of Leghorn. This demand was granted by the Grand Duke, on the faith (it is alleged) of Montanelli's plighted word to do his utmost to restore order and peace. If such a pledge was given, it was badly kept by Montanelli; for his words and acts were ill-calculated to calm down the excitement of the popular mind. From his balcony in the public square of Leghorn, he harangued the people in favor of an Italian constitution, the plan of which he had drawn up. Little as it may be supposed the Grand Duke approved of the newly elected Governor's proceedings, he was not, or did not feel himself in a position to cancel the appointment made. Destitute of that firmness of character which is so essential for a ruler to possess in critical times, his deficiency in this particular was not supplied by the advisers whom he called to his side. Frightened at the aspect of affairs, Gino Capponi, the president of the Tuscan Cabinet, resigned; and an unsuccessful attempt to form another Ministry, under another head, was followed by the hazardous step of devolving this task on the democratic Governor of Leghorn. Accepting with alacrity the offered post, Montanelli called on Guerrazzi to aid him in his work. The Chamber of Deputies, which had given a strong support to the late Ministry, was dissolved; and in all the posts vacated by the Duke's adherents, supporters of the revolutionary cause were placed. The Ducal rule was virtually at an end. Impelled by fear, and coerced by pressure from without, Leopold allowed the reins of government to slip from his trembling hands; and it was easy to perceive that it required but a slight collision to hurl him from the seat he so insecurely maintained.

On the 9th January, 1849, the Representative Chambers of Tuscany were opened in person by the Grand Duke. The session commenced with clamor and dissension; the echo as it were, of the voices that prevailed outside. The discussion that ensued on the draft of the "Italian Constitution," submitted to the Chambers for approval by Montanelli, grew violent in the extreme. A strong party arrayed itself in opposition to the creation of the federal power which Montanelli proposed; but a powerful party out of doors gave a clamorous support to the Minister's plan. The populace and the journals were on his side; and, yielding to the democratic voice, the Italian Constitution received the assent of the Legislative Assembly.

This triumph, however, was far from allaying the fevered spirit of excitement which prevailed out of doors. Day by day, disorder and disturbances increased in Florence. With difficulty could Guerrazzi restrain within bounds the revolutionary club of which he was the chief. Drunk with the excitement which a startling series of events and a new-born consciousness of power are so likely to produce in minds unused to reason and reflect, new grievances, new demands, speedily took the place of those to which concession had put an end yesterday. The revolution, not only in Tuscany but in all Italy, came to be looked upon in the light of a drama enacted upon the stage: and a paucity of events, or a slight delay between the acts, gave birth to cries of impatience and discontent. "Onward—onward!" was the cry; and those who, from their talents or position, might have possessed the power to check the headlong progress of democratic violence and unrest, allowed themselves to be swept onward with the stream.

Renewed disturbances took place at Leghorn; the populace of that town clamorously demanding that a Republic should be at once proclaimed. The Governor, appointed by Montanelli, openly declared his sympathy with the popular views. On the last day of January there ran a rumor through the streets of Florence, that the Leghornese were on the eve of marching on the Tuscan capital, in arms. Penetrating to the recesses of the Pitti Palace, that rumor, fraught as it was with scenes of approaching violence and bloodshed, determined the Duke to withdraw himself from the peril he was powerless to avert. His family had some months previously retired to Sienna; and thither now, with haste and secrecy, Leopold repaired.

The fugitive monarch was welcomed with enthusiasm by the Siennese. In place of the tricolored insignia of revolution, the white and red flag of Tuscany was publicly displayed; cheers for the Grand Duke resounded through the streets, and clamorous demonstrations of attachment, in words and acts, were unmingled by revolutionary cries.

The republicans of Florence, ill-satisfied with this state of things, called upon Leopold to return ; fortifying their demand with the intimation that, in case of his refusal to comply with the public wish, his dethronement would be proclaimed. Hastening to Sienna, Montanelli sought an audience of the Grand Duke, to urge a compliance with the popular desire. But Montanelli's mission proved fruitless ; for Leopold, terrified by the ever-darkening aspect of affairs, fled with his family to the seaport town of San Stefano, on the morning of the 7th of February. Two official letters announced to Montanelli this proceeding of the Duke, and the Minister immediately returning to Florence, communicated to his colleagues the event that had occurred.

Florence was instantly in commotion on the receipt of the news. The official letters of the Prince were sent to all the civil and military authorities of the State ; and by Guerrazzi's orders the tocsin of alarm was sounded, the garrison was called to arms, and the Chambers were convoked. The storm, that had been so long looming in the distance, darkening the horizon, had burst over Tuscany at last.

Terror, consternation and confusion prevailed at Florence. No sooner had the deputies assembled to deliberate on the state of affairs, than their proceedings were interrupted by the unlicensed intrusion into the Chambers of a deputation from one of the revolutionary societies of the town. The leader of this band, a man of the name of Niccolini, immediately commenced a harangue—" Citizens, legislators!" he exclaimed, "the people of Florence——"

" Silence!" interrupted the President of the Chambers; "it is not for you to speak within these walls. If you have a petition, it will be received by the Secretary of the Assembly, according to proper form."

" I bear not a petition, but an order from the people!" said Niccolini; who then proceeded to state that nothing else but a Provisional Government, composed of Guerrazzi, Montanelli, and Mazzoni, would satisfy the inhabitants of the town.

The tumult increased; the President put on his hat and declared the sitting at an end. A considerable number of deputies left the hall; at seeing which, a deputy of the name of Socci, rising up and striking his hand violently on the desk, called out after his departing comrades—" Stay! let us die upon our chairs."

The President Zannetti gave the signal for the sitting to be resumed, and then followed a debate of the most tumultuous kind. Some deputies tried to still the clamor that prevailed; but amidst the cries that penetrated to the chamber from without—cries of "Viva il Governo Provvisoria; viva Montanelli, Guerrazzi, e Mazzoni!"—cries which stimulated their partizans in the Assembly to exhort compliance with the popular demand—every expostulation, every appeal to reason was in vain.

"Let us respect the voice of the people," said the deputy Trinci; "as for me, I have full confidence in the men who would form the government proposed."

With words such as these resounding in tones of menace from different portions of the hall, the adherents of the fugitive prince finally gave way to the popular demand; and by a vote of the Chamber, a Provisional Government, composed of Guerrazzi, Montanelli, and Mazzoni, was installed.

Passing from the Chamber of Deputies, the triumvirate presented themselves before the Senate, to have the election of the Lower House confirmed; their appearance was received in silence; indicating plainly consternation, disapprobation, and distrust: the Duke of Casigliani alone gave utterance to the sentiments generally felt by the senators.

"This new power," he said, "cannot be ratified by us, since it does not profess to govern in the name of the Prince."

"Elected by the people, I shall govern in the name of the people," returned Guerrazzi; and however distasteful this reply might be to the Assembly, fear was a too predominant sensation amongst their members to admit of their putting themselves in opposition to the popular will. The vote of the Chamber of Deputies was confirmed.

Tumultuous popular demonstrations of joy in Florence accompanied the instalment of the Provisional Government. Under the leadership of the same Niccolini who had invaded the precincts of the Representative Chamber, a crowd of people traversed the city, and in every public square proclaimed the deposition of the Grand Duke. Trees of liberty were planted in every street, in every lane, in the vicinity of every church, amidst cries of joy and enthusiastic *Evvivas*, mingled with the martial strains of the revolutionary hymn of France. The statues of Leopold were thrown down, and his heraldic insignia injured or defaced.

The first act of the Provisional Government was to dissolve the Chambers, and to call a new Parliament; but before the latter had entered upon its duties, speedily as the elections took place, the tide of popular feeling had begun to turn in favor of the old form of government, which had been so roughly overthrown. In truth, it was no wonder it should be so; for, from the day that the Provisional Government was installed, riots, dissensions, and commotions prevailed throughout the most part of Tuscany. Irritated with the aspect of affairs, the Government had recourse to stringent measures to restore order and calm. Arrests were made upon suspicion; and the prisons were filled with persons charged with political crimes. Too impatient to wait for the opening of the new Parliament, which was to decide upon the form of government Tuscany should have, the citizens of Leghorn, on the 17th of February, with the concurrence of their Governor, proclaimed the Republic with sound of trumpet through the streets of their town.

The Grand Duke of Tuscany, in his retreat at San Stefano, had received tidings of the movement in Leghorn; and the report of cannon at Orbetello, fired in honor of the republican victory, reached his ears. The sound was one that brought terror and perplexity to him; for he had been informed that Montanelli had given orders to the Tuscan troops to march on San Stefano without delay, and obtain possession of his person by every practicable means. It was, therefore, absolutely necessary for his safety that he should leave his present abode; but with that indecision which is the characteristic of weak minds, Leopold could not determine in what direction he should bend his steps. Unable to act in this exigency for himself—hesitating to accept the offer that was made him of an asylum in Piedmont—he resolved to seek the counsel of the Pope. Communication with the Pope, at that time a refugee at Gaeta, was difficult; but through the gallantry of a young officer, who undertook a voyage of a hundred and eighty miles in a small fishing-boat, the difficulty was surmounted and in conformity with the advice received, Leopold embarked for Gaeta, to share with Pius the protection of the Neapolitan King.

To the courage and resolution which the Grand Duchess displayed, she was alone indebted for the means of joining her husband in his flight. Being apprised by Leopold of his intention to embark for Gaeta, she set off instantly for San Stefano, accompanied by her children, two ladies of honor, and two officers belonging to her suit. Without troops, without guards, without any means of resisting popular violence, the attitude assumed by the populace of Orbetello, a city through which she had to pass, was one calculated to strike her with alarm. Scarcely had her carriage entered the town, when it was surrounded by a crowd that effectually blocked up the way; while from every side resounded cries that plainly indicated to the Princess the intention of the people to prevent her from journeying on. To move them from their purpose, she tried remonstrances and entreaties; but in vain. Suddenly, however, changing her bearing, at the moment when the cries around her had reached their highest pitch, she started to her feet, and with a queenlike gesture, look, and tone of voice, cried out—"Back! I *will* pass on. *Now*, I no longer entreat—I command." Surprised, confused and overawed—acted on by the magnetic influence of a resolute will—the crowd with one accord drew back, and the Grand Duchess proceeded triumphantly on her way.

The new Parliament, convoked by universal suffrage, opened its deliberations at the end of March. The first act of this body was to nominate Guerrazzi head of the executive power, and to invest him with almost dictatorial sway. As between him and Montanelli, one of his late colleagues in office, much dissension and altercation had prevailed, Guerrazzi profited by his new dignity to free himself from the presence of a formidable rival, by sending Montanelli on an embassy to Paris. But though supreme in Tuscany, and placed in a position grateful to an ambitious spirit like his, Guerrazzi was too clear-sighted not to feel that his reign could not last long. Signs of a reactionary movement grew more apparent every day. The Florentine populace, lately such ardent republicans, grew so lukewarm in the cause, that Guerrazzi considered it necessary to draft to Florence a band of staunch adherents from the democratic town of Leghorn to execute his commands. This measure, however, was productive of results little in conformity with the projector's views. Instead of strengthening his hands, it weakened them in an eminent degree. His popularity with the Florentines, already on the wane, dwindled away rapidly day by day, through the malpractices of the Leghornese. Composed of the lowest of the people, the dregs of a seaport town, excited by evil passions, the wish to tyrannize, and a thirst for gain, this band soon drew upon itself the hatred of every class within the town. Threats of vengeance for insults offered, and injuries inflicted, were daily uttered by the Florentines. Scowling looks and contracted brows awaited the band of mercenaries on every hand; in the public-houses where they refused to pay, in the streets, where their rude, insolent bearing was conspicuously displayed. So evident was the danger of a collision between the hostile parties, that the municipal authorities of Florence solicited Guerrazzi to withdraw the band of strangers from the city. Assenting to this request, Guerrazzi ordered his unpopular adherents to depart; and, in obedience to this command, the Leghornese, on the 11th of April, marched in a body towards the station of the railway that led to their native town.

But even in the moment when the danger of a conflict seemed to be at an end, the long-brooding mischief occurred. To which of the opposing parties was attributable the blame of precipitating the fray is not known. Both, probably, in this respect, were equally in fault—both, probably, burned with the same desire to come to blows; the Leghornese, exasperated by the triumphant looks, words, and gestures of those around—the Florentines, by the desire to seize on the last opportunity that remained to them to chastise the offending band. Where such feelings exist, where such inflammable materials prevail, the smallest spark is sufficient to kindle a devouring flame. In the Piazza of Santa Maria Novello, the combat between the Leghornese and Florentines began. A general consternation prevailed, for a horrible massacre seemed likely to ensue. The National Guard were called to arms, and repairing to the scene of battle, they put an end to the conflict before long: overpowered by numbers, the defeated Leghornese took to flight.

This victory exercised an important influence in Florence over the course of events. Several members of the municipal council, emboldened by the defeat of the Leghornese, decided at once to put themselves at the head of the reactionary movement that had begun, and which showed itself unmistakably in the acts of the populace of the town. Loud as had been the cries of "*Viva la Republica!*" amongst which the emblems of democratic power had been reared on high, were now the shouts of "*Viva Leopoldo Secondo!*" amongst which those obnoxious symbols were overthrown. A more striking instance of the fickleness of popular feeling can scarcely be afforded in the records of any nation than that which at this period took place in the Tuscan capital. In two months' time, an unreasoning enthusiasm for republican sway had passed into an equally unreasoning enthusiasm for despotic rule. Victims of their own extravagant expectations, which had made liberty appear to them a synonym for plenty, cheapness, idleness, ease, they now trampled under foot the tricolored insignia of the goddess at whose shrine they had so lately bowed—victims, too, of the fatal error which had raised to power a man unfit to hold the helm of a State in troubled times, they now revenged themselves for their mistake, by heaping on their late worshiped chief epithets of hate and scorn. Voices which had grown hoarse a short time before, in leading the chants in Guerrazzi's praise, were now the loudest to demand his expulsion from the seat he held. "Abbasso Guerrazzi!" was the cry that, caught up by hundreds of voices, now resounded through the same squares and streets which had but a few weeks previously re-echoed with his praise.

Those members of the upper classes who had only given a reluctant or forced consent to the deposition of the Grand Duke, were not slow in availing themselves of the reaction of public opinion in his favor to restore him to his throne. In the name of Leopold, one of the members of the municipal council assumed the reigns of government; and several influential persons, amongst others the commander of the National Guard, ranged themselves on his side.

However disheartened Guerrazzi might be at the aspect of affairs, he met the danger with an undaunted mien. Summoning to his side three hundred of the National Gnards as a protection against popular violence, he at the same time convoked the Chamber of Deputies. Sixteen members alone, however, of the legislative body responded to the appeal. From these few still faithful adherents, Guerrazzi demanded the impeachment of the municipal council, as a body guilty of treasonable acts and designs. The discussion on this momentous question had scarcely commenced, when the deputies were startled by the sudden appearance before them of one of that very body whose acts had been arraigned.

"Gentlemen," said the intruder, "you have taken the resolution to impeach us—*You!*" he added, in a tone of scorn. "Nevertheless, I come here in the name of the municipality, to assure you that your cause is hopeless, and that unless you change your views and conduct speedily, we will not answer for your lives."

At these words, some of the deputies made a movement to reply, but before they could execute their intention, the bold speaker had resumed—

"Open the windows!" he said; "look at that throng of citizens; listen to their cries. They are demanding their sovereign; they are calling down curses on your heads!"

Looks of fear and disquietude were visible in the faces of many of the deputies at these words, and four of their number, rising from their seats, declared their adhesion to the monarchical cause, and offered the aid of their services to the municipality to effect the restoration of Leopold. Disheartened by defection, Guerrazzi, abating his pretensions, sought now to effect a compromise with the monarchical party. Demanding and obtaining an interview with the municipality, he offered, on certain terms, the aid of himself and his adherents to forward the object proposed. Much time was spent in negotiations on this head, for the deliberations of the assembly were influenced in a great degree by the aspect of affairs outside. Both parties, republican and monarchical, awaited with anxiety a more undoubted, a more universal manifestation of the public will than had yet occurred; so a wordy debate dragged on till evening, when the partizans of the Grand Duke, forming the majority of the assembly, assured by intelligence received that theirs was certainly the victorious side, refused point-blank the compromise proposed.

With the standard bearing the ducal arms, and in solemn state, the members of the municipal council repaired to the Palazzo Vecchio, from the ancient walls of which had issued Guerrazzi's mandates during his ephemeral reign. Amidst shouts a thousand times repeated of "Viva Leopoldo Secondo!" "Abbasso Guerrazzi!" the municipal authorities took possession, in their sovereign's name, of this seat of republican rule. At the foot of the same dark walls which have witnessed so many mutations of popular feeling in their day, where only two months before the ducal arms had been trampled in the dust, a cry for a bust of the absent Prince clamorously arose; and when, in compliance with this demand, an effigy of the Duke was shown, the air was rent with enthusiastic cheers.

Guerrazzi, deserted by his former zealous adherents, and rudely dispossessed of the authority which, with popular sanction and approval, he had so recently assumed, though conscious that his cause was hopeless and his power at an end, refused to take any measure to assure his safety by flight, and calmly surrendered himself up to the officers of justice, who came to execute the decree of arrest issued by the new authorities against him. Brought to trial, and pronounced guilty of treasonable practices against his sovereign, he was condemned to expiate, by a long imprisonment within the walls of the fortress of the Belvedere, the triumph of the brief term of power and popularity he had enjoyed. With the day that witnessed his arrest, the revolution of which he had been the chief animating spirit, may be said to have terminated; for, notwithstanding the Leghornese contested with arms the entrance into their town of the Austrian troops whom Leopold had called to his side, the conduct of Leghorn in this particular was not imitated by any other large city of Tuscany; though many towns, both small and large, were well known to look with disfavor on the Grand Duke's recall. In truth, the restoration of Leopold to his throne, seems to have been brought about, not by a love of the Government that had been overthrown, but by a hatred of that anarchy which had resulted from democratic rule. In the minds of the respectable classes of the land, of all those who were interested in the security of life and property, the government of the Grand Duke was viewed simply as preferable to the government of the mob. Of the two kinds of despotism, the former seemed the best—the least of two evils, between which there appeared to many no alternative but to choose.

Though the authority of the Grand Duke was nominally established in Florence on the 12th of April, the day after the expulsion of the Leghornese, Leopold did not return to his capital until the 28th of July, when not only Florence, but every town in Tuscany, had its good behavior fully secured by the presence of Austrian troops. Throwing himself thus avowedly on a German army for support, and declaring thus openly how little dependence he placed in the affection and loyalty of the people over whom he ruled—augmenting taxation, too, in various ways, to defray the cost of supporting that large band of foreign soldiers, on whose aid he leaned—it cannot be a matter of surprise that the reactionary feeling in his favor, which gave him back his throne, has died out utterly, and that whatever feelings may now be found operating in favor of the maintenance of his rule, affection is not one. Even to the stranger, this is evident, who happens to be present on some public occasion, when the Grand Duke is brought into immediate contact with the inhabitants of Florence. Amidst the crowd that lines the streets on St. John's Day, to witness the grand parade of Grand Ducal and aristocratic equipages, the few hats uplifted, as the sovereign passes, serve but to make more marked, more striking, the absence amongst the general mass of any kind of courteous salutations.

To the thought of the future of Italy, who does not turn with interest?—who would not proffer their best wishes for the prosperity of a country the parent land of European law, art, literature and civilization? In the progress which the world is making at this present day, Italy, so blessed by Providence, so bounteously endowed by nature with everything that can minister to a nation's riches and prosperity —a country that shone out so brightly during the prevailing darkness of the middle ages—Italy, surely, is not destined to lag behind in the rearward ranks of onward marching nations. Throughout the whole Peninsula, there are many signs that the existing state of affairs will not be of long continuance: and the termination cannot come too soon of a state of things which blights both heart and mind, which blasts all intellectual growth, fosters idleness and self-indulgence, and is fatal alike to private and public virtue. Brought up in a state of intellectual slavery, as Italians were, unused to liberty of thought and speech, unhabituated to the exercise of self-government—no wonder it was they abused those privileges when, a few years ago, they wrested them from their rulers. Remembering the source from which the errors of the revolutionary period flowed, they should be treated leniently, as the errors of children, who, from being perpetually guarded, checked at every step, hedged in by restrictions, suddenly, at one bound, find themselves emancipated from control. Though individuals will sometimes, from the strong bent of nature, rise superior to the power of circumstances, yet as a general rule, it may be said, national institutions form the national character.

It was of Italy Napoleon declared: "Out of eighteen millions of people, I have, with difficulty, found two men." As it was half a century ago, when these words were spoken, so it is now: the same influences are at work to make men rare in Italy—men in the full sense of the word—reasoning, reflective, intelligent, strong-willed, high-principled, active, energetic human beings—capable of taking fortune at its tide, of bending circumstances to their will, and of pursuing, in the face of opposing obstacles, a fixed aim and a definite course of action. But natures such as these, fitted to guide and govern, to reassure the timid, to overawe the turbulent, in times of popular commotion — such natures are not the products of a country where thought is shackled, speech is gagged, and every path is closed to honorable ambition. Evils act and react upon one another: an unworthy government makes an unworthy people, and an unworthy people perpetuates an unworthy government. But Italians, long as they have been trodden down, and heavy as is the yoke fixed upon their necks, have now awakened fully to a sense of their abased condition; and with that consciousness will come regenerating influences: a patriotism which, purified from selfish aims, will make politics something else than a trade, or a market of competing venalities.

Italy, now more than twenty-five millions strong, has but to will to be free—to will unanimously, determinedly, self-sacrificingly, to be free—to become so speedily. Relying now too much on foreign aid and foreign intervention for an amelioration of their condition, the people as yet do not fully see or feel, that freedom, to be lasting, must be attained by their own efforts; and that the wail of inability on their part to win liberty for themselves, involves a confession of their incompetency to maintain it, if gained by them through the means of foreign succor. "Aide-toi et le ciel t'aidera," is a proverb embodying sterling truth and sage counsel. For Italy to take her place amongst the foremost nations of the world—to cover the seas with her merchant ships, to rear emporiums for human industry, and to produce such minds as will extend the landmarks of human knowledge — minds which, penetrating into Nature's secrets, will turn its mysteries to man's profit—minds exerting by wisdom, learning, fancy, pathos, eloquence, wit, an enduring dominion over the intellect of succeeding generations; to do all this—an ambition to which she may well aspire—Italy must not receive her freedom as a gift, but must work it out by her own energies, through the purifying agencies of suffering, sacrifice, devotion and perseverance.

In the present juncture of affairs, when a collision between France and Austria seems imminent, it behooves Italians to act with caution; for the expulsion of the Austrian from their land, if accomplished by foreign aid, would be an act from which they could not reasonably hope to derive the least advantage. The freedom of a nation has never yet been achieved, nor ever will be obtained, through the assistance of a despot. Philanthropy abides not with the wearer of an imperial crown, nor hatred of oppression with the master of the lives and fortunes of millions. To uproot one tyranny merely to have another planted in its stead, would be no gain to Italy. On the contrary, the yoke last imposed would prove, in all probability, more grievous than the one that it succeeded. The fable of the horse which asked the man to mount him, to avenge him on his enemy, affords a salutary warning, in reference to the course which would inevitably be pursued by France in the character of avenger of Italian grievances; for the service done, the position occupied by its doer would still be retained, and Italy, curbed by the strong hand of her selected champion, would find, ere long, that there could exist for her a still greater evil than the rule of Austria. To invite assistance is, on the part of nations, to invite oppression. A people who cannot win freedom by their own exertions, must resign themselves to a state of servitude and dependence; for the well known "Rob Roy good old rule,"* though banned and scouted in private life, is the doctrine still acted on by kings and nations; and whilst Might makes Right in their estimation, weak states will ever fall victims to the stronger. In this, however, as well as in other affairs of life, we may in general trace a law of retributive justice; for in a nation which consists of millions, weakness is a disgrace, a degradation.

There is a Nemesis ever attending on human error, either as regards states or individuals. No fault or folly can be committed that does not involve some penalty, and Italy is now not one nation chiefly because its millions have no unity in thought, feeling and aspiration; for throughout the land, miserable petty jealousies divide the inhabitants, not only

* "That those should take who have the power,
And those should keep who can."

of states but of cities, from each other. During the late revolution in Tuscany, Leghorn, with a view of establishing itself as an independent republic, rose up in arms against Florence; and Genoa, enjoying a large measure of liberty under the rule of the King of Sardinia, is ready now to fight, as it fought a few years ago, to attain a distinct national existence. Florence is jealous of the pretensions of Rome, and Naples has no true sympathy with either. Whilst such a state of things continues, the dream, so dear to the Italian patriot, of making Italy something more than "a geographical expression," can certainly not be realized. Without unity of thought and action, resistance is hopeless; but, with community of aim and purpose, the overthrow of foreign or domestic tyranny would be unfailingly and speedily accomplished.

In the next attempt which Italians make to acquire the privileges of freemen, let them avoid those errors which blighted the fair promise that characterized the commencement of their last endeavor. The wisdom derived from suffering and experience should now be theirs; and if they profit by its teachings, Italy will exhibit, in the succeeding century, a picture differing widely from the aspect it presents in this, of a people burning with resentment and hatred towards its rulers, and rulers regarding with terror and distrust the millions beneath their sway.